THREE ORDINARY GIRLS

TIM BRADY

is also the author of—

HIS FATHER'S SON
The Life of General Ted Roosevelt, Jr.

A DEATH IN SAN PIETRO
The Untold Story of Ernie Pyle, John Huston,
and the Fight for Purple Heart Valley

TWELVE DESPERATE MILES
The Epic World War II Voyage of the SS Contessa

THREE ORDINARY GIRLS

THE REMARKABLE STORY *of* THREE DUTCH

TEENAGERS WHO BECAME SPIES, SABOTEURS,

NAZI ASSASSINS—AND WWII HEROES

TIM BRADY

CITADEL PRESS
Kensington Publishing Corp.
www.kensingtonbooks.com

CITADEL PRESS BOOKS are published by

Kensington Publishing Corp.
119 West 40th Street
New York, NY 10018

Copyright © 2021 Tim Brady

All rights reserved. No part of this book may be reproduced in any form or by any means without the prior written consent of the publisher, excepting brief quotes used in reviews.

All Kensington titles, imprints, and distributed lines are available at special quantity discounts for bulk purchases for sales promotions, premiums, fund-raising, educational, or institutional use.

Special book excerpts or customized printings can also be created to fit specific needs. For details, write or phone the office of the Kensington sales manager: Kensington Publishing Corp., 119 West 40th Street, New York, NY 10018, attn: Sales Department; phone 1-800-221-2647.

CITADEL PRESS and the Citadel logo are Reg. U.S. Pat. & TM Off.

ISBN-13: 978-0-8065-4038-2
ISBN-10: 0-8065-4038-9

First Citadel hardcover printing: March 2021

10 9 8 7 6 5 4 3 2 1

Printed in the United States of America

Library of Congress Control Number: 2020945350

Electronic edition:

ISBN-13: 978-0-8065-4040-5 (e-book)
ISBN-10: 0-8065-4040-0 (e-book)

To Susan,
Ti amo.

Chapter 1

YEARS AFTER THE GREAT DEPRESSION, Truus Oversteegen re-called the miseries and struggles of those times as if they were still happening outside her window in Haarlem. She remembered standing in long lines with her mother and neighbors, waiting for the government dole to be parsed out. There were more lines outside the factory gates at Hoogovens, the blast furnace manufacturers, where laborers waited to find out who might or might not be given work within the plant on any given day.[1]

Her parents knew precisely who was to blame for the worldwide woes: it was the capitalists, as they had informed her time and again. The owners of the factories who profited off the sweat of labor.

Truus remembered taking her father's hand, as a five-year-old, as they marched in demonstrations and protests. She remembered the drums pounding, the red flags fluttering in the breeze. She remembered what it felt like to

---

1. Truus Menger, *Not Then, Not Now, Not Ever*, 1982, orig. Dutch title, *Toen niet, nu niet, nooit*. English trans. Rita Gircour, 1998. Nederland Tolerant: Max Drukker Stichting, p. 11.

be surrounded by a sea of grown-up legs and chanting voices.

On one indelible occasion she and her father, Jacob Oversteegen, marched with a wave of protesters through Haarlem, until they crashed into a second wave of counter-protesters. These newcomers to the throng were angry men, shouting at the group in which she and her father were encircled. "String up the socialists!" they called out. "Hang them from the street lamps!"

Then the mounted police arrived, and suddenly Truus was lifted out of the crowd and onto the back of a horse, between a police officer and the saddle horn. As the police officer carried her away, her father disappeared from view, swallowed by the circling fury of protesters and counter-protesters. Disappearing was a thing he did quite often during those days when the family was living on a houseboat in the canal, as many families did in Holland.

At the police station, she was given a bowl of porridge, which she was too upset to eat. Finally her mother, Trijntje van der Molen, arrived, and Truus began to feel a bit better. As she and her mother walked home, she looked up at the streetlights, the angry voices from the demonstration—"Hang them from the street lamps!"—still ringing in her head. She asked her mother if they were socialists. Trijntje replied, "Yes, we are socialists," and Truus could hear the fierce pride in her mother's voice.[2]

Truus Oversteegen was born in 1923. Her younger sis-

2. *Not Then*, p. 12.

ter, Freddy Nanda, or Freddie, as she was called by every-one, arrived two years later. The girls were thick as thieves growing up, even after their father left the houseboat. In truth he had never provided much to the family in terms of stability anyway. He was a drinker and a womanizer who contributed little to the family's financial needs, and in fact was likely more of a drain.[3]

The breakup of their parents' marriage and subsequent divorce was not something either of the girls remembered as traumatic. In fact, when her father left, Freddie re-membered him singing a French farewell song to the family from the bow of the canal boat. The girls would continue to see their father around Haarlem for years to come.

Trijntje took the girls to live in a flat, where they shared a bedroom furnished with straw mattresses that Trijntje made herself. It was an impoverished existence, but they were a loving family and this pulled them through. They loved, in particular, to make music together. They had a whole string section in the family—Trijntje played the mandolin, Truus played the guitar, Freddie played both the ukulele and the zither, and they sang to their own ac-companiment.

The Oversteegen family was a large one, with a tradi-tion of being active in leftist circles in Haarlem. One uncle, George Oversteegen, an anarchist, had even earned

---

3. *Vice* online magazine interview, May 11, 2016.

a seat on the Haarlem City Council in the late 1920s.[4]
Trijntje was also raised with leftist values, and the economic uncertainties of the Great Depression sharpened
her critique of the miseries that capitalism visited on the
working class. For Trijntje, Truus, and Freddie, their political, social, and cultural lives revolved around the family
association with leftist causes. The girls were members of
the AJC (Arbeiders Jeugd Central) a socialist youth movement that emphasized education, physical conditioning,
folk dance, music, and camping, all pursued in the context of a working-class atmosphere and socialist structure.

When the girls were still young, Trijntje gave birth to a
brother named Robbie,[5] and the flat they shared became
even more crowded. Neither did his addition help in pars-
ing out the government dole—the Dutch welfare stipend—
on which the family lived. It amounted to precisely 13
guilders and 75 cents a week and the rent alone took 3½
guilders. Inspectors from a state organization called Social
Help in Practice would periodically come by to check in the
family cupboards and underneath beds just to make sure
the Oversteegen girls and their mother and Robbie were
not trying to hide a hoard of riches. Fat chance of that![6]

4. Eveline Buchheim, *Under Fire: Women and World War II*; Ellis Jonker,
"Freddi and Truus: Sisters in Arms." In *Under Fire*. Amsterdam:
Verloren Publishers, 2014, p. 143.
5. Truus refers to Robbie as her stepbrother and never addresses his
paternity in her memoirs. Robbie's paternity appears to have been
left a question mark in the life of his sisters, at least through the
war. Documentation at www.geni.com/boboversteegen states that
Robbie's father was Jacob Oversteegen.
6. *Not Then*, p. 14.

They also wanted to make sure Trijntje wasn't entertaining any men in her home. There was none of that, but what she *was* doing was holding leftist meetings in the apartment, which included men. When the fact that she was hosting gatherings was discovered, it was enough to get the family cut off from the dole. Afterward, they were forced to go to friends and neighbors begging for soup.

In desperation, Trijntje went down to the welfare office with the girls in tow to demand that the officials rescind their decision and give her and the family back their food stamps and stipend for rent. She yelled, she remonstrated, she refused to leave. Finally, the police were called. When an officer grabbed Trijntje to force her out of the office, Truus jumped in and bit him at the same time as Freddie kicked him in the shins. These little girls were not wallflowers!

Unfortunately, when they left the government office, they still had no food stamps and no stipend for rent. For the next six weeks they ate brown beans.

When she was fourteen, Truus began working as a domestic for wealthy families in the Haarlem area. It was not work that suited her; her sense of independence usually overtook her willingness to follow orders. Later she would recall "children who were often little tyrants" and "lord[s] of the manor [who] wanted to pinch my buttocks."

She took a position with one family who had a villa in the well-to-do Haarlem suburb of Bloemendaal, "the bastion of the rich in Holland," Truus called it. Bloemendaal was near the sandy dunes of South Kennemerland, which was the area that ran along the coast of northwestern Netherlands. Truus was to be a live-in servant, but things didn't work out as planned. She spent her very first night there homesick in an attic room thinking of Freddie and Robbie at home. Trijntje had packed peppermints and peanut brittle to ease the transition, but they only made Truus feel more homesick.

She was awakened the next morning by an unsympathetic German maid named Kathe, who greeted her at breakfast with a bowl of watered-down porridge. Truus had no stomach for the gruel to which Kathe said, "Zen you will eat nothing," and sent the girl off to wash windows, make beds, and vacuum the house.

At one point, Truus took her shoes off to have a cup of coffee. When she was ready to put her shoes back on, she discovered that one of the children of the house had put a thumbtack in the heel. Nice kids! She was then ordered by Kathe to empty a chamber pot filled to the brim with the family's evacuations from the previous night. To top off her morning, she had an encounter on the stairs with the master of the house, who stopped Truus on a landing and gave her a long lascivious look before blatantly trying to grab her crotch.

Truus wound up kicking the chamber pot down the staircase in front of the whole family, retrieving her suitcase, and racing out of the house back toward home in Haarlem. Her mother told her it was too bad about the money she would have received for the job, but to make sure Truus understood whose side she was on, Trijntje quickly added, "I would have done exactly the same!"[7]

7. *Not Then*, pp. 13–15.V

* * *

The family was far from sheltered from the political upheavals of Europe in the 1930s. Aside from Trijntje's
meetings and the girls' participation in socialist youth
groups, the girls did things like make dolls for the refugee
children of the Spanish Civil War. They were also fully
aware of who the Nazis were and who were their sympathizers. In the Netherlands there was a party known as the
NSB, the National Socialist Movement (Nationaal Social-
istische Beweging). It was headed by a moon-faced, civil
engineer named Anton Mussert, who had earned the con-
tempt of Dutch progressives even before his political career began, when he married his mother's sister—his own
aunt.

While Mussert and the NSB remained a relatively minor
force within the Netherlands' political structure during
the 1930s, there were other factions in the government
who were more than willing to reach out to Nazi Germany
to reassure them that Dutch allegiances leaned more
right than left. It was even rumored in leftist circles that
the queen's son-in-law, Bernhard, a German prince by
birth, and newly wed to Princess Juliana, had secret ties to
the Nazi Party.

Truus and Freddie learned early that it was not enough
just to sneer at Mussert. In fact, Trijntje's communist leanings placed her and her daughters in the thick of the
struggle. She not only kept the girls well-informed of what
was happening in Germany and elsewhere, but she also
brought anti-fascist refugees into the house through her
membership in a communist relief organization called

Red Aid. As early as 1934, Trijntje welcomed German left-ists fleeing from Hitler's oppressions into their home. There would be a late-night knock on the door, and a Dutch neighbor from Party meetings would be there with one or two shivering souls on their way to asylum in Eng-land. Trijntje would let them in for an overnight, and the next day the Dutch neighbor would be back to take them on their next leg toward freedom.

Early on, the girls learned to keep quiet about the visi-tors and to keep quiet about the activities their mother was involved in. Even before the Germans came to occupy their country, Truus and Freddie knew that talking was dangerous. They knew what the Nazis were and what they were capable of. They knew the meaning of betrayal.[8]

As Hitler and the Germans flexed their muscles through Europe from the mid- to the late 1930s, remilitarizing the Rhineland, establishing the Anschluss in Austria, annex-ing the Sudetenland, grabbing Bohemia and Moravia from Czechoslovakia, with no signs of stopping and ap-peased all the while by Western Europe, it became more and more apparent that a second World War was immi-nent. But the Dutch people, who had been spared the horrors of the first World War by the simple expediency of staying neutral during the bloodbath, remained largely convinced, or deluded, into thinking that the same thing would hold true during the next conflict. The country even served as the exile home of Kaiser Wilhem II, who was spending his final days in relative harmlessness, chop-

8. *Not Then*, p. 13.

ping wood on an estate outside the town of Doorn in Utrecht. Maybe that was all these fierce tyrants from Germany wanted from the Kingdom of the Netherlands: a place to contemplate fate and furiously work up an old man sweat.

On September 1, 1939, two days past Truus's sixteenth birthday, Germany invaded Poland. For Great Britain and France, there were no more cards to play, no more attempts to appease Hitler. The newsreels down at the theater off the Grote Markt in Haarlem showed footage of the German people triumphantly heil-ing Hitler, while the newspapers told of Wehrmacht tanks sweeping across the Polish landscape as the Polish cavalry charged on horseback into the deadly fire.

The Dutch government had ordered a mobilization of its armed forces just a few days before the German blitzkrieg swept through Poland, but it hedged its bets by declaring the intention to stay neutral in the coming conflict, after the British and French declared war. Despite the government's best intentions for the country, the war had an immediate and harsh economic impact on the Netherlands. A British blockade of Dutch ports effectively ended trade between Germany and the Netherlands. It also underscored the value of the Dutch coastline to Hitler and the Third Reich, further reducing the likelihood that the Kingdom of the Netherlands would be able to remain neutral throughout the coming war as they had during the first World War.

To say that the Dutch military was unprepared to defend itself against the German war machine would be a gross understatement. While nations across Europe had been building military forces over the past few years to try to keep some pace against the money being poured into the Wehrmacht by Germany, the Dutch still didn't possess a single tank in its entire arsenal until 1940. Military spending, which was actually doubled in 1938, still represented just 4 percent of federal spending in the Netherlands, compared to 25 percent in Germany.[9] The only expansion of its army between the wars was the creation of two regiments of bicyclists, one of which included a military band with specially designed handlebars that could be steered while playing an instrument. The regimental motto was "Swift and Nimble—Composed and Dignified."[10]

The nation's chief defense strategy was one that had been in existence since the seventeenth century. It involved conceding territory to the northeast and south in the Netherlands, while at the same time flooding the lowest lying areas of the country—those already beneath sea level and including many of Holland's major cities, including Dordrecht, Utrecht, Haarlem, and Amsterdam— along a line running from the northwest near Lake IJssel, southeast to the Amstel and Rhine Rivers. The Germans could enter the country but would immediately be stymied by sluggish water, too shallow for boats and too muckish for foot or vehicle travel. The cities inside the

9. Wikipedia, "Netherlands in World War II."
10. Pete Jordan, *In the City of Bikes.* New York: HarperCollins, 2013, p. 159.

line were fortified by newly built bunkers and fortresses, financed by the slight increase in the country's defenses spending.

Life for the Oversteegen family in Haarlem went on as usual, with the added intensity of war drums looming on the horizon. One day Trijntje asked Truus and Freddie to pick up a boy and girl from another safe house in Haarlem and bring them back to their apartment for an overnight stay. The girls, who had been squabbling with each other just before the request, felt put upon and rebelled at the idea of taking more visitors into their cramped quarters. Trijntje was having none of it. These children had escaped from Germany without their parents, she told them. They were lonely, frightened, had no idea what their future held. How could Truus and Freddie be so selfish, petty, and self-pitying?

The girls, hardly more than children themselves, were abashed and did as their mother asked.

Truus took a housecleaning job with a family of Jewish immigrants from Germany, who owned a furniture store in town. They had left everything behind to escape the Nazis. One day, she overheard a visitor to the family from Germany urging them to continue on to America, sure that Hitler would soon come to the Netherlands as he had Poland.

Truus wondered if her own family should go to America too. That night she asked her mother about this. War was coming, couldn't they find a way?

"You need money for that," Trijntje reminded her daughter. "And what would we do there anyway?"[11]

Truus had no answer for that.

On May 10, 1940, the Oversteegen family, along with everyone else in the neighborhood, awoke to the ominous droning of planes overhead. Everyone rushed out into the street in their pajamas to look up at the planes passing over Haarlem. The day was gorgeous and clear, the skies a crystal blue. It seemed impossible, unreal, that those planes were actually carrying bombs, and that Dutch antiaircraft weapons were now shooting at the German bombers. Then one of the gray-green bombers started to smoke. Moments later, it was falling out of the sky, the green cross near its tail twirling as it dropped. There was nothing unreal about the shudder of the earth following the crash and the explosion of the plane as it burst into flames.

Someone put a radio in a windowsill and cranked up the volume. The broadcaster was transmitting what sounded like gibberish over the airwaves. Everyone would later understand the nonsense to be coded messages, probably directed across the English Channel, but at that moment it added to their confusion. Finally, a government official came on with the actual news in understandable Dutch: they were under attack by the Germans. The Germans were invading the Kingdom of the Netherlands on multiple fronts.

11. *Not Then*, p. 20.

A woman cried out, "Oh Jesus, where can we go now!?"[12] and all around her, neighbors stood clutching one another, trying to comprehend what this all meant for them. Truus, Freddie, and Trijntje were also trying to make sense of all that was happening. It was at this moment that the girls' brother Robbie, out of simple nervous energy, started to sing the song "Naar de bollen," a popular song by the famed cabaret Dutch singer Louis Davids.[13]

Eventually everyone went back into their homes to listen to their own radios and track news of the invasion in their living rooms.

Trijntje quickly swung into action. It was time for all of her left-wing books, her paintings, her photos of socialist gatherings, her pamphlets, leaflets, anything that connected her with the cause, to go into the stove, and now. The four of them spent most of the day gathering and burning any tangible evidence of their leftist past.[14] There could be no visible hint of their politics if the Nazis knocked on the door.

Hitler had authorized the invasion of the Netherlands only the day before. Up to the moment of the invasion, many Dutch people remained so sanguine about the possibility of avoiding a German attack that one newspaper

12. *Not Then*, p. 21.
13. The translation of the title was roughly "Tiptoe to the tulips," though the song was not the same as the American tune, "Tiptoe Through the Tulips," which was also current at the time. *Not Then*, p. 21.
14. Pauline Broekma, *Historisch Nieuwsblad*, June 20, 2016.

headlined its morning edition on the day of the invasion, TENSIONS DEFUSED. EXPECTED EVENTS NOT TO OCCUR.[15]

Soldiers in the Royal Netherlands Army fought valiantly, including those bicycle regiments, which actually performed as well as could be expected. But German firepower would quickly prove overwhelming. Trying to circumvent the anticipated flooding of Dutch lowlands, the Germans landed paratroopers at a number of airports and at The Hague, home of the Dutch government. They were challenged by Dutch forces wherever they appeared, and the fighting between the armies was hot. Many more German troops were pressing from the south and east, however, through the provinces of Limburg and Noord-Brabant.

The Germans also employed trickery in the invasion. Near the Dutch border with Germany, a group of Wehrmacht soldiers dressed in the uniforms of Dutch military police strolled across a bridge with a contingent of German "prisoners of war." Once they'd passed the real Dutch defenders guarding the crossing, they immediately turned on them and attacked. Some of the paratroopers were also said to be posing as Dutch forces, and to counter the threat, soldiers of the Royal Netherlands Army near The Hague started to challenge strangers that they encountered by asking them to pronounce the name of a local seaside town, Scheveningen, which was notoriously difficult for Germans to get right.[16]

15. Russell Shorto, *Amsterdam: A History of the World's Most Liberal City.* New York: Vintage Books, 2013, p. 263.
16. Ben Coates, *Why the Dutch Are Different.* Boston: Nicholas Brealey Publishing, 2015, p. 116.

The Dutch desperately needed assistance from Allied forces, but both Great Britain and France had problems of their own dealing with Germany, and no help would be forthcoming. In addition, German forces focused on cutting off any possibility of Allied aid through Belgium in the west by concentrating units near The Hague around the area that separated Zuid (South) Holland, and its provincial capital of Rotterdam, from Noord-Holland and Amsterdam.

In aiming at The Hague, the Germans were also clearly maneuvering to capture the queen and the Dutch government. Their efforts were foiled, however, when two days into the invasion on May 12 Crown Princess Juliana, her children, and her husband Bernhard all fled to England on a British destroyer. The Commander-in-Chief of Dutch Armed Forces advised Queen Wilhelmina that he could no longer guarantee her safety in the Netherlands, and the next day, May 13, 1940, she, too, fled to England. The rest of the government followed suit later that day.

When she arrived in London, the queen issued a defiant statement, telling her people to keep on struggling and that she could best work for the Kingdom of the Netherlands in the safe arms of the British. From here, she could fight against Nazi tyranny as well as guard against threats to the Dutch East Indies, the colonial engine of the national economy, which was already being pressured by the Axis power lurking in the Far East, Japan. Wilhelmina declared London to be the new seat of the Kingdom of the Netherlands, to be supported by a new government-in-exile.

The speed with which all of this happened left most of the Dutch population with their heads spinning. The

Oversteegen family, hardly sympathetic to the royal family and the conservative government to begin with, felt misled by the reassuring pronouncements they'd heard just prior to the invasion. Now, just four days after the attack, they were being told that their queen and government had abandoned them to the Nazis and were safe in London. Worse news was coming the next day.

The Dutch continued to fight even after the government left The Hague, but they were already squeezed into the area known as Fortress Holland, centered around the large cities in the western part of the nation. By Tuesday, May 14, Germany was threatening to bomb the city of Rotterdam if Dutch authorities persisted in defending what was left of the nation. The Nazis set a 3:00 P.M. deadline on the afternoon of the fourteenth for the Royal Army of the Netherlands to surrender, terms to which the Dutch commander agreed.

German bombers, however, were already in the air, prepared to carry out the attack when the agreement was reached. German radio operators ordered the strike to be aborted, but they were only partially successful in turning the wave of bombers from the target.

Fifty-four Stuka planes unloaded their bombs on the city, and a rain of death and destruction swept over Rotterdam. According to the Dutch historian Loe de Jong, "Fires started here, there and everywhere and in less than twenty minutes more than two square miles of city blocks were turned into a blazing hell of death and devastation."[17]

---

17. Loe de Jong, *The Lion Rampant*. Trans. William W. F. Stoppelman. New York: Querido, 1943, p. 3.

Hundreds of people were killed with the impact of the bombs; hundreds more died in the devastating smoke and fires; thousands upon thousands were left homeless and without shelter. All roads out of Rotterdam were jammed into impassable human dams packed solid by the press of desperate refugees trying to escape the burning city. Some of the first German bombs landed on the city's water main, which subsequently made fire hydrants and fire crews across Rotterdam useless against the spread of flames. The city's zoo was destroyed by fire, setting free scores of exotic animals into the chaotic streets of the burning city. There were reports of patients in the upper floors of a burning Rotterdam city hospital choosing to jump to their deaths rather than face the searing flames spreading toward them.[18]

The fires were still burning the next day when the terms of the capitulation of Holland to German forces was signed. There were still Dutch forces fighting in Zeeland, in the far northern corner of the country, but theirs was a lonely battle that would not last long. Nine million Netherlanders were suddenly under the heel of the Reichstag boot. In the words of de Jong, "In five days, a struggle which had been expected to last five months had come to its end."[19]

The full meaning of that change would come in time, but some of the dreaded consequences of Nazi rule were immediately anticipated, particularly in Amsterdam, which housed the largest portion of Jewish refugees from Germany in the Netherlands. The number of suicides on

18. *Why the Dutch*, p. 137.
19. *The Lion*, p. 4.

that day when Hitler and his minions occupied the country was so large that the Amsterdam city department of health was not capable of gathering all the bodies in its ambulances. They hired trucks and drivers to help.[20]

The first act of the new regime in the Netherlands was to free all of the NSB members who had been jailed by the supplanted administration. These were the same right-wing thugs, including Anton Mussert, who had been imprisoned by the Dutch government prior to the invasion for their collaborations with the Germans. They were now free to puff out their chests and strut around the streets of Amsterdam, Haarlem, The Hague, and the still smoldering ruins of Rotterdam like preening cocks.

The final toll of death and destruction in Rotterdam was 900 dead and more than 10,000 homeless, along with the destruction of 31 department stores, 13 banks, 19 consulates, 2 museums, 4 churches, 22 movie theaters, and 517 cafés. The city was essentially leveled.[21] In Great Britain, which was about to face its own long siege of bombing from the German Luftwaffe, Rotterdam represented the supreme destruction that Germany was capable of inflicting on any civilian population in Europe.

On May 15, Germany's 207th Division entered Amsterdam from the southeast side of the city, crossed the Amstel River, and then continued west toward Haarlem.

It wasn't until the following day in Amsterdam that the German Wehrmacht made its grand entrance into the city, motoring in like the conquering nation it wanted the

20. *The Lion*, p. 4.
21. *Why the Dutch*, p. 139.

world to see, complete with two divisions of Panzer tanks, endless motorcycles, trucks, and halftracks hauling anti-aircraft weaponry. A squad of Mercedes-Benz brought the German officer corps and deposited them at the finest hotels in the city where they immediately commandeered all of the best rooms.

Meanwhile in Haarlem, Truus Oversteegen went down to the Grote Markt to witness the arrival of the Germans. There in the center of the city, by the Grote Kerk, by the statue of Laurens Janszoon Koster, the fourteenth-century Haarlem citizen—said, by every good Haarlemmer, to have created and printed with movable type before Gutenberg—a long convoy of German tanks and military vehicles rumbled and thundered up the pavers of Grote Houtstraat.

A number of Dutch fascists, the NSBers, were there to greet them with *Sieg Heils* and the accompanying stiff-armed salute. The women from that crowd threw flowers at the tanks and one of the belching, treaded monsters stopped just in front of Truus. A German soldier opened the hatch at the top of the tank to look out, and as he did, she noticed that the tank had blood in its tracks; the red stain didn't go unnoticed by other Dutch patriots in the crowd either. One of them yelled, "Murderers!" and others picked up the chant until the police arrived to disperse the crowd.

Truus went home in a foul mood. "The scum is here," she said to her family and their two young Jewish visitors when she arrived at the dinner table.[22]

---

22. *Not Then*, pp. 23–24.

Chapter 2

HAARLEM, AN ANCIENT AND PROUD CITY, grew up between the river Spaarne and the coastal dunes along the North Sea beginning around the tenth century A.D. It blossomed into one of Holland's major cities during medieval times, rivaling Dordrecht, Delft, Rotterdam, Leiden, and Amsterdam as a center of commerce and culture.

The city center, the large cobblestone-covered market square, known as the Grote Markt, was dominated by the massive Gothic presence of the Grote Kerk—the Great Church—in the heart of Haarlem. Resting like a massive bulwark of righteousness amid the hustle and bustle of human commerce in the square, the church dates back, after various repairs, renovations, and religious upheavals, to the early years of the thirteenth century. It was initially consecrated as a Catholic church and named for Saint Bavo, who is said to have saved the city of Haarlem from a coastal people, the Kennemers, in earlier times. The church was subsequently converted to Protestantism with the Reformation in the sixteenth century. It became noted for its huge organ, which was the largest in the world during the 1700s and played by Mendelssohn, Handel, and a ten-year-old Mozart in 1766.[1] One of the great artists of the Dutch Masters' era, Frans Hals, a native Haarlemmer, was buried beneath the stone floor of the church, along with many other city notables.

Haarlem lies just to the west of Amsterdam. The two municipalities have been twenty minutes apart from one another since soon after train travel became the principal means of transportation in Western Europe in the nineteenth century. The trip is not much longer than that by bicycle, which has been, more so than any other nation in Western Europe, the chief mode of getting around for Dutch people since early in the twentieth century.

Haarlem endured and mostly thrived through all the years of rich and unique Dutch history to the present. It was built like the whole of the Netherlands in lowlands near the sea. In the Middle Ages, its major industries were textiles, shipping, and beer. It endured multiple fires, the plague, which visited Haarlem in 1378 and wiped out about half of its population, as well as a lengthy siege by the Spanish army in the sixteenth century.

Tulips began appearing in the polders around Haarlem during the early seventeenth century, and the city subsequently became the epicenter of the crazed period that arrived soon after. During this phase of "tulip mania," bulbs of this still exotic flower (its European origins were from Turkey, where the flowers had arrived by way of the trade route from central Asia) were traded in the first fu-

1. Wikipedia, "Haarlem."

tures market the world ever knew. During the 1630s rare and prized bulbs were bought and sold for amounts equivalent to the price of a new house. A big one. The market in Haarlem grew up around the many taverns that had been built in the city to accommodate travelers. A newly built canal, the first tow canal in Holland, linked Amsterdam and Haarlem by means of passenger boats, which were pulled along the river. Traders would come to the smoke-filled taverns of the city—pipe-smoking was an endemic Dutch pastime—drink heavily, and trade bulbs to the wee hours of the morning.[2]

Tulips remained an important component of Haarlem's economy through World War II, and into the present. The city remains surrounded by tulip beds, stretching from Alkmaar in the north, south toward The Hague and Rotterdam. From the first bloom of crocuses in mid-March, through daffodils and hyacinths a few weeks later, to the spectacular variety of delicate colors that come with the tulip bloom in late April and into May, a spring bicycle ride on the polder roads around Haarlem is like a spinning pallet of colors.

To the north of Haarlem, along the North Sea Canal, are several commercial and industrial communities—Velsen-Noord, Velsen-Zuid, IJmuiden, Velserbroek, Santpoort-Noord, and Santpoort-Zuid. The canal was built in the nineteenth century at the narrowest point in Holland between Amsterdam and the North Sea. It provides the fi-

2. See Mike Dash, *Tulip Mania.* New York: Crown Publishers, 1999, pp. 135–140 for a vivid description of a Haarlem tavern during the mania.

nancial and business capital of the Netherlands with far quicker access to the ocean and all the commerce it brings.

Above the canal and toward the sea, villages like Beverwijk, Heemskerk, and Noorddorp dot the landscape. Farther inland, among the lacework of canals that mark the interior, yet more villages fill the map, including Limmen, Akersloot, and Krommenie.

To the west and north, Haarlem is flanked by towns, which have become part of a metropolitan area that joins with Amsterdam to the northeast to create the densest population center in North Holland. Toward the sea, on the west side of the city, suburbs and resort communities like Overeen and Zandvoort line the seacoast, along with the wealthy community of Bloemendaal, replete with resplendent villas and mansions. It was and is home to some of the richest families in the Netherlands.

The center city of Haarlem maintained its medieval flavor well into the twentieth century. Densely constructed with compact cobblestone streets lined by a mix of shops, cafés, and tightly pressed homes whose doors front thoroughfares that contain the inevitable Dutch mix of foot and speeding bicycle travel, Haarlem also has its surprises. A plethora of hidden gardens dot the city, many contained within the properties of the various almshouses that were built by the wealthy through the centuries to accommodate elderly women in need.

There are also a number of woods in Haarlem, including the Haarlemmerhout, a small forest on the southern edge of the city, which was said to be the oldest public park in the Netherlands, dating back to the 1500s. A number of the spacious villas in the city were built with their backs to the woods, along the Wagenweg, the old "wagon road" to the west of the trees. To the east, the River Spaarne wound north into the old central city and upward to the North Sea Canal.

To the east of the Spaarne, near Haarlemmerhout, was a neighborhood called Schlacthuisbuurt (Slaughterhouse), which was home to many of the more modest apartments and homes in town, including those occupied, at different times, by the Oversteegen family.

On the west side of the river, northwest of the city center in the general direction of Bloemendaal, a more upscale part of town had grown up around a neighborhood called Kleverpark.

It was here that young Jannetje Johanna Schaft, Jo Schaft, to her parents, and Hannie Schaft to history, grew up like a Dutch girl out of Hans Brinker, in a pleasant row house across from the park on Van Dortstraat, near a windmill.

Each morning, with her books clutched tight to her chest and her wavy red hair tossed over her stylish cardigan sweater and down her back, Johanna walked timidly through the pleasant green neighborhoods on the north side of Haarlem on her way to primary school on Tetterodestraat.

Johanna's hair and freckles made her self-conscious in a way that most redheads know. There was no doubt about its color, no blond blending in with the red to possibly classify it as strawberry. It was red only, and would be called only red for all her days, and her classmates from the first day of school forward let Jo Schaft know that she stood out.

that first year to take part in the more carefree activities of a first-year university student, like rowing on the River Amstel, and riding horseback in the countryside. But Jo's natural inclinations and the tenor of the times quickly steered her in the direction of deeper concerns.[9]

She became a devotee of the teaching of a humanist philosophy professor on campus named H. J. Pos, who had helped found a group called the Vigilance Committee in Amsterdam. The Vigilance Committee sponsored lectures, seminars, and conferences and published pamphlets intended to counter the National Socialist Movement of Anton Mussert in the Netherlands. Jo also volunteered to collect donations for Spanish refugees of the Civil War, and in the process met a Jewish student named Philine Polak. The two became fast friends and were soon joined by another student, who like Philine was Jewish, Sonja Frenk, as the pair became a trio of lunchmates and confidantes.

Jo's second year at the university was no less full of politics and studies. Germany's invasion of Poland in the fall of 1939 brought increased tensions to Amsterdam as it did everywhere in the Netherlands and Europe. Jo sent parcels via the Red Cross to captured Polish officers, and along with two friends, Annie van Calsem and Nellie Luyting, formed a women's political club, which they would eventually name *Gemma*.

When the invasion of the Netherlands came in May, Jo went home to Haarlem to be with her parents. But after the bombing of Rotterdam, after the terror of the attack

9. *Hannie Schaft*, p. 32.

had calmed down and a certain normalcy returned to Holland, she went back to her studies in Amsterdam in order to be with her Jewish friends, Sonja and Philine. Eventually, they all returned to their classes and she took and passed her final exams for the year.

Of course, nothing could be quite the same under Nazi control. There was an intense struggle undertaken by the new regime to make life in Holland in that summer of 1940 feel like it had not been changed by what began on May 10. The stifled outrage of Dutch citizens, however, as they faced the everyday presence of German troops in the streets was hard to bear. Jo's politics grew increasingly radical, and despite the presence of NSB reactionaries on campus, more vocal. Even the queen's decision to run to England, leaving the nation to its own devices, left a bad taste in her mouth.

That fall, Jo decided to live in Amsterdam with her friends and fellow Gemma-ites, Annie van Calsem and Nellie Luyting. They shared an attic flat on Michaelangelostraat, and Jo, for the first time, felt the liberty of being outside her parents' ever-watchful eyes. She dressed more stylishly, in greens and browns to enhance her red hair. Though they socialized with guys on campus, they didn't feel free enough to invite them into the apartment. It was still a conservative age. And in the first few weeks after the move, her parents were frequent visitors, just making sure that everything was all right.

Still, Jo was growing more assertive, stronger-voiced, and occasionally even sharp-tongued, especially when it came to political topics. The women read underground newspapers and listened to Radio Oranje, the voice of

Dutch resistance, which was broadcast from England (the Germans had quickly banned all radio broadcasts not emanating from the Third Reich).[10] Beyond that, there was little that Dutch students, or anyone else, could do in the face of the overwhelming German presence, aside from turning away from Wehrmacht soldiers in the street and giving them a cold shrug if they asked for directions. If they went to a theater or a concert and it was crowded with German troops, they would quickly make an exit.

The Oversteegen girls—Freddie was now fifteen years old, and Truus was about to turn seventeen—tried to resume everyday life in the wake of the invasion. When the war was just a month old, they decided to go camping with some friends at Noordwijkerhout, in the dunes southwest of Haarlem toward The Hague. They knew a farm there, owned by a man named De Wit, which had campgrounds that they had used with other members of the Dutch Youth Federation, their socialist group. Along with friends from the organization, they packed their bikes and set off on the ride to De Wit's farm.

They were greeted with somber news. Mrs. De Wit told them that a young couple, frequent visitors to the campground from Rotterdam, had died in the bombings of that city. When they were joined by fellow Youth Federation campers from The Hague and Rotterdam, their spirits were lifted. But the downcast mood of one of the newcomers, a friend from Rotterdam named Joop, soured

10. *Hannie Schaft*, p. 37.

their feelings again. It turned out that Joop's girlfriend, Elske, who had come to the De Wit farm as well, was pregnant. Like Truus and Freddie, they were still teenagers: Joop, eighteen; and Elske, just a month older than Truus.

Their lives were completely changed, not just by the pregnancy. Joop and Elske described what had happened to them during the bombing. At the height of the attack, he had looked for her in the midst of all the rubble, finally found her, and was able to steer them into a cellar, where they huddled as the explosions and chaos continued to rain down around them. So here, the two young lovers waited, terrified and lonely, expecting death to come crashing in on them at any moment. But the explosions finally stopped. The debris quit falling and they had survived, but here they were now faced with a life full of uncertainty. A child on the way just as the Nazis were sweeping over their homeland, changing all that had been familiar to them.

The dunes at Noordwijkerhout, so familiar from their youthful trips, now seemed foreign as they repacked their bicycles for the trip back to Haarlem. The country had changed irrevocably. Their youth was being robbed from them by the Germans.

It would be the last trip the girls made to Noordwijkerhout. The Nazis soon declared the dunes off limits and set up antiaircraft guns all along the coast. An airfield would soon follow near Noordwijkerhout, and the De Wits were forced to leave their farm and move to The Hague.[11]

11. *Not Then*, p. 26.

Chapter 3

THE FIRST STEPS that the Nazi occupation took in the Netherlands were primarily administrative. An Austrian named Dr. Arthur Seyss-Inquart was appointed to be the new Reich's commissioner of the country, basically supplanting the government of the Kingdom of the Netherlands in one fell swoop. Seyss-Inquart, a tall, balding, Viennese lawyer, eyes encased by thick-lensed, horn-rimmed glasses, was a longtime bureaucrat and looked it. He was an early convert to the National Socialist Party thinking espoused by Hitler, next door to Austria in neighboring Germany. Seyss-Inquart played a crucial role in formulating the Anschluss agreement, which essentially turned his native land over to Hitler and the Germans. As a consequence, he earned a reputation in Berlin as a diplomat and was sent to Amsterdam to apply those skills to the governance of the Netherlands.

The initial measures taken by Seyss-Inquart and the occupiers were intended to be conciliatory, but that was a governmental disposition that was far from second nature to the Nazis. As a first gesture toward letting bygones be bygones, the German high command decided to release all Dutch soldiers captured in the five-day war. Unfortunately, the soldiers came back to Holland underfed and poorly cared for. As well, the hard fact was that there were no jobs available to them. To alleviate the problem of an increase in unemployment, the new administration decided to employ many of these ex-soldiers in an expanded police force, which would soon come in very handy in the increasingly repressive regime that was to soon evolve.[1]

The Germans, while understanding that there would be some initial resentments in Holland, essentially viewed the Dutch as Germanic cousins and hoped ultimately that Netherlanders could be coaxed into seeing the advantages of becoming happy partners in the Third Reich. The fact that Seyss-Inquart was an Austrian was itself intended to be a concession to the Dutch, who were presumed to be more amenable to having an Austrian at the head of their government than a German. Netherlanders eyed the governance of Seyss-Inquart with more than a little skepticism right from the start. In Dutch, the pronunciation of his name sounded almost exactly the same as the pronunciation of 6¼—*zes en een kwart*—and so he quickly acquired a vaguely mocking nickname.[2] Soon after he assumed power, Seyss-Inquart traveled to devastated Rotterdam to announce that in consideration of Dutch kindnesses extended to Austrian children after World War I, he had arranged a program that would send

1. *The Lion*, p. 18.
2. Cornelius Ryan, *A Bridge Too Far*. New York: Simon & Schuster, 1974, p. 20.

20,000 children of Holland to spend the summer being well-fed and cared for by caring Austrians. While highly publicized and exploited by the Nazis, with correspondents following after the children to report on their well-nourished and sun-splashed summers, the relief effort's propaganda value was dimmed considerably by the fact that only 6,000 of the announced 20,000 children actually made the trip, and most of these were the kids of Dutch fascist NSBers.[3]

The Germans quickly established their own police system, which functioned parallel to and in command of the already existing Dutch system. Appointed by Hitler himself, the police chief was another Austrian, Hanns Albin Rauter, who came to the Netherlands as a favorite of Himmler's. He had worked as a part of the Nazi underground in Austria prior to Anschluss and subsequently rose in the ranks of Himmler's SS (Schutzstaffel) until he was given the appointment in Amsterdam.[4]

The police system that was established in the Netherlands had two central components: the Sicherheitpolizei or Security Police and the Ordnungspolizei or Order Police.

The Security Police included a State Secret Police, comparable to the Gestapo, which was designed to punish political crimes. This security service (Sicherheitsdienst), known as the SD, was the investigative branch of the Sicherheitpolizei and pointed the Gestapo in the direc-

3. *The Lion*, p. 18.
4. Werner Wambrunn, *The Dutch Under German Occupation*. Redwood City, CA: Stanford University Press, 1963, p. 40.

tion of transgressors. In time, the SD employed large numbers of Dutch undercover agents known as V-men, who infiltrated resistance groups looking for enemies of the Reich.

The Order Police (OD) were the most visible branch of the police force. Dressed in green uniforms that quickly earned them the nickname "Green Police," they were a near constant presence on the streets of Dutch cities, quickly arriving at mass raids, large-scale arrests, or battling strikes, and maintaining order at public executions. In the words of one historian, the Green Police "became the incarnation of German police terror."[5]

In the beginning these tools of fascist oppression were sublimated as Seyss-Inquart and Rauter let the Dutch people grow accustomed to the circumstances of the new regime. In keeping with the gradual assimilation of Dutch society with German values that the Nazis envisioned at the outset of the occupation, Seyss-Inquart announced that media in the Netherlands would only be subject to German guidance, rather than strict censorship. Newspapers were invited to publish an announcement that they would be free to print whatever they wished.[6] Instead of overbearing Nazi control, news copy would be filtered through a government press division, which would offer "recommendations" about appropriate subject and content. The same division would soon offer a range of topics that members in a newly established Netherlands Journal-

5. *Dutch Under*, p. 41.
6. *The Lion*, p. 271.

ists Association were encouraged to choose from. It was in this fashion that Dutch newspapers soon became dotted with stories far more sympathetic to the German way of doing things, and overt propaganda began to appear as a substitute for daily news.

Seyss-Inquart argued that for too long the Dutch had been influenced by a national press that was prejudiced against Germany and its führer. It was now time that the Dutch people were introduced to the real Hitler and his beneficent leadership. Seyss-Inquart printed and distributed a pamphlet featuring a multitude of photos that illustrated a kindhearted Adolf Hitler going about the business of leading a happy and smiling German people. There were lots of images of the führer with dogs and many groups of happy schoolchildren, relaxing at his home in the Bavarian Alps, feeding a horse, greeting a lovely woman of Berlin society. In distributing this revisionist view of Hitler to the Dutch people, Seyss-Inquart included a note that sounded more like a plea than an introduction to his beloved leader: "All I desire with this booklet is to give you a true picture of the humane being the Fuehrer is—an inexpressibly great and magnanimous man who can be hard, too, but only when necessary."[7]

Netherlanders responded by returning thousands of copies of the publication back to Seyss-Inquart's office in Amsterdam, many with postage due.

There had been some hope among Dutch Jews that they might be spared some of the horrors visited upon

7. *The Lion*, pp. 37–38.

other European Jews. German Jews had already experienced the terror of Kristallnacht and the anti-Semitic "cleansing" of the nation—the camps already constructed at Dachau and Buchenwald. Polish Jews were already being slaughtered at Auschwitz. But when the occupiers first arrived in the Netherlands, they persuaded the Dutch that they would deal with the "Jewish problem" in the country once the war was over. It was unnecessary to worry about these things immediately.[8]

In August, less than four months into the occupation, the Germans instituted their first anti-Jewish measures when they banned all Jewish religious services and rituals. Two months later, the Seyss-Inquart regime required that all government employees sign a decree declaring that they were of Aryan descent. A month later, Jews were banned from all civil service jobs in the country.

The persecution of Jews was felt intensely in Amsterdam at the university. A professor named Paul Scholten drafted a petition that would be sent to Seyss-Inquart stating that there was no Jewish problem in the Netherlands and that the measures instituted by the occupiers were diametrically opposed to Dutch values that supported religious and racial tolerance in the nation. Not only did the petition fall like water off Seyss-Inquart's back, the great majority of faculty at Amsterdam and other Dutch universities dutifully filled out the required government forms asking for verification of their Aryan ancestry.

8. *Dutch Under*, p. 62.

In November, after the dismissal of Jewish civil servants, of which university faculty members were a part, students at universities in Leiden and Delft went on strike. In Amsterdam, despite increasing unrest including protests in the central city and fights breaking out between NSB-ers and angry students, there was no strike.[9]

For Jo and her Jewish friends Sonja and Philine, the question became what outrage would take place next? And when? It was clear that anti-Semitic oppression was not going to abate anytime soon. Studying was almost impossible under the circumstances, but Jo struggled on with her classwork. She was so incensed, however, while attending a lecture taught by an accommodating professor, who allowed two NSB members to loudly express their fascist opinion, that she walked out of the classroom along with most of the other students attending. Unfortunately, this was about the extent of what she could do.

Meanwhile in Haarlem, the Oversteegen women— Truus, Freddie, and Trijntje—began their own forms of resistance that were very much in keeping with what they had done before the Nazi occupation.

The girls' connections to the socialist youth movement brought them into contact with Kees Broekman, the publisher of an anti-Nazi magazine aimed at young people called *De Koevoet*. He asked if they would be willing to distribute his journal around town, and they agreed to do so. They were already passing around copies of *De Vonk* (The Spark) and *De Waarheid* (The Truth—a banned organ of

9. *Dutch Under*, p. 148.

the Communist Party in the Netherlands, which continued to publish underground after the occupation). Meanwhile Trijntje, who had long used stenciling equipment that she kept at home to create fliers for the Party, continued to create leaflets announcing this or that meeting, which Truus and Freddie distributed to likeminded leftists in the Haarlem community.

One day late that fall, Broekman approached Truus and Freddie with a plot he was hatching. Anton Mussert, the fleshy-faced leader of the Dutch NSB, was scheduled to be in Haarlem to give a talk to his black-shirted minions in the National Socialist Party. The rally was to be outdoors, held in the Haarlemmerhout, the old city park on the south side of town. Broekman's friend, Wim Groenendaal, had borrowed a pair of wire-cutters from an electrician friend, and the two of them planned to cut the speaker wires to Mussert's microphone just as he was to begin his speech.

Broekman asked Truus and Freddie to spread the word among Haarlem's teenagers, and tell them to show up with their thumbs on their bicycle bells. When Mussert approached the stage they were to ring their bells as loudly and as long as they could.

The plan worked perfectly. When the young Blackshirts of the NSB marched in with great pomp and ceremony, followed by Mussert, an equally sizable group of Haarlem youth let loose with the bicycle bells. Mussert went to the microphone to calm everyone down and deliver his speech, only to discover the microphone had no sound.

Meanwhile, the cacophony of the bicycle bells continued like a roar.

It didn't take long for the Blackshirts to realize what was happening, and they proceeded to maul some of Haarlem's teenagers, including a fourteen-year-old boy who wound up in the hospital. They also wrecked his bicycle.

Truus and Freddie, who were of course attending the event, did their best to steer clear of the ruckus and to help their friends get away.

All in all it seemed a fine prank to play on the NSB and its mini-Hitler.[10]

But resistance in the Netherlands would soon get much more serious.

10. *Not Then*, p. 32.

Chapter 4

BY THE TIME NEW YEAR 1941 rolled around, Amsterdam had become the epicenter of unrest in the Netherlands. The city held the great majority of the nation's Jewish population (approximately eighty thousand, or three-quarters of Holland's Jews lived in Amsterdam), as well as communists, and both groups were repugnant to the Nazi overlords and their Dutch minions. Mussert's shock troops, the black-shirted members of the NSB youth organization called the WA (for "Weer-afdeeling" or weather department, an allusion to Germany's storm troopers), began to ramp up their street tactics of intimidation, stomping and elbowing their way through the Central City in Amsterdam like bully boys.

At the same time, the occupied Dutch government of Seyss-Inquart was continuing to put the screws to the Jewish population of the country. On January 10, 1941, the government decreed that all Jews needed to report to and be registered by the Bureau of Public Records, which was largely understood to be preparation for the creation of a Jewish ghetto in Amsterdam.[1]

Other official discriminatory measures were instituted like a ban on Jews visiting the cinema, while unofficially the NSB sent its black-shirted troopers out to local cafés and restaurants to encourage, with a twist of an arm here, and a fist in the face there, that NO JEWS ALLOWED signs be placed in the windows of the businesses.

Some young Amsterdam Jews began to form their own defense gangs to protect, as best they could, the Jewish quarter in the city. Inevitably there were violent clashes between these groups. Inevitably someone was killed in the ensuing melees, and it happened to be a Blackshirt named H. Koot.

The NSB immediately turned the deceased rabble-rouser into a martyr. There were loud cries and hand-wringing among the right-wing leaders of the country. H. A. Rauter, the chief of police, even claimed to Himmler, his boss and counterpart in Germany, that "a Jew had bitten through Koot's jugular vein and sucked his blood."[2] A huge demonstration in the streets of Amsterdam followed Koot's funeral. Soon thereafter, authorities shut off the Jewish quarter from the rest of the city. They also created a Jewish Council, composed of Jewish leaders chosen by the new government for their pliability and willingness to accept the fascist regime—as a means to

1. Ad van Liempt, *Hitler's Bounty Hunters*. Oxford: Berg, 2005, p. 8.
2. *Dutch Under*, p. 107.

maintain order among Jews within the city (the council would subsequently prove enormously helpful in assisting the Nazis in hijacking the wealth and treasure of Dutch Jews for export to Germany).

More fighting between the Jewish groups and the NSB followed that February until Rauter, after consultation with Himmler, determined that decisive action was needed to put a stop to all of the brawls. Of course, the jackboot came down squarely upon the Jews rather than the NSB thugs. In mid-February, the green-shirted OD, the official Order Police of the Dutch state, swept into the Jewish quarter of Amsterdam and arrested 425 young men between the ages of twenty and thirty-five and sent them off, in short order, to German concentration camps.[3]

Aside from the invasion itself, this was the first large-scale act of aggression against the Netherlands population by its occupying government. It left much of the Dutch populace stunned and incredulous—unaccustomed as it was to such oppressive acts against its own people.

Dutch communists, who had been looking for a pretext to take some action against the Seyss-Inquart government, now organized a strike, focusing their efforts largely in Amsterdam, and centered mostly around municipal workers in city transit jobs, where the Communist Party (CP) had a great deal of strength. On the morning of February 25, streetcar operators all over the city shut down, and by noon the city itself was at a standstill. Workers from private industries began to walk out of their jobs. Soon word

3. *Dutch Under,* p. 106.

of the action spread outside of the city, and workers in Zaandam, Haarlem, and Utrecht stopped working as well.[4]

The strike took the German authorities by surprise: no one went on strike in Hitler's Third Reich. Seyss-Inquart had been so sanguine after the mass arrest, assuming that it would stifle any action from the Dutch people, that he'd gone home to Austria for some rest and recreation, leaving Rauter in charge. After the initial shock, authorities made an attempt to rein in the strikers through the office of the Amsterdam mayor and the newly created Jewish Council, but to no avail. As day one of the strike moved into a second day, Rauter decided again to come down hard on the Dutch and once again turned to Himmler and the German SS for assistance.

The Germans arrived in force. By noon of the second day of the February Strike, SS officers began patrolling the streets of Amsterdam to restore order in the city. They were issued live ammunition and given permission to fire if they felt the need. They did feel the need, and nine strikers paid the price with their lives. There were a thousand arrests and numerous deportations. One hundred strike organizers were detained, and twenty of these were executed.[5]

Also executed after a trial in The Hague was Bernardus IJzerdraat, a tapestry artist from Rotterdam who had organized what many consider the first resistance force in the Netherlands. Calling themselves De Geuzen (the Beg-

4. *Hitler's Bounty Hunters*, p. 10.
5. *Hitler's Bounty Hunters*, p. 10.

gars), after the Dutch nobles who organized to fight the despotism of Spain in the sixteenth century, IJzerdraat had kept a list of its members in his home, which the Germans discovered in a raid. IJzerdraat was quickly dispatched, by rifle, in March.[6]

The strike would turn out to be the only such action taken against the Nazi regime in direct response to its treatment of Jews in all of Europe during the entirety of World War II. To leftists, and others who participated, it was a symbol of revolt, which would continue to inspire resistance long after it was over. That its root cause was the pogrom against the Jews of Amsterdam was emblematic of a continuing fight against German anti-Semitism and the programmatic measures against Jews stemming from the Nazi regime.

Of course the ferocity of the measures taken to squash the February Strike were also instructive. If it hadn't been clear before, it was now: any actions taken against the new government in the Netherlands would be met by the full force of the German police state. And the full force of the German police state was an awesome power. Fighting it in the streets of Amsterdam or any Dutch city was a losing proposition.

If there was to be resistance, it needed to be stealthy. It needed to watch its own back.

At the flat on Michaelangelostraat in Amsterdam, Jo Schaft and the Gemma club sisters lived in the midst of

6. Wikipedia, "Bernardus IJzerdraat."

the unrest of that January and February. The continuing measures taken against Jews angered and frightened Jo and her Jewish friends Sonja Frenk and Philine Polak, and the chaos in the streets raised the level of fear and anxiety as well.

On a visit home just before the February Strike, Jo spoke with her parents about Sonja and Philine and the possibility that they would need to get out of Amsterdam soon if measures were taken directly against Jewish students at the university. The tug of activity in the city soon brought her back to Amsterdam where she arrived the day before the strike. Despite her continued concerns, she felt emboldened by the action and took to the streets like so many others to protest the exportation of Jews in the wake of the murder of the thug Blackshirt Koot.

After the strike and the ensuing repression of the protesters, schoolwork and university life seemed tame, and Jo became more and more involved in the work and debates centered around the Gemma club. Under the influence of Sonja Frenk, Jo was growing even more leftist in her critique of the circumstances that led the nation and the world to this state of fascist dominance.

Her sense of history led her to be encouraged by the German invasion of the Soviet Union in June 1941. She recalled for her fellow Gemma club members the history of Napoleon's ill-fated attack of "Mother Russia" and predicted the German assault would likewise be bogged down in the morass of that massive nation.[7] Of course, any

7. *Hannie Schaft*, p. 44.

possible repercussions from that hoped-for eventuality were well into the future.

Meanwhile the restrictions against Jews continued: first, they were barred from going out in the evenings; then they were banned from public parks. As the year progressed, the school work of all the young women at Michaelangelostraat continued to suffer—how could it not under the circumstances?—and their parents began to notice. By the end of the school year in 1941, Jo's mother and father decided that they couldn't afford to pay for her share in the flat any longer, and Jo had to come home to commute to the university from their home in Haarlem. When Sonja and Philine and every other Jewish student were prohibited from attending the University of Amsterdam, they became frequent guests at the Schaft house as well.[8]

The restrictions were becoming ever more onerous: Jews were prohibited from riding public trams or trains; then they were restricted from using bicycles; then they were forced to stay indoors between the hours of eight in the evening until six in the morning. They were banned from libraries, concert halls, and restaurants. Jews were prohibited from having sex with non-Jews. Like cattle herded into barns for the evening the entire Jewish population of the Netherlands was penned indoors by the authority of the Dutch government.

The Jewish Council, created in the wake of the February Strike, became a convenient tool for the authorities to

8. *Hannie Schaft*, p. 44.

use to announce and promote the new laws. A peculiarity in Dutch social customs aided the methods of the Seyss-Inquart regime. Instituted in the late nineteenth century as a means to organize political groups and religious denominations into separate facets of the national society, the Pillar System existed well before the Nazis arrived. The system was created to deal with potentially fractious elements in the community of the Netherlands. All were encouraged and allowed a full range of expression within their individual groups. Catholics, Protestants, liberals, and socialists all lived within both the structures of the national government and their own pillar. Individuals within each pillar listened to their own radio stations (the Dutch Christian Radio Association or the Catholic Radio Broadcasting Organization or Left Broadcasting), joined that group's political party, had their own labor unions, their own newspaper, even their own sports' club.[9]

Jews in the Netherlands had never had their own pillar prior to World War II. As a group they were just too small in number to merit that distinction, so they were folded into the socialist pillar. When the Jewish Council was created at the behest of the Seyss-Inquart regime, no matter how coerced its decrees might be, they were perversely legitimized within the context of the Pillar System. From then onward, whatever transpired through the auspices of the Jewish Council were matters of the Jewish community and best handled within that "pillar."

The tradition of cataloging citizens allowed a kind of

9. See discussion in *Amsterdam*, p. 266; see also *Dutch Under*, pp. 61–68.

acquiescence among others in Dutch society to the dangerous distinctions that were isolating and threatening Jews in the Netherlands. When the Germans determined that all Dutch citizens needed a new personal identity card, few batted an eye when it was ordered that all Jews have a large J stamped on their IDs. Of course the new identity cards made it much easier for the Nazis to locate Jews. It also helped enable the next measure to come.

In Amsterdam in the spring of 1942, a young Jewish girl named Anne Frank, her sister, and all members of the Frank family were required to pin or sew a yellow cotton star on their coats so that all the world knew that they were *Juden*. Why not make it immediately obvious to every person on the street or in a shop or on the tram, who and who was not a Jew?

It was just the most glaring of a string of attacks on her and all the Jews of Holland. A year earlier, Anne and her sister Margot were forced out of the school that they'd attended since their education began. They were sent, again by decree, to an all-Jewish secondary education high school.

Her father, Otto Frank, a Jewish veteran of the German Army in World War I, had been forced to transfer control of his business to Aryan partners months earlier. In preparation for what he sensed was to come, Otto had arranged for a hidden annex behind his business on the Prinsengracht, one of the series of semi-circular canals that mark and ring the City Center, to be converted into a living quarter for his family. He knew by this time, as did every

Jew in the city, that there would be no exceptions in liberal-minded Holland to the German solution to what Hitler and all his followers had long ago labeled "The Jewish Problem" in Europe.

That summer, in response to all these measures, and to aid her two Jewish friends at the University of Amsterdam, Johanna Schaft committed her first *illegality*. At a public pool in Amsterdam, as two young women of similar age to Sonja and Philine were swimming laps, Jo snuck into the changing room, rifled through their lockers until she found their identity cards, and then pocketed them. No doubt, she hurried from the pool with her head down and her hands in her pockets, not daring to look left or right. A friend of a friend would know how to make counterfeit cards. Jo would soon hand them off and in return get counterfeits for Sonja and Philine.[10]

In a matter of days, the first large-scale gathering of Jews to be sent off to labor camps in Germany began in Amsterdam.

10. *Hannie Schaft*, p. 44.

Chapter 5

IN HAARLEM, THE OVERSTEEGEN GIRLS, along with their mother Trijntje, had been involved in *illegalities* for months. Even before the February 1941 strike, Truus went with her mother to a potato-seller in the Grote Markt named Rinus Hoebeke, a good Communist Party man. He took Trijntje aside and pulled a wrapped package of fliers from beneath his vegetables. Could she use her stencils to make more of these announcements of the coming strike? And then could the girls distribute them at the tram garage, a stocking factory, and a couple of other small manufacturers in Haarlem? "Don't get yourselves caught" were his parting words of warning to mother and daughter.

Trijntje cut the stencils and rolled out the ink for the fliers, and the girls dutifully distributed them to the workers around Haarlem, along with their friends Jan Heusdens and Wim Groenendaal. The strike didn't have as massive an impact in Haarlem as it had in Amsterdam, yet many people had taken to the streets. Trijntje took Robbie, and Freddie went out with some women from the Leiden Gate neighborhood in Haarlem, and they joined a number of strikers from a local shirt factory. Kees Broekman and his wife tried to rally workers at Hoogovens steel plant with mixed success.

Meanwhile, Truus—curious about what was happening in Amsterdam—pedaled to the city the afternoon of the strike along with other Haarlemmers, wondering how the strike was going at its epicenter. She found groups of people everywhere, cheering, raising signs, and debating with one another. She helped a man distribute strike pamphlets in mailboxes up and down the canals and streets. Truus started to worry about the fact that there were no Germans on hand to thwart any of this, and she found herself warning others about an impending visit from the SS. But she had little effect: Who was she but a teenage girl passing out strike literature?

Soon enough the German motorcycles with their tidy little sidecars came roaring into the city, and the crowds were dispersed.

Truus pedaled home exhausted and found her mother and Freddie waiting for her, frantic with worry because she'd neglected to tell them that she was going to Amsterdam.[1]

The girls continued to distribute anti-Nazi pamphlets as well as the leftist newspapers *De Vonk* (The Spark) and *De Waarheid* (The Truth). Just before Queen's Day at the end of April, Freddie and Truus rode their bikes around town

1. *Not Then*, p. 33.

putting up homemade banners over the German posters calling for Dutch workers to help in Germany. The banner said: "Don't go to Germany! For every Dutch man working in Germany, a German man will go to the front!"[2]

Trijntje and the girls continued to hide undocumented families, the *onderduikers*, literally, the undercovers, of Dutch society, including German Jews. They had moved from their flat to a house, which afforded them a pair of tiny attic bedrooms they used for their guests. While Truus slept on the couch, Freddie slept on two chairs pushed together beside her sister in the living room, and Trijntje and Robbie slept in a bed in the front room of the home. Since the Oversteegens were still subsisting on Dutch government welfare, a Jewish charity offered a little extra cash to help subsidize the safekeeping of those families who came through.[3]

In the summer of 1941, the Kaufman family arrived and stayed long enough for the girls to get to know them and learn some of their traditions. The father was Jerrit, the mother was Hannah, and they had two little boys. Another woman, Mrs. Frank, was staying with the family at the time. Trijntje had taught Truus and Freddie to say *gut shabbes*, which pleased the Kaufmans. The girls had learned a song in the socialist youth camp that Truus called "a Yiddish tearjerker." When they sang it for their guests, giving it their best dramatic performance, their botched pronunciation prompted snickers that swelled

2. *Under Fire*, p. 143.
3. *Under Fire*, p. 143.

into gales of laughter. Truus and Freddie didn't mind. It lightened everyone's mood.

The Kaufmans kept kosher, and their food and utensils were supplied by the same Jewish organization that was subsidizing their expenses. On Friday nights, Truus and Freddie would light the candles for the family and listen to Jerrit singing the prayers upstairs for his family. On at least one occasion, the Kaufmans shared their cake with the Oversteegens as thanks for all their considerations.[4]

The dangers of housing *onderduikers* became more acute as the year progressed. One evening, during the Kaufmans' stay, there was a knock on the door. Trijntje instantly went on high alert, looking hurriedly around the room to see if there was any evidence visible of the family in the attic. Of course Truus, Freddie, and Robbie followed suit, but they saw nothing that would give away the Kaufmans.

There was another more insistent knock. Taking her time, Trijntje rose from her chair, peeked outside through a window, and only then opened the door.

A large man, an acquaintance of Trijntje's from her meetings, stood in the doorway with a smaller man shadowed behind. Their mother let the pair in as Truus and Freddie, all watchfulness and nerves, huddled together in the living room.

The first man, the big one, spilled out the story of the second man to the Oversteegens. The Huns were after

4. *Not Then*, pp. 36–37.

him. He needed a hiding place. Did Trijntje know anyone
who could take him in?

After some discussion, it was determined that he should
be escorted downtown to a shopkeeper who lived above
his own radio and gramophone repair store. It was always
better under these circumstances to send a man with a
woman than to pair two men together. At this time of
night in particular, it was seen as more natural. Truus was
given the assignment of guiding the man there. Their instructions were to lock arms as if they were a couple and
to proceed with caution. In Truus's estimation, proceed
with caution was hardly explicit advice.

They bumped into each other as they stepped into the
night, trying to get the rhythm of their locked arm walk.
The night was still, every sound exaggerated. Truus felt
the double unease of the chore that had been given her
and the fact that her arm was locked with a young man of
about her own age.

Suddenly, Truus sensed a presence behind them. She
stole a backward glance and saw a man keeping pace with
them a few meters to their rear. "Run!" she said to her
companion, pulling her arm out of his. The two of them
took off on a dead sprint through the streets and alleys of
downtown Haarlem. Through backyard gates and tightly
wound streets, over cobblestone and canals. It seemed
like miles before Truus finally felt safe enough from the
shadow for them to sit and catch her breath. She was
breathing hard and sweating and so was the stranger she
was helping. She remembered that he'd been introduced

to the family as Arie. They looked at each other, bound by their own terror. Arie took her hand at that moment, brought it up to his lips, and kissed it with gratitude.[5]

Between the terror of the moment, the fear in Arie's eyes, and the sensitivity of that kiss on her teenage hand, Truus was a puddle of conflicting emotions.

"This is Arie," she said to the shopkeeper when they arrived at his store a few moments later, urging her companion forward. She didn't want to look Arie in the eye. "Can he stay with you? The Big Man"—meaning the tall man who had brought Arie to her home earlier—"will take care of things." She meant that the Big Man would explain to the shopkeeper when Arie would need to be taken to his next stop after the shopkeeper.

"Are you Trijntje's daughter?" the shopkeeper asked.

He only meant it as a means to be certain about who was certifying the bona fides of this exchange, but the question made Truus nervous. "Yes, but you aren't allowed to talk about that," she said.

"Okay, okay," the shopkeeper said, smiling, obviously more at ease than Truus was. She stole a final glance at Arie, still feeling his kiss on her hand, understanding, but not quite fully, its meaning. She said good-bye. Good luck. Her face was still flush when she got home that night.[6]

"Everything all right?" her mother asked.

"Everything went fine," Truus said.

5. *Not Then*, p. 38.
6. *Not Then*, pp. 37–39.

She slept again on the couch that night. Freddie lay beside her in the two pushed-together chairs with the Kaufmans upstairs in the attic.

Not long after, it was time for the Kaufmans to move on. The Jewish charity had determined that Trijntje's leftist activities made her home too great a risk for hiding families.

They would learn later that the Kaufman family was ultimately discovered and shipped to the camps. They did not survive the Holocaust.[7]

Like most sisters, Truus and Freddie did not always get along. Truus, as the older of the two, was more assertive and dictatorial, and felt she was entitled to boss Freddie around. Freddie on the other hand was eager to display her independence. Freddie had grown into a pretty young woman with soft curls in her hair, a dimpled chin, and a smile that was both mischievous and fetching. She moved with the lightness of a dancer and flitted about Haarlem like a sprite on her bicycle.

Truus was more of a tomboy than her younger sister, particularly when she put her hair up under a cap to bike. Her mannerisms were like a guy: she would sit with her knees apart, taking more than her share of space on the couch, while Freddie's legs were always carefully crossed and unobtrusive. The truth was that Freddie could be an annoying little sister, a bit of a tagalong, and more than willing to let Truus take the lead when it suited her, the

7. *Under Fire*, p. 143.

better to carp at her decisions later. And Truus could be a bit of a bully with the casual arrogance of a big sister.

Still they worked well together. To distribute the *Trouw* newspapers, they worked as a team. One of the girls would serve as a lookout while the other stuffed the paper into the bags of strangers riding the bus or walking on the street. To advertise itself, the paper, which was published by the Party, devised bold slogans cut from stencils made by Trijntje and pasted on the walls by the girls. They felt free to paste right over the German announcements posted all around the city. One of the girls would stand blocking the view of passersby while the other worked on the wall.

After the German invasion of Russia, the girls were given a large banner to place directly over some government announcements on a wall by the side of the train tracks to Heemstede. It was a tribute to the Brave Russian People, which was a lot of words to plaster up on a wall under duress, but working together, the girls managed it. They were particularly pleased with this one. The bold sign became the talk of Haarlem, and the girls took pride in their joint labor.[8]

They were of similar mind on another matter too: when Frans van der Wiel showed up at their front door—tall and slim, and wearing a fedora and long wool coat over a jacket and tie—both could appreciate his movie-star looks.

It was Trijntje who went to the door at his knock. She

8. *Hannie Schaft*, p. 57.

knew who he was through her Party connections, and immediately let him in. Meanwhile, Truus and Freddie were peeking through the sliding glass doors to the entryway, whispering and elbowing each other. They tried to be cool when their mother opened the doors and introduced him to her daughters.

Frans was quite formal, taking off his hat and shaking first Truus's hand and then Freddie's. He introduced himself, and much to Truus's chagrin—she didn't want to seem *déclassé*—sat in the lumpiest chair in their living room. She and Freddie were surprised when their mother excused herself and left the girls alone with their guest.

Her reasons quickly became apparent when Frans announced the purpose of his visit. Frans was putting together a resistance group in Haarlem and had heard from members of the Party that Truus and Freddie were intrepid activists in the movement. What he had in mind was a lot more subversive, a lot more violent, and a lot more dangerous than anything they had been doing before. Their tasks would include acts of sabotage and the use of weapons. He mentioned the Russian partisans as an example of the sort of organization he had in mind. The first rule of the group would be that they could not breathe a word about what they were doing to anyone, not even to their mother.

In the Soviet Union, women and girls had been fighting the Germans since the invasion began. The Huns typically underestimated women, and the last thing they expected was for young women to be fighters. Which would make Truus and Freddie especially valuable to the Dutch cause.

Truus and Freddie might be called upon to blow up bridges and trains. They would have to learn how to use a pistol, throw grenades, and detonate bombs. As Frans lit a cigarette and fixed the girls with a sobering stare, he asked, "Do you think you could shoot someone?"

It was an extraordinary question to put to two teenage girls. Then again, with Holland occupied by a foreign nation, the streets filled with black-shirted thugs, and helmeted Germans roaring around on motorcycles and sidecars, these were hardly ordinary times.

Freddie was first to respond. "I've never done that before!" she blurted out, which was obvious enough already.

Truus was more circumspect, genuinely considering the question, as if she had been mulling over the possibility for a long time. And, in fact, both of the Oversteegen sisters had been reared on the fringes of radical political behavior. They had been part of their mother and father's political lifestyle from infancy onward. She thought about the day earlier that year when she thought she and Arie were being followed. If she had had a weapon and they had been apprehended by the man in the shadows, what would she have done? Would she have been able to pull the trigger?

Yes, she told Frans, she thought she could kill "a real fascist, a swine who takes people from their homes to have them executed." But she hesitated over other possibilities: not all Germans soldiers were Nazis after all.

Frans assured her crisply that in his resistance group they would make certain that any executions would be Gestapo or blatant traitors. There would be no mistakes.

He mentioned the Guezens, the first Dutch resistance group. He said that they'd been betrayed from within, that there might be circumstances when the girls would be asked to take action against one of their fellow Dutch citizens, a traitor to the cause. Could they do that?

As for the idea that not all Germans were bad, Frans was almost contemptuous. The Nazis controlled Germany and they had invaded Holland. They actually thought they were being kind to the Dutch, but what was to come would only get worse. They would cut back on liberties; they would reduce food and clothing. They would take everything that wasn't nailed down.

The interview came to an end when Frans stood up. The sound of shuffling chairs brought Trijntje back to the living room. Acting formal again, he tipped his hat and bid the girl's mother adieu. Truus and Freddie walked him to the door, where he whispered that he'd need an answer in two days.

He added an ominous note: once they were in the group, there would be no turning back.

Back in the living room, Trijntje quizzed her daughters about what exactly he had asked of them. Although she knew he was from the Party, she did not know what his plan was for her girls.

Truus lied to her mother. She told Trijntje that Frans wanted them for some simple errands suitable for girls. Nothing dangerous.

There must have been something in her face or Freddie's that suggested this wasn't the full truth. Trijntje was suddenly very quiet. Then she told them that she would check with others in the Party about the reliability of this Frans van der Wiel.

What she said next would stay with them for the rest of their lives. "You are free to undertake anything against the Nazis that you feel is right," she said. "But be careful and don't let each other down when things get dangerous."

Then she spoke from a deep spot in her heart: "I couldn't be without you. I hope you'll never do anything mean or anything against your better judgment. Stay human always and under all circumstances."[9]

The girls and Trijntje went back to Rinus Hoebeke, the potato seller in the Grote Markt, to get some sense of who Frans van der Wiel was and whether or not he could be trusted. Rinus was somewhat reassuring. He said that he didn't know where van der Wiel was from but that he was a good man. On the strength of that partial endorsement, and with nothing else to go on, the girls nervously agreed to meet with Frans when he sent a message with directions to a home on Wagenweg.

The girls bravely rode their bicycles to the address on Wagenweg, which turned out to be an outright mansion, right on the boulevard. Two white columns and a tiled Mansard roof distinguished the house, as did a beautiful stretch of woods that grew on all sides and behind it. A pair of marble sphinxes stared impassively out at them

9. *Not Then*, pp. 40–43.

from either side of the front door. This was not the sort of home Freddie and Truus were accustomed to in Haarlem unless they were there to do housework.

They had been told to meet Frans at a pond in the back. As they pushed their bikes down a path around the side of the gray brick mansion, they passed a room full of glass windows like a greenhouse built onto the side of the house. Later they would learn that this was the estate of Mari Andriessen, one of Holland's best-known sculptors, and the glass room was his studio.[10]

"Hello, ladies," Frans said from out of the shadows of a dusky winter's eve, startling Truus and Freddie. His movie star looks were starting to wear thin, Truus thought.

In the shadows they could now make out a pond overgrown with weeds and algae; beside it was a moldy stone bench. Frans indicated that they should sit.

As he had when visiting them at their home, Frans got quickly to the point. He described his vision for the resistance group—that it would be quite small and autonomous from other resistance organizations and that the girls would be a crucial part of whatever action they were taking. Here he paused in his description. "By the way," he asked, "can you give me the address of Karel Mok?"

Both Truus and Freddie were silent. They knew Karel Mok through their mother's Party connections. They knew that he was not only a communist, but Jewish as well,

10. Mari Andriessen, in *Woord en Beeld, Librariana,* online, April 26, 2018.

and despite these two very dangerous strikes against him, he continued to work within the Party. Both of the girls knew his address, but they would be damned if they'd give it to this near stranger, no matter if he was certified—sort of—by Rinus Hoebeke.

They tried changing the subject. Whose pond was this anyway? Why were they meeting here?

Before they could get another word out, Frans had pulled a revolver out of his coat pocket and pointed it directly at them. The movement was so quick and unexpected that the girls were left speechless, their minds lagging behind an immediate understanding of what was happening.

"The address, please," he said, waving the gun at both girls at once. "I'm sorry to tell you this, but I am Gestapo and I need to know where Karel Mok lives." He pulled some papers out of his coat pocket and flashed them in their direction long enough so that they could see they were covered in stamps and swastikas. He tucked them back into his coat pocket.

"Bastard," Truus said. "Let me see those one more time."

As he reached back into the pocket, Freddie sprang at him as did Truus, an instant later. She kicked at the pistol and hit his wrist, sending the gun flying. Freddie went for his throat and Truus got on his chest. Their combined weight pinned him to the ground beside the pond, where they continued to throw punches and elbows at his head and ribs.

Frans suddenly went limp, no longer resisting. "Stop! Stop!" he cried, no longer the cocksure, hat-tipping movie star. "They told me to do it!" he said, instinctively holding up his arms against blows that had stopped coming. "They wanted me to test you."

Slowly the girls eased off him, surveying the damage they had done: Frans had a bloody nose, a cut lip, a bruised eye that would turn black by the time they next saw him.

The girls were also battered, particularly Freddie whose blouse was ripped, to go along with a strap broken on her shoes, a bruised finger, and a bleeding knee.

A steady string of apologies mixed with more explanations spewed from Frans as they all stood up and caught their breath. He had orders to test how dependable the girls would be. He was so sorry, but he had to do it. It was what was expected of a resistance fighter. This was serious business. How can we ever make it up to you?

Truus put the pistol in her own pocket and spat at Frans's hand when he offered it.

"Well, are you happy?" Freddie asked him.

Still catching their breath, exhausted by what had just happened, the sisters shared a glance of disbelief. What kind of business was this? What kind of operation was this guy running?

As they picked up their bikes and started to walk out of the woods, their dignity began to seep back into their carriage. By the time they were out of the trees and brush, they ignored all aches and pains and walked straight, heads held high, to Wagenweg. For all their outrage, the simple fact of the matter was that the sisters had just teamed up to kick the hell out of a guy who'd pulled a gun on them.

In another age, they might have given each other high fives as they started to pedal home. But a hard question was also roiling around in their minds: if Frans was actually serious and legitimate, if the test had the genuine purpose of testing their readiness for the difficult tasks of resistance, did they really want to be part of this?[11,12]

11. *Not Then*, p. 47.
12. This scene, including interviews with Truus and Freddie, is dramatized in the German documentary television series, *Schottenkampf: Europas Resistance gegen die Nazis, 1941–1942.*

Chapter 6

WITH A FEW DRAMATIC EXCEPTIONS—the general strike in 1941 being the most notable—resistance efforts in the Netherlands in the first couple of years of occupation were largely made up of nonviolent, covert underground activities that were already familiar to the Oversteegen sisters. A broad and lively anti-German press continued to publish a number of papers, including *De Waarheid* and *De Vonk*, which Truus and Freddie continued to distribute, as well as papers like *Trouw* (The Faith), *Vrij Nederland* (Free Netherlands), and *Het Parool* (The Motto). In all forms, including local edition papers, single broadsheets stenciled in kitchens, religious papers, neighborhood news bulletins, and more, it is estimated that almost thirteen hundred illegal newspapers were printed and distributed during the occupation.[1]

An underground press was a crucial need during the occupation. As one observer put it, "In the legal news-

1. Verzets Resistance Museum, Amsterdam. Online exhibit: Themes WWII Resistance: "Illegal Press."

papers there was nothing but propaganda; the Germans won just about everything there was to win. Reading the illegal newspapers was important to the course of the war. It gave you strength. I got *Trouw* from someone living in my street, and *Het Parool* was delivered to the door. My father, being Jewish, refused to have anything to do with it. He was afraid. That's why we read the newspapers on the sly."[2]

The tenor of resistance began to change, however, the deeper into war the world plunged, and the greater the stakes of life and liberty in the Netherlands. As the United States entered the war in Europe after Pearl Harbor and fighting on the Eastern Front took on a massive scale for the Germans, the Third Reich entered a new phase of intensity in its efforts to wage war on multiple fronts. In Holland, Germany began to strip its conquered territory of resources in order to finance and produce the all-encompassing war that it had begun.

The Reich began to exploit the Netherlands in new and ominous ways. In December 1941, winter clothing was demanded from Dutch manufacturers to help keep German soldiers from freezing in Russia, never mind how it might leave the needy in the Netherlands. A lack of scarce metals led the Germans to confiscate Dutch currency; copper, nickel, and silver coins were replaced by zinc. And soon began raids on one of the dearest of possessions for the citizens of the Netherlands: the green shirts began to round up and confiscate Dutch bicycles for the use of Ger-

2. Verzets online exhibit: "Illegal Press."

man military men. By the end of 1942 more than a hundred thousand bicycles had been stolen from Hollanders
for Wehrmacht use, primarily on the Eastern Front. And
parts like rubber tires, spokes, and chains were as scarce
as hen's teeth.[3]

Even more unsettling demands began in the spring of
1942 when the Germans started drafting labor from
many different occupied countries in Europe. In the
Netherlands, it had relied primarily on coerced, but still
essentially voluntary, labor in the first couple of years of
the occupation. Then a series of measures were begun
that would eventually lead to a full exploitation of Dutch
workers.

In typical German fashion, it was all done systematically
and in a careful step-by-step process. First, all unemployed
persons between the ages of eighteen and forty were
forced to register with employment offices. Then Dutch
employers were forced to seek permission to hire new
workers under the age of forty. Soon after, German authorities began sending special forces to the Netherlands
to round up skilled workers to help build weapons in German armament industries. Hollanders unwilling to go to
the Reich were sent to labor camps or directly to Deutschland. All told 162,000 workers were deported from the
Netherlands to Germany in 1942.[4]

Even as the screws of Nazi oppression were turned

3. *Dutch Under,* p. 71.
4. *Dutch Under,* p. 74.

tighter, armed resistance was slow to develop in the Netherlands. There were a number of formidable obstacles. The swift and overwhelming victory of German forces in the invasion stifled any initial ideas of resistance with a sense of hopelessness. And the fact that the queen and government had abandoned the country left any resistance movement without a central rallying point within the Netherlands itself.

The overbearing proximity of Germany to the Netherlands, along with long-standing cultural ties, which Germany continually tried to exploit, led many in Holland to reject the most drastic measures of rebelling against the oppression. As the strength of the NSB in the Netherlands suggests as well, many in the country were sympathetic to the ideas of German nationalism. There was also an inescapable feeling of defeatism among many, a sense that the future might actually reside in the tenets of fascism.

Another element of geography also slowed the growth of the resistance, according to a historian of the Office of Strategic Services (OSS), the World War II precursor to the Central Intelligence Agency (CIA) in the United States. "The lack of mountainous and forested terrain prevented the establishment of hiding areas for large groups of *maquis*." The flat terrain, and the many bodies of water and waterways, "confined movement to the established railroads, road networks, and bridges which were easily controlled by the Germans, who established checkpoints to curtail freedom of movement. Gasoline was scarce, and many Dutch used bicycles for transportation, sometimes riding on the rims because of a shortage of rubber for tires."[5]

Slowly, however, in largely independent groups that in time would coalesce with other like-minded resisters, a number of resistance groups emerged in the Netherlands. Some focused on continuing efforts at underground work dedicated to weakening the stranglehold of Nazi oppression in the Netherlands. Others focused on the increasing need to shelter the most endangered members of society from roundups, arrests, and deportations—Jews, communists, workers, and soon Dutch Army veterans.

Along with the need to hide hundreds of thousands came a concomitant need to feed and care for those in danger who couldn't help themselves. A fact that gave rise to the sort of dangerous *illegalitie* that Jo Schaft had first participated in when she stole identity cards from the gymnasium in Haarlem for her Jewish friends—and one that Jo soon began making a habit of in Haarlem and Amsterdam as she commuted back and forth between her parents' home and her strained but continuing education at the university.

Beyond stealing IDs and stamps, hiding *onderduikers*, and participating in the production of underground papers and journals, however, there were some Dutch resisters, like Frans van der Wiel, clamoring to strike violently at their German oppressors.

5. Stewart Bentley, "The Dutch Resistance and the O.S.S." Central Intelligence Agency, Spring 1998, cia.gov/library.

* * *

It was an odd assembly that gathered in Kenau Park on a spring evening in 1942. Two full-grown adult men, two younger men, and two teenage girls, most smoking cigarettes, as they talked quietly in a corner of the park off the winding paths—not far from the canal that circled lazily through the greenery. The Oversteegen girls knew Jan Heusdens from other actions. He was a small man on the lam from the Nazis for vague, unspecified reasons having to do with activities in Rotterdam. They also knew Cor Rusman, an older man, a bricklayer from Haarlem, who had prior associations with the communists of the city, including the girls' mother. Wim Groenendaal, their old Haarlem friend was in the park, too, along with the leader, Frans van der Wiel, whose two earlier encounters with the girls were still vivid.

In time a few others would join the group: two hard-handed laborers from Hoogovens: a handsome, curly-haired young man named Jan Bonekamp and his workmate Jan Brasser, who went by the *nom de guerre* Witte Ko (the White Cow); along with Henk de Ronde and Frans's brother, Alexander. But at the first gathering it was just Freddie, Truus, and the four guys.

Heusdens and Groenendaal had been, along with the Oversteegen girls, part of the *Trouw* and *Waarheid* group in Haarlem, members of the team that had done small jobs for the people involved with the production and distribution of the papers. Though they themselves were not necessarily communists or Party members, they would eventually emerge as the core of the local branch of the sabotage team that would eventually call itself the Haarlem Council of Resistance, the Raad van Verzet, or RVV.

The Haarlem RVV was ultimately linked to a wider organization of the same name, whose hallmark was a willingness to perform duties of armed resistance. "Most of the members of this Haarlem team [were] ordinary boys, workers, all driven by resistance from left-wing political views," remembered Truus Oversteegen. "I don't think you can say that our team, especially the later Council of Resistance, was a communist group. It contained communists, but also what we called at the time: members of the Freethinkers' Association, Anarchists, Trotzkyites, Socialists. It all blended together." The distinction would become more important in time, both as the war progressed and afterward.[6]

Frans van der Wiel was the unquestioned leader of the group. He recruited the members, he organized the meeting, he took the lead and issued directives that were less commands than strong suggestions that the others were allowed to debate and question, but usually follow. Frans had served as a corporal in the Dutch army before the war, and in civilian life marketed honey in Haarlem.[7] On his own initiative he began to organize this group a few months before he approached Truus and Freddie. To the girls, he quickly evinced a couple of obvious traits that were both powerful and a little disconcerting: he seemed

6. *Hannie Schaft*, p. 56.
7. *Hannie*, p. 42.

to have a deep hatred of Germans and little fear on his own behalf, or on behalf of the members of the group in pursuing risks in attacking this enemy. He wanted men and women saboteurs with similar characteristics. They sensed quickly that they would need an enormous amount of courage and perseverance to remain a part of Frans's cell.

The subject of their gathering was weaponry—specifically, their need for it. The pistol that Frans had employed in his charade with the girls a few weeks earlier was the only firearm currently in the group's possession. And it was, in fact, a pretty miserable representative of firearms in general. Truus described it as "dating back to the time when the hunter/gatherers came to settle."[8] It had been dug up from a hiding place in the garden of a Dutch army officer, and no one was absolutely certain whether it would fire forward or backward or if it would fire at all.

In the early stages of the resistance, the only real source for weapons in the community was their enemy: the Germans. Of course, getting arms from the Wehrmacht wasn't as easy as simply asking for them. They would have to be taken, and discussing that necessity, and how to achieve it, was the reason Frans had gathered them in the park.

He had something to show them all that he felt would help in their task. He went to his bicycle and retrieved two bundles, revealing their contents as if they were treasure. Wrapped in the first of the packages was a heavy bayonet acquired from a backyard dig at the home of a veteran,

8. *Not Then*, p. 48.

similar to the old pistol's procurement. Inside the second bundle was a wicked-looking kris, a twisting, corkscrew-style knife of Indonesian tradition and origin, which was no doubt a souvenir of some Haarlemmer's visit to the Dutch East Indies colony in the distant or not so distant past.

There was more than a little incredulity among the stalwarts gathered in the park when the gist of Frans's plans for these daggers became apparent. His idea, basically, was to use these knives to "trade up" in weaponry. Some members of the group would have to kill armed Germans with the kris or bayonet and then grab their sidearms in order to build the RVV's arsenal.

Tonight, their job was to go out and look for German targets. Get the feel of trailing the enemy. Look for marks. Look for opportunities to attack. If they saw one, take it.

Freddie might have been a fierce fifteen-year-old girl, but standing all of five feet tall, she was hardly a match for a burly "green sleeve"—the green-uniformed police in the OD. She could be forgiven for openly expressing her doubts about the plan. "You see, he is crazy," she said to her sister.

Jan, too, was full of doubts. "He must have read too many cowboy stories," he said.

But Frans was unfazed. When a group of strollers happened by too near to their business, he quickly resorted to the unlikely cover that he had suggested earlier to the others as a means to disguise what they were doing together in the park: they were to pretend to be a fitness group and he would pretend to be their coach. He loudly gave them a few exercise instructions and then told his group of would-be assassins to meet back there on Sunday in sports clothes.[9]

The passersby could have cared less about what they were doing.

Jan was hardly much taller than Freddie, which was one of the reasons that Frans wanted to send the two of them out together, posing as a couple, to scout potential victims. The only problem was that Wim, who would have otherwise been paired with Truus, was in charge of the collection at his church that night, which meant that Truus and Jan were the ones who went out together looking for SS officers to shadow. Freddie followed behind them at a discreet distance on her bicycle.

Frans had mapped out a route for Truus and Jan to explore, and it wasn't long before they actually happened upon an SS officer walking through the city. They followed at a safe distance for a time, then got close enough to the German for Truus to smell the sweat of his body—though she wondered later if it wasn't her own sweat she was picking up on. Quicker than she wanted it to happen, she actually saw Jan pull the kris from inside his coat. Was he really going to do it? Truus came to a halt and shut her eyes, not daring to look or breathe. A grateful moment later she realized Jan was still at her side, that he hadn't plunged the awful knife into the back of the German.

Freddie biked up to them afterward, also thankful that

9. *Not Then*, p. 49.

nothing had happened. "We aren't tough enough for this," she said to her sister and Jan.

Truus had caught her breath. Her heart was still racing, but she was feeling somewhat braver. "If the bastard had attacked us it would have been a different story, but I really can't do it this way," she said.[10]

Sometime later that night, they all caught up with Frans and returned the unbloodied knife to him.

"Well, this means we'll have to figure out a different way to get some hardware," was all he said.

"We didn't sign up to be SS," Truus said to him in parting.

Later Frans would tell her that he never really expected them to do the job. Obviously, he liked to play these testing little games with his recruits.[11]

10. *Not Then*, p. 51.
11. *Not Then*, p. 51.

Chapter 7

STILL STUDYING IN AMSTERDAM, Jo Schaft existed in the middle of a chaotic world that combined law school studies, looking out for her Jewish friends—Sonja and Philine—and her continued *illegalities*, at which she had become so proficient that the underground women to whom she'd brought the first stolen IDs for Sonja and Philine were now making specific requests of Jo. Erna Kropveld said she could ask Jo to get a card for a forty-year-old woman, and just hours later, Jo would return with the same.[1]

That summer and fall of 1942, the terrible times really began for the Jewish community in the Netherlands. In June, an agency called the Zentralstelle for Jewish Emigration informed the Jewish Council that the Reich needed Jewish labor in Germany and deportations of Dutch Jews were to begin immediately. The carefully maintained Bureau of Population Records was consulted, including records of the special Jewish census conducted the year before, and the roundup of Jews, primarily from Amster-

1. *Hannie Schaft*, p. 46.

dam, began in full force. More than six thousand Jews were forcibly gathered in raids conducted in July and shipped to transit camps at Vught in the southern Netherlands (Vught would be turned into a full-fledged concentration camp a year later) and at Westerbork in northeastern Holland, only twenty-five miles from the German border.

The camp at Westerbork was originally built by the Dutch in 1939, well before the Nazis arrived. It was intended to house the influx of Jewish refugees arriving in the Netherlands from Germany at the time to serve as a refugee way station toward acclimation in Holland.[2] That it would wind up now as a way station for shipment to Auschwitz was a simple, yet horrible, historical irony.

The camp was built in a desolate corner of Holland in an area of scrubby trees and heathland. The first large-scale arrivals in the late summer and fall of 1942 were generally kept for several months as more and more Dutch Jews began to fill the camp to overflowing. An overflowing Westerbork meant a steady shipment of individuals and families to the camps in Germany.

It was at this time in Amsterdam that the family of Otto Frank, including his teenage daughter Anne, began their long stay in the hideaway behind Frank's office building near the Prinsengracht. Anne began keeping her famous diary that June, and the family entered its hiding place in the secret annex on July 9. They carried school satchels and shopping bags from their old home in the Jewish sector of Amsterdam. "We got sympathetic looks from people

2. *Why the Dutch*, p. 142.

on their way to work," Anne wrote that night. "You could see by their faces how sorry they were they couldn't offer us a lift; the gaudy yellow star spoke for itself."[3]

In the densely populated Netherlands a segment of the population became active in the difficult task of hiding Jews, workers, and others sought by the Nazis, while another group, many of them connected to the NSB, were just as interested in turning *onderduikers* over to the authorities (this group would soon be incentivized when the "Final Solution"—the extermination of all Jews in Europe—was fully implemented and the *Zentralstelle* in the Netherlands decided to a put a bounty on the heads of all Jews who were still unaccounted for in the rolls of Dutch Jewry). A game of cat and mouse developed between the two sides as the numbers of those hiding and those being sent to the camps both grew.

A group of like-minded Dutch resisters called the LO, the National Organization for Aid to Those in Hiding (Landelijke Organisatie voor Hulp aan Onderduikers) evolved out of efforts of a housewife named Helena Kuipers-Rietberg and a minister of the Reformed Church in the Netherlands named Frederick (Frits) Slomp. Slomp was an early resistance leader, who became an itinerant preacher against the occupation in 1942. Fearing capture on public transportation, he traveled across the country by bicycle, giving illicit sermons against the Nazis to Dutch churchgoers, among whom in Winterswijk in southeast-

3. Anne Frank, *Diary of a Young Girl.* New York: Doubleday, 1967, p. 16.

ern Holland, were Helena Kuipers-Rietberg and her husband.

An organization like the LO was needed to help organize efforts at supporting those who had disappeared. But more assistance was necessary to keep *onderduikers* safely undercover. Over the years, Germans introduced all sorts of official documents to keep the Dutch under control: work exemptions, bicycle permits, identity cards, food stamps, and so forth. One of the principal concerns of those helping to hide Jews, workers escaping forced labor in Germany, and members of the Communist Party was— just as Jo was doing in Amsterdam—stealing and forging papers that would give invaluable identity to those in hiding as well as resistance people who were aiding them. To get food, you needed ration coupons; to get ration coupons you needed to identify yourself; to be out in public, IDs were necessary in case you were stopped; to travel anywhere you could be asked for identity at a moment's notice.

A whole cottage industry of forging papers sprung up to fill the need. A group called the Persoonsbewijzencentrale (PBC, Central Office for Identity Cards), founded in 1942 by the Amsterdam sculptor Gerrit van der Veen, became the country's largest forging organization. A year later, a second group was formed— the Falsificatie Centrale (FC, Central Office for Forged Documents) an offshoot of the LO.[4]

4. Verzets Resistance Museum, Amsterdam. Online exhibit: Themes WW II: "Hiding Aid."

It was a delicate and painstaking job to recreate passable documents. Early forgery attempts were primitive compared to what would develop: in 1941 and 1942, a penknife was used to scrape off the "J" for Jew. Every identity card had a fingerprint on the back of the photograph on which a transparent seal was placed with a special type of glue. The stamp of the issuing municipality, laid over the photograph, had to be carefully removed with acetone fumes in order not to damage the printing on the document. Then a forged stamp needed to be put back on the replaced photograph in exactly the right place. Special tools were required for a relatively simple forgery.[5]

Similarly, those involved in housing *onderduiker*s developed ways and means of taking on the dangerous and fearful task of hiding Jews. In Haarlem, the daughters of a local watchmaker, Corrie and Betsie ten Boom, began to help Jews in need of hiding, beginning in May 1942. A stranger appeared at their door one day and asked for their help. She said that she was Jewish, that her husband had recently been arrested, and that her son was off in hiding elsewhere. She'd heard that they'd helped Jewish neighbors of the ten Boom family and asked them if they would be willing to do the same for her. The ten Booms not only welcomed her into their home, they ultimately created a room in the house that they called "The Hiding Place" which would hide scores of *onderduikers* through the course of the war (or the part during which they were

5. Verzets online exhibit: "Hiding Aid."

active. The ten Booms were informed on and arrested in 1944; Corrie would survive Ravensbruck concentration camp in Germany, Betsie would not).[6]

An architect helped fashion for them a secret room off of Corrie's bedroom, large enough to hide six individuals at a time. It had its own ventilation system, and a buzzer warned refugees if a security sweep was in progress. Corrie was acquainted with the head of the local ration-card office and was able to get ration cards from him to keep her guests fed. Corrie's book *The Hiding Place* became a bestselling memoir of those war years.[7]

The Oversteegen sisters began performing one of the most dangerous chores of underground work: ferrying Jewish children from one safe hiding place to the next. One of Truus's first assignments of this kind was to take a shy and frightened ten-year-old girl named Louise from a safe house in Haarlem to a more permanent location in the country. While en route, Truus explained to Louise that they would also need to pick up another child for delivery to a second home, and Louise looked even more frightened at the prospect.

The second child was a fourteen-year-old boy named Fritz, who had been too much of a handful for his elderly safekeepers. He wanted to go outside; he wanted to turn up the radio; he wanted to be a fourteen-year-old boy

6. Corrie ten Boom House, Haarlem, www.corrietenboom.com.
7. Corrie ten Boom House.

again. Of course, none of this was possible in the safe house or for its owners. Nonetheless, when Truus picked him up, Fritz politely thanked the couple for watching over him and seemed sincerely appreciative. He later gave Truus money to buy flowers for the elderly pair.

Truus, Louise, and Fritz rode their bicycles toward Hillegom, a small town southwest of Haarlem where both would be staying. Fritz had his charms and Louise gradually warmed up to him and their circumstance. Well before they had reached their destination, Truus saw that the weeks of inactivity while in hiding had left both children out of shape, so she decided to risk stopping to let them catch their breath. While they sat on the side of the road, Fritz regaled both Louise and Truus with stories that made them laugh. For those moments, they were just three youngsters, pausing on a bike ride in the country and having a good time.

But soon after they started again, Truus realized she'd left her bag at the stopping place along the road, and told her companions to wait while she went back to get it.

By the time she got back the mood had changed drastically. A squad of German troops had passed while she was gone, and one in particular had given Fritz and Louise the hairy eyeball. The carefree atmosphere was gone, and Louise had turned back into the pale, jittery child she'd been before.

Fritz was delivered to a farm, where he could work outdoors and expend some of his boundless energy. It was a nice family. When Truus confided in the farmwife about

Fritz's troubles at the prior safe house, the woman just laughed it off. She had an adolescent son of her own. "We'll manage."

Louise was well-placed as well, with a childless couple who looked after her through the war like she was their own. In fact, Louise's parents would never return from the camps, and this couple would ultimately take her in permanently.[8]

Around that time, the horrors of the Jewish pogroms in Amsterdam were beginning in earnest. In conjunction with their continuing roundup of Jews, the Nazis had begun to barricade Jewish neighborhoods in urban areas in the Netherlands. They would simply force Jews from their own home and herd them into a designated area, where they were left to their own devices to find housing.

Truus was on a tram to Amsterdam one day, when at a stop, four German OD officers carrying submachine guns came aboard and quickly took up posts at all four exits in the car. The driver was ordered not to stop. Nervously, Truus got up and went toward the rear platform to where one of the helmeted Germans approached her. She guessed him to be around forty-five years old. He glanced in her direction and offered a cigarette, which she took, saying, "*Danke*," but she was afraid to look at him.

They were traveling through Amsterdam into the heart of the city, when suddenly the driver put on the brakes. Looking outside, she immediately saw the reason. A

8. *Not Then*, p. 55.

crowd was streaming toward the tracks carrying all sorts of luggage, desperate to get away from German soldiers armed, as the men on the tram, with submachine guns. They could hear the burp of a gun in the distance, and then another. A woman on the tram stood up with tears streaming down her face.

The gunfire got closer, and from her place by the rear platform, Truus could see a young mother being dragged from her home with a baby in one arm, and a little boy tightly gripping her hand on the other. The woman wasn't moving fast enough for the Nazi prodding her forward. Without warning, he hit her in the back of the knees with the butt of his gun. She fell forward and as she did, the baby's head slammed into the curb. He lay there apparently lifeless.

Everyone on the tram was now screaming as the car lurched forward. The chaos of the scene continued around the woman as she cradled her baby, still being prodded by the green-sleeved German. The two of them grew smaller as the train continued on.

"*Mein Gott,*" Truus heard the German soldier next to her saying from beneath that menacing turtle-shell helmet. "That's no way to fight a war."[9]

If only she had a pistol, Truus thought. If only she had a pistol, she would have shot the German who'd beaten the mother . . . and maybe the one who offered her a cigarette too.[10]

9. *Not Then*, p. 66.
10. *Not Then*, p. 66.

Chapter 8

LATER THAT FALL, Frans gave the girls their first real assignment. He had identified an SS officer who frequented a restaurant popular with the Germans called the Heerenhek. According to Frans, the officer was a code reader, someone who had intercepted and interpreted transmissions between the Dutch underground and British Military Intelligence. The British and Dutch underground had made connections early in the year and established a link that allowed for the escape of some British flyers who had been downed on bombing raids over German territory in Europe. This SS officer was part of the effort at disrupting this crucial means of getting downed pilots safely back to Britain.[1]

Frans took the girls down to the plaza near the Central Station, where he had just seen his SS soldier, and discreetly pointed him out to the girls. As Frans outlined his plot to the girls, he made it all sound pretty straightforward. Truus and Freddie were to head to the Heeren-

1. *Not Then*, p. 57.

hek café dressed in their most seductive outfits, with a coating of makeup and high heels and something other than their usual schoolgirl wool socks. They were supposed to look like women of the street, lure the mark out of the restaurant and down to the woods off of Wagenweg, near their group rendezvous place at Mari Andriessen's home. Here, Cor would take over and do the murderous deed.

Of course, the simplicity of the plan was not so simple when put under the microscope. The first and perhaps insurmountable problem was that neither Truus, nor certainly Freddie, looked like a "Hun whore" as Truus would later describe their costumed persona. Freddie got rid of her pigtails, but her baby face and teenage frame still made her a dubious prostitute. But then again, to state a sordid fact, there were men who liked just that sort of juvenility.

The next question was, could they actually pull off the disguise? Could they act like "Hun whores"? To get in the mood, Truus and Freddie went to the Haarlem cinema to see what Truus later described as a "sticky-sweet love picture." Back at the Andriessen hideaway, in the company of the others, Truus and Freddie practiced their roles to the amusement of all. Even after Frans painted her face with bright red lips, powdered cheeks, and arched eyebrows, and doused her in a fog of cheap perfume, Freddie was openly laughing and Cor couldn't contain his snickers. As Frans pointed out, however, the SS officer had been seen with a variety of women near the Heerenhek; she and Freddie just needed to show up to be noticed.

To further stoke their courage and practice in their heels, they walked in the park for a bit, and then finally headed toward the restaurant together.

A number of German soldiers occupied tables inside, but there was no sign of their German SS officer. The two girls, feeling more than a little conspicuous in their makeup and heels, found a table next to a German soldier sitting with a glass of gin and a lovely Dutch girl nursing an ice cream sundae.

Frans had given them ten guilders to help them kill time until the mark showed up. With those coins burning a hole in their pockets, the sundae seemed like an awfully tempting way both to make time pass and fit in. The waiter spotted them quickly for what they were—teenagers in cheap dress-up—and gave them a long glance down his nose. Nonetheless he dutifully took their order, and soon enough Truus and Freddie were spooning their own sundaes.

It all ended on an embarrassing and frustrating note. The SS officer didn't come in, and to kill more time as they waited, the girls ordered a second sundae. When the waiter came back with a bill that read 13 guilders and 80 cents, Truus and Freddie panicked. Despite digging in their pockets for every cent they could find, all they came up with amounted to 11 guilders and change. The girls apologized, the waiter called them dirty sluts, and the crowd in the restaurant jeered as the Oversteegen sisters were physically hustled out of the café.[2]

2. *Not Then*, p. 58.

* * *

Two days later, they ran headlong into the SS officer just on the street near the Heerenhek. No makeup this time, no high heels. Just the girls and a few teasing smiles. In the blink of an eye, Truus was sitting inside the café next to the code-breaking SS officer. Truus sent Freddie off, as an older sister to a younger sister would—*Go play somewhere*—for the benefit of the German. Truus knew that Freddie would hang around and at the right time run to Frans and Cor with word that the mark was in play.

The Hun had a beer in the restaurant while Truus nursed a soft drink for what seemed to be hours. She flirted with a sense of unease: he reeked of age and authority. Probably fifty years old. All his smiles were lurid enough to make her slightly ill. She smoked a cigarette and it made her feel worse. Behind his round glasses she caught a glimpse of his eyes twitching down and lingering on her breasts. The nausea continued, but he wanted to talk about the medals on his chest, which she dutifully admired.

Truus was ready to get on with this. She told him about her "uncle's private woods" on Wagenweg. "Only a ten-minute walk, and so romantic," she promised. He started laughing and said in German that Truus probably wanted to learn a thing or two. The two of them got off their bar stool. The owner of the joint made a gesture to the Hun that made everyone roar with laughter. Truus blushed like a naughty child.[3]

3. *Not Then,* p. 59.

When they got outside, Truus spied Freddie not too far away with her bicycle in hand. Just a glance was enough to signal her sister that the plan was happening, and Freddie immediately sped off to alert Frans and Cor to be prepared.

Truus led the SS officer through the park and off toward the woods, continuing her flirtations despite her disgust and misgivings. Years later she would still remember the hardness of his mouth and hands. She had trouble pretending to be enamored because of her fear.[4]

She batted his groping fingers away as they continued their clumsy stroll toward the Wagenweg and night began to fall on Haarlem. "It was getting dark and I had great difficulties getting the guy into our woods. Any bush in *De Hout* [the wooded avenue leading to the house on Wagenweg] would have been fine with him," she remembered.[5]

Finally, they reached the Andriessen property marked by a pair of statues just off the street in the front of the home. Truus led her German through the gate at its side, and then back into the dark recesses of the estate, toward the pond where Frans had tested she and Freddie several months earlier. The German turned to her expectantly and pulled her hard against his body. Her fear was intense, but she knew that Frans was there in the shadows, just as he'd been before, and this time Truus was never more grateful to hear his voice.

4. *Not Then*, p. 60.
5. *Not Then*, p. 60.

"What are you doing here? What is this?" Frans barked, emerging from the shadows. He started to speak in German, saying to the SS man in a hard, proprietary voice that this was private property. Frans was playing the perfect outraged "uncle" to his "niece" Truus. He would have to notify the officer's commander if he didn't leave immediately.

The German was startled, but quickly gathered his composure. Clicking his heels, he apologized. As he turned to walk away, Frans came up behind him, put the old prehistoric pistol to the back of his head, and pulled the trigger.

The shot echoed in the still of the woods and the SS officer slumped to the ground. Cor and Freddie came rushing out of the shadows, while Truus turned to vomit on the ground near the pond.

Working quickly over the warm body, Frans and Cor stripped the German of his uniform and bundled it for future use, pausing only to allow Frans to tell Freddie, in a furious voice, that she needed to get out toward the street to see if anyone was coming. When they were finished taking the officer's clothes, Frans and Cor dug a hole in the woods, dragged the naked body to its tomb, and rolled him into it. When the SS man was covered with dirt, they swept it with a branch and added a layer of leaves to make it look as inconspicuous as possible.

Just as they were finishing, Freddie came racing up from her post on the street to say that a German car had pulled up and was stopping along Wagenweg. The gang immediately took off into the depths of the woods. As they broke through the trees, they came across a high fence surrounding a tennis court—a barrier that Freddie and Frans were quickly able to surmount. Unfortunately, Truus and Cor were stymied and only found the adrenaline to make it over the top when they heard hounds howling in the woods behind them.

Freddie beat her sister home. Both felt lucky that their mother and stepbrother Robbie had gone off to Amsterdam for a few days to stay with an aunt. They curled up together and cried.[6]

6. *Not Then*, p. 61.

Chapter 9

THE NUMBERS OF PEOPLE involved in the resistance in Haarlem and surrounding communities had grown substantially through the summer and into the fall of 1942. They included dozens of others beyond the little cell established by Frans van der Wiel. The LO, the group that specialized in hiding *onderduikers,* had become increasingly active in the area, especially as it became clear that the Germans wanted to forcibly take young Dutchmen to Germany to work in the factories for the war effort.

Also active in Haarlem was the Ordedienst (OD), which was an organization established by former soldiers soon after the capitulation. Early in the occupation, this group had anticipated that the Germans would not stay in Holland. Their intent, with the legal Dutch government in exile in the U.K., was to fill the power vacuum in the country and maintain military order when the Nazis left. When the Germans not only stayed, but imposed their overbearing regime on the nation, many members of the OD themselves became active in the resistance.

Besides these groups, there existed in Haarlem a number of small independent resistance groups, and cells, usually linked to factions of the underground press. Members associated with *De Vonk* (the Spark) were generally affiliated with socialist causes; those associated with *De Waarheid* were generally Communists. There were also groups in nearby communities and neighborhoods within the city like Saantpoort, Velsen, Bever Heemsted, and Krommenie.

Given the variety of resistance cells and ideologies, it wasn't surprising that multiple tactics developed in fighting the Germans and their collaborators, ranging from the quiet but effective tools developed in the LO for hiding *onderduikers*, to the violent resistance favored by Frans van der Wiel's group.

Naturally, as the size and diversity of the resistance grew, the possibility of conflicts within in its ranks also surfaced. And outright betrayals of its members to the German authorities grew as well. A large section of the Dutch population remained sympathetic to fascism; Anton Mussert's NSB was not only still the largest single native Dutch political presence in Holland, but Mussert was even then, in October 1942, lobbying with Hitler himself to become a more active force in Dutch governance (a Dutch presence to rival the German regime of Seyss-Inquart). The dynamics of this previously stable society had suddenly turned combustible under the boot-heel of Nazi occupation. The outcome was felt in the smallest of Dutch communities and neighborhoods and ultimately in the most interpersonal of forms.

So it was, in Haarlem in the circle of CP activists in the wake of the arrest of a man named Joseph M. Gerritsen.

Gerritsen was taken into custody earlier in the summer by the SD. He was soon released and rejoined his comrades in the leftist circles of Haarlem. Through the later summer and fall, however, more and more members of the resistance in the area were found out by the authorities and suspicions were rife that an informer was revealing the names of members of local CP resistance cells. Whispers about Gerritsen emerged. The fact that he'd been pulled in by the SD and released suggested that maybe he had developed a relationship with the police.

Truus was there at the advisory meeting called by the local CP to discuss Gerritsen's case. Emotions ran high; they were desperate for a solution. Their people were being arrested one after another, taken in by the SD, and sent off to the camps or worse. None of the local CP trusted Gerritsen, and yet he was still a comrade. Could he really have betrayed them at such a level? It seemed unthinkable, and yet they had to face the truth. Gerritsen needed to be eliminated.[1]

The job was assigned to one of the Oversteegen girls, but whether it was Truus or Freddie remains uncertain. According to one account, Freddie was chosen along with the "commander of the group," presumably Frans van der Wiel.[2] The details of the assassination are unknown, but we do know that Freddie was upset for weeks afterward,

1. *Hannie Schaft*, p. 60.
2. Verzets Resistance Museum, Amsterdam. Online exhibit: Three Girls in Resistance: "Liquidations."

and only able to rationalize what happened years after the fact in an interview: "You don't shoot at a person, but at your enemy, someone who betrays other people."[3]

Truus, however, offered a different story: it was Truus herself who pulled the trigger. According to her, she excused herself while at a CP meeting attended by Gerritsen. Instead of going to the bathroom as she said she was going to do, Truus went through Gerritsen's jacket pockets where she found a gun, a sure sign that he was working with the SD. No one was assigned weapons in their group but commanders. There was only one means for him to have a pistol and that was if it had been given to him by the secret police.

Afterward, Truus made a date to meet Gerritsen in the woods down by the Burgwal canal. There she accused him of betrayal. Sensing what was to happen, Gerritsen pulled out his weapon, but she or some other CP member had already emptied the pistol of cartridges. He raised the gun and pulled the trigger—on an empty chamber. It was then that Truus raised her own weapon and fired, killing the traitor.[4]

"The shooting of people was terrible. I remember that we cried violently, Hannie, Freddie, and me. Arms around each other. It's not a nice job, but it had to happen. At some point, traitors will be found out in your group and they must go. You can't put them in prison. You have to find a solution and that solution is: he must be liquidated."[5]

3. Verzets online exhibit: "Liquidations."
4. Jack Kooistra and Albert Oosthoek, *Recht op Wraak Liquidaties in Nederland, 1940–1945*. Leeuwarden: Penn, 2009, pp. 66, 167.
5. *Under Fire*, p. 145.

Chapter 10

NOT FAR FROM WHERE the Frank family was hiding in Amsterdam that fall, Jo Schaft continued her dual life as a student and activist, helping Jews who had gone underground from Nazi detainment. When the raids began in July, she helped Sonja and Philine shift through a revolving number of safe homes, both in Amsterdam and Haarlem. She hung out at public places including swimming pools, theaters, concert halls, and cafés, looking for opportunities to swipe ID cards from unsuspecting strangers. Jo also collected canned food and gifts for those who had already been transported to Westerbork. Her cousin Aaf Dils later described being taken to a hidden room in the Schaft house that was full of preserves and little presents for those in the camps that Jo had collected for distribution to the *onderduikers*.[1]

The strain of drifting between the *illegalities* and her law studies, between life in Haarlem and life in Amsterdam, was starting to wear on Jo. It was difficult to find safe

1. *Hannie Schaft*, p. 49.

places for Sonja, who balked at the confinement and talked frequently of trying to get out of Holland despite the dangers involved in escape. She stayed at the Schaft home in Haarlem, as well as in the Oostzaan neighborhood of Amsterdam, using the fake identity of Hannie van de Bijllaard at the home of a friend of Jo's named Dien van Biel. Sonja couldn't bear to be locked up, so Hannie and "Hannie" would go out to roam the streets together.[2] Which endangered not only themselves but the families housing the refugees.

When Jo took Sonja to the home of her friend Nellie Luyting in Alkmaar, north of Amsterdam, Nellie's parents were horrified by Sonja's comings-and-goings, often dragging Nellie along for company. According to Nellie, her parents got into a shouting match with Jo about the problem. Jo thought there was nothing wrong with letting her friends be free to roam and had a hard time understanding Nellie's parents' good intentions. There was a screaming match between Jo, Sonja, and Nellie's parents in front of the Luyting house.[3] Jo and Sonja claimed that the parents were locking Nellie up, that she had a right to get out with her friends. But they were not persuasive. In the end the Luytings booted Sonja out of their home and sent a letter to Jo's parents telling them what happened. The Schafts wrote back to apologize for their daughter's behavior, but in Nellie's eyes it was all indicative of the stresses Jo was feeling. It was not the way she normally acted.

2. *Hannie Schaft*, p. 50.
3. *Hannie Schaft*, p. 50.

Students all over the country were feeling similar pressures. At the university in Amsterdam that November 1942, rumors began flying that the Germans were planning a labor draft of seven thousand Dutch students to work for German companies in Deutschland—students had previously been exempted from these call-ups. A month later, in an effort to appease Anton Mussert and the NSB who had been clamoring for a more active role in Dutch governance, Hitler gave Mussert the title of "Leader of the Dutch People" and gave him permission to form a sort of shadow cabinet, apart from the German administration of Seyss-Inquart. One of these newly appointed cabinet members, the Secretary-General of Education, Science and Protection of Culture, asked university officials to prepare lists of students for this draft in December.

The request was met with immediate resistance from students all over the Netherlands. Rectors at every Dutch university but one refused to comply. At the University of Utrecht someone firebombed the office of the registrar, and the university was quickly shut down. Debate about whether or not to shut down all Dutch universities after the Christmas holidays began to spread across the country. The Germans realized that a labor draft would cause Dutch colleges to close, and they decided to take a step back from their plans.[4]

Life remained unsettled at the universities when students, including Jo, began drifting back to classes after

4. *Dutch Under*, p. 150.

the holiday break in January. Larger events, however, quickly superseded the arguments over the draft.

In February two attacks were committed in The Hague that would have immediate and major consequences for university life throughout the Netherlands. On Friday, February 5, General Seyffardt, commander of the Dutch Volunteer Legion and another of Mussert's cabinet-level appointments from December, was shot in his home.

Seyffardt had grown up the son of a Dutch minister of war and served in the Dutch army until his retirement in the mid-1930s. When the Germans invaded the Netherlands, Seyffardt, a fierce anti-communist, helped found the Dutch Volunteer Legion. The Legion was a group of former Dutch soldiers who offered to help Germany in its fight against the communist menace to the east. Regiments from the group were sent to the Eastern Front in 1942 to battle side by side with the German Wehrmacht.

Seyffardt stayed in the Netherlands, got appointed to Mussert's cabinet, and was shot dead in the most high-profile and brazen act of Dutch resistance to date on February 4, 1943.

The group that organized the assassination was known as the CS-6 (named for a street number on Corellistraat in Amsterdam). It was headed by Dr. Gerrit Kastein, a Dutch neurologist, who was one of the earliest members of the communist resistance. CS-6 was formed almost immediately after the German occupation and was well known in the underground resistance of Amsterdam, including among student groups at the University of Amsterdam. In fact, a number of students were members, including the person who pulled the trigger on Seyffardt, a student named Jan Verleun, who escaped and went underground (he would be captured and executed about a year later).[5]

The assassination of Seyffardt had been triggered by fears among CS-6 and other Dutch leftists that Hitler's appointment of Mussert as "Leader of the Dutch People," and Mussert's creation of a cabinet, signaled the beginning of a National Socialist government in the Netherlands. It was assumed that Mussert would institute a general conscription of Dutch citizens for service with the Germans on the Eastern Front.

The fears mounted and a second shooting of yet another of Mussert's new cabinet members came quickly on the heels of the Seyffardt assassination. This time the victim was H. Reydon, Minister of Public Information and Arts, who was also shot in The Hague, along with his wife. Reydon's wife was killed instantly, but Reydon would linger for months afterward until finally succumbing to his wounds.

The gun used in the second shooting was soon traced to Kastein. In fact, it had been given to him by a member of the secret police, who had infiltrated the CS-6 cell. Kastein was subsequently arrested and committed suicide by jumping from a prison window in The Hague just weeks after the second assassination.[6]

The killing of Seyffardt and Reydon set off a fierce string of reactions from German authorities. Dutch SS

5. Frank Meijerink, *Traces of War*, "Seyffardt, Hendrink," 12/18/2012, www.tracesofwar.com.
6. *Traces of War.*

head Hanns Albin Rauter used the fact that a student had killed Seyffardt to crack down on universities across the country. Raids were conducted at several colleges with young scholars being arrested by the score. In Amsterdam alone 120 to 130 college students were picked up for interrogation.[7]

Hannie Schaft was likely aware of the CS-6 organization in Amsterdam, but there is no evidence that she was a part of it. If she had been, she probably would have been rounded up in the sweep that followed the second assassination and executed as many of the CS-6 members were.[8] But other measures instituted by the authorities in the wake of the *liquidities* had a deep impact on her schooling. The ministry in charge of higher education quickly set a limit on the number of students eligible to continue studies at universities and colleges. It also decided that every graduate would have to work for a time in Germany and sign a declaration of loyalty to the fascist regime. The oath required students to declare that they would "solemnly obey existing laws, decrees, and other rules in all honor and conscience." They had to swear that they would "refrain from all actions directed against the German Reich, its armed forces, or the Dutch authorities, as well as from actions and utterances that will endanger public order at the universities and technical institutes."[9]

Students were given one month to decide if they would or would not sign the oath. Students not signing the oath

7. *Hannie Schaft*, p. 51.
8. *Hannie Schaft*, p. 51.
9. *Dutch Under*, p. 151.

would be considered unemployed by the authorities, subject to immediate labor drafts, and could thus quickly find themselves working in some munitions or arms factory in Germany.

Faculty at Dutch colleges were divided about what to do: at Delft, professors advised students to sign in order to keep the university functioning; at the University of Amsterdam, faculty encouraged their students to decide for themselves. Among those in Jo's circle, there was almost universal agreement to resist signing the oath. At a gathering of her Gemma group, just one girl wanted to sign the oath and continue her schooling. Jo took the lead in putting intense pressure on this recalcitrant girl to not sign the oath, arguing that this was a matter of solidarity, Dutch patriotism, and consideration for those groups, beyond the student body, who were facing far worse measures of repression.

In the end, the young Gemma woman was not swayed; she wound up signing the oath.[10] Even so, 85 percent of students across the Netherlands were convinced by arguments like Jo's and refused to sign the oath.

The loyalty pledge essentially marked the end of university instruction in the Netherlands. With so many students failing to sign, thus ending their college careers, enrollment dropped to next to nothing and faculty quickly became superfluous. On May 5, Rauter called up all male students who had not signed for the labor draft. Many went into hiding, and their families were subse-

10. *Hannie Schaft*, p. 52.

quently threatened with deportation. Ultimately about 31 percent of non-signing students reported for duty in the German labor camps. The number of students who enrolled in colleges and universities for the academic year of 1943–1944 was 10 percent of what it had been the year before.[11]

At the University of Amsterdam through the course of the spring, a few professors offered illegal, off-campus lectures and exams in cafés and public places. Jo continued to go to a few of her classes, trying to complete her studies in law, but it became more and more difficult to continue after a time. She decided it was time to go back to Haarlem and get more deeply involved in the resistance. And she brought her Jewish friends, Philine and Sonja, with her, home to the Schaft house at 60 Dordstraat in Haarlem.

11. *Dutch Under*, p. 152.

Chapter 11

HAARLEM WAS ITSELF in the midst of its most restive and violent moment of the war since its beginning. The bloodiness stemmed initially from action almost certainly taken by the CP cell of Frans van der Wiel. Of course, the Nazis trumped all acts of violent resistance with breathtaking cruelty. And so it was in Haarlem in February 1943.

Troubles began in the city in late January when a Wehrmacht officer on the local medical staff named Alois Bamberger was found dead in Bloemendaal, just outside of Haarlem, with a bullet in his back. The German high command in the Netherlands was outraged that an officer, serving in a non-enforcement position, should be so brutally shot down. Even before an investigation began, Hanns Rauter became involved and proclaimed the assassination the work of a communist resistance group. He announced a series of punitive measures in Haarlem, Heemstede, and Bloemendaal. Bicycles were impounded, a curfew was set, and over a hundred citizens were arrested and shipped off to prison.[1]

The worst was to come. On February 2, seven Haarlem Jews along with three communists from Velsen were executed by Rauter's SS out on the dunes of Overeen by order of German general der flieger Friedrich Christiansen. There was no pretense of a charge against them, no attempt to actually connect them with the murder of Bamberger. They were driven out to the windswept dunes and shot down.[2]

Of course, the happenings in and around Haarlem were essentially simultaneous with the killings and attempted killings of the NSB cabinet members in The Hague, which served as added justification for the reprisals in Haarlem.

The growing cycle of violence and retribution was shocking to the citizens of Haarlem. The occupation, the war, the increasing number of bombing raids sweeping over the Netherlands from England toward Germany, and the awful roundup of the Dutch Jewish population had all been terribly alarming to the majority of the populace in the city, but there had not yet been this kind of killing in Haarlem—executions of the citizenry. Perhaps not surprisingly, many in the town blamed the resistance for bringing the heavy fist of the German police down on Haarlemmers. An editorial in one local paper, the *Haarlemsche Courant*, wondered how a resistance cell could murder a German officer knowing full well that the

1. Bas von Benda-Beckmann, *De Velser Affaire*. Amsterdam: Boom, 2013, p. 150.
2. *Recht op Wraak*, p. 228.

reprisal would be doubly brutal. The editorial went on to suggest that the assassins were supremely selfish, inflicting misery on the citizenry at large by means of a cowardly individual execution committed as a faceless crime in the dead of night. In a conclusion certain to gain approval from Rauter, the paper actually finished its opinion by saying that the response by German authorities was "strict but fair."[3]

All of this turmoil was having its effect among resistance leaders in Holland who had much larger followings than Frans van der Wiel and his tiny cell in Haarlem. It wasn't so much the violence of the actions that was disturbing; it was the chaos of the movement and the lack of a unified strategy. The resistance was made up of communist groups, workers' groups, student groups, and groups comprising former soldiers; there was the LO and there were groups committed to violent resistance, like van der Wiel's; and there were the groups that specialized in forgeries and producing documents for the *onderduikers*. Each operating separately, none of them knowing what the others were doing.

In the case of Bamberger, for instance, there was no clear motive for his liquidation. Rumors would later surface suggesting that the murder was part of a domestic situation, that Bamberger had been involved in a love affair and was killed by a jealous lover. This was never substantiated, however, and a number of resistance actions had taken place in Haarlem just before the execution, includ-

3. *Hannie Schaft*, p. 64.

ing an attempt to blow up the mayor's office (he was an NSBer) with hand grenades, suggesting to the Germans that the killing was part of a string of attacks. And in fact, van der Wiel himself would later (in post-war testimony) suggest vaguely, and without claiming responsibility, that Bamberger had been murdered because he was "dangerous to the young men in the city."[4]

This sort of vague rationale was hardly inspiring as a justification. But it didn't really slow down the Haarlem group. At least, not initially.

On February 10, 1943, Hendrik Bannink, a member of Haarlem's WA—the NSB Blackshirt defense group—was gunned down in the city while bicycling home from the funeral service for Hendrik Seyffardt in The Hague. It was near 7:00 P.M. on a winter's evening when Bannink's body was found on an empty street with the bike nearby as well as a 9mm shell casing. An investigation by local police came up with no clues as to who the killer was (in time, Jan Heusdens would claim to have done the deed).[5] Only the fact that Bannink was Dutch, not German, seemed to spare the people of Haarlem from immediate retaliation.

What evolved from all of this mayhem was twofold: On the large scale, Dutch leftists who saw the need for violent resistance began to organize a group based in Amsterdam that called itself the Raad van Verzet (RVV), or Council of Resistance. Its goal was to coordinate resistance in the re-

4. *De Velser Affaire*, p. 151.
5. *Recht op Wraak*, p. 136.

gion without taking away the independence of action among the various cells involved in the cause. The RVV began to help coordinate the distribution of IDs and stolen food coupons, and the printing of illegal presses. The organization also established radio connections to the Dutch government in London. It became one of the principal links between the underground in the Netherlands and Allied forces across the North Sea.

The second, smaller scale change that occurred in the wake of Bannink's murder in Haarlem that February was that Frans van der Wiel began to lead his group with a more considered strategy. Instead of targeting Germans for liquidations, they would focus their sabotage and violence on Dutch traitors, which was drawing a more tepid response from the authorities.[6]

Weapons became more available to the Haarlem group with its new association with the national RVV. Most of these were coming by way of Dutch citizens sympathetic to the fight and suddenly willing to offer their firearms to the cause. It was never easy to move the weapons from one needy cell to the next and once again, it was handy to have a pair of young, seemingly innocent girls on bicycles to transport weapons over Dutch highways. Which is what Truus and Freddie were assigned to do.

One morning Truus was asked to take a load of pistol parts to a resistance couple, Bob and Annie, in Amsterdam She knew them well from other assignments, and in

6. *De Velser Affaire,* p. 152.

fact, she had gone so frequently to their place in Amsterdam that she'd grown extremely close to an old Flemish Jew whom they housed there. "Granny," as they all called her, had been a professor at a Belgian University before going underground. She and Truus were drawn to each other for disparate reasons; Granny, isolated and fearful in her hiding place, was amazed by Truus's stories of derring-do in the resistance. She was intellectual and interested in the psychological effects of this sort of work on a teenage girl like Truus and listened attentively to her stories. For her part, Truus took great comfort in these conversations with Granny. It was the first time anyone had considered how it felt to a girl like Truus, who was doing so many things that went against her character.[7]

Granny asked about other aspects of her life too. "She asked me about the time before I joined the underground, what kind of school I had gone to, what our family was like." They talked for hours and Truus loved it. She shyly confessed that she had only gone to elementary school, and that her sister and she found it very difficult to sit through discussions that were above their heads. They felt left out because they couldn't understand those fancy words.[8]

Granny taught her German as they peeled potatoes or cut cabbage for dinner. Truus brought books to the Belgian woman in exchange. "The progress I made [on the

7. *Not Then,* p. 71.
8. *Not Then,* p. 72.

language studies] and the feeling I wasn't so stupid after all, made me really enjoy going there."

It was a rare pleasure to spend an afternoon with Granny that spring. Allied bombing runs were coming more and more frequently. The Germans had not only armed Haarlem and its surrounding communities with antiaircraft batteries to meet the waves of B-17s flying from England, but they had also begun to prepare the countryside for an Allied invasion from the sea. The war was gradually turning: the Germans had been checked by the Soviet Union on the Eastern Front and were currently being swept out of North Africa by the Allies. The news offered a measure of hope in the Netherlands, even in the midst of its struggles, which now included, here in Haarlem, being caught beneath frequent air battles. Truus had recently watched in horror as sweeping German spotlights caught a bomber in the crossing beams of a pair of arc lights and sent a stream of illuminated tracing flak into the sky. It caught the poor British flier right in the plane's belly. She prayed for the crew as the aircraft burst into a ball of flames and came screaming down onto some unknown polder out in the countryside.

The encroachment of the broader war caused tensions at home. Truus and Freddie and all the others in the Haarlem RVV were being advised to beware. The linking of Frans van der Wiel's communist cell to the nation's wider RVV movement had precipitated more comings and goings around the Wagenweg hideout. Rumor had it that the increased activity meant that their gathering place at the Andriessen home was being viewed with suspicion by local eyes. The group was starting to look for other places to meet, and it was under these circumstances that Truus, Freddie, and Kees were preparing for their various missions one morning.

Truus and Freddie were both delivering weapons and firearm parts, which arrived at the hideout in a bag carried by Cor Rusman. Each of the girls had sewn extra deep pockets into their overcoats, which allowed them to carry some of their contraband on their person. Some of the pistols were put in bags attached to the bicycles, which made the rides wobbly and easily unbalanced. The girls and Kees set off together, with Freddie soon veering off on her own. Truus and Kees continued on toward Amsterdam, but once there, they went their separate ways— Kees on an assignment to trail a collaborator.

Truus rode on in a misty rain to the home of Bob and Annie, where she gave a practiced warning knock to announce her presence. She knocked again. It was taking too long for an answer, a sure sign of trouble, and when Annie finally came to the door, she was sobbing and unable to say what was the problem.

Soaked to the bone by this time, with her bike listing this way and that from the weight of her load, Truus finally bulled her way inside, imploring Annie to catch her breath and say what was the matter. When it finally came out, it was like a punch to the gut.

"Granny is dead," Annie sobbed with tears streaming down her face.

It took a moment for the news to sink in. Now it was

Truus who couldn't speak. The old woman, her mentor, her teacher, the person who listened to her, who understood what she was going through, was gone in the snap of a finger. How do these things happen? "All of my visits to this house flashed in a moment. I would never laugh again with her about her Flemish way of talking. I would never hear that 'That's it, girl. You'll get the hang of it.' Never again: 'When this war is over, I'd love to meet that mother of yours.'"[9]

Annie took Truus up to Granny's bed to show the girl the proof of what she'd said. Truus fussed for a moment with the dead woman's long, gray hair, reminded for a moment of a little dead bird she had found once as a child, picked up, and held gently in her hands.

"When shall we have the funeral?" she asked Annie without thinking.

Annie was aghast. Of course, there could be no funeral. The Gestapo would be on hand before the casket got closed. Before a shovel was turned. They would be pounding on the door of Annie and Bob two minutes later, ready to haul them off to Vught or Westerbork.

Truus realized that this was the way things were now. This was life and death now. You die alone in some stranger's bedroom in a stranger's city. This was the way things were in Holland under the Germans. The realization that there would be no funeral, no honorable way of saying good-bye, hit Truus like a second punch in the stomach. "What are we to do?" she asked Annie.

9. *Not Then*, p. 73.

As it turned out, Annie had the same question of her.

Bob was not there to help them figure things out. He'd gone off with their son to North Amsterdam and knew nothing of what happened to Granny. Truus went into the kitchen and washed her face. She saw a comb by the sink and suddenly had the impulse to brush her hair. Maybe it was because she'd just been fussing with Granny's hair; maybe it was because combing her hair always gave her a moment to think.

It helped. She was soon steering Annie back upstairs to where Granny lay. They took off the old woman's clothes and wrapped her in an old blanket. They took off her only jewelry, a ring, using a bar of soap to loosen it, so that there would be nothing to identify her to the authorities when the body was found. Then together, Truus and Annie carried Granny down the stairs to where Annie had placed the old lady's wheelchair.

It was Truus who pushed her outside into the moonlit night; Truus who struggled pushing the chair on Amsterdam's cobbled streets; Truus who eyed the canal nearby and then decided she would have to take the body farther from Bob and Annie's house, so no link could be made to the resistance. She walked and pushed, down the streets, glancing occasionally at her load, trying not to deeply consider what she was doing.

There was a shadowy spot along the water. The lip of the canal was right there. Truus created a little momentum with the chair and then pulled back quickly, like a brake on a streetcar as the wheelchair hit the curb above the *gracht*. Granny spilled into the water, leaving a widening circle as her body disappeared.

The moonlight was too bright on the street as Truus stood watching the ripples in the water that had once been Granny. Where was she now? Where had that sweet old lady gone? Then suddenly in the middle of the splash, on the surface of the canal, her hair appeared, floating up on top of the water, fanning out like a patch of gray algae.

Truus took a deep gulp of air. Looked frantically left and right. She had to run, she had to get out of there, but her feet were leaden. Oh, please old lady! Please, sink!

With a final whirling gulp, the canal took Granny to its depths and Truus was finally able to move. She started to hurry down the street, but then remembered, not too fast to draw attention, and she forced her pace slower.

She couldn't resist a final, backward glance, however. The water was still; no hair floated on its surface. Poor Granny was gone.[10]

10. *Not Then*, p. 75.

Chapter 12

Jo Schaft returned to a Haarlem that had changed drastically from the one that she'd left just a few years earlier. The war made the town grim and gray. The atmosphere of distrust was palpable, not only because of the German presence, but because of the stark split between the collaborators and the resistance. The sense of fear was almost tangible: Jews continued to be herded off to Westerbork, on their way to the death camps to the east in Germany, and so, too, were an increasing number of Dutch resisters, who were being arrested in the wake of the recent assassinations and attacks against the occupiers.

There was an awful quiet in the city, a carefulness in language and tone that had never been required before. A wrong word said to the wrong person could prompt a late night visit from people who a citizen of Haarlem did not want to see at his or her door at any time of day. Neighbors looked on neighbors with a side-eye glance, watched through slits in curtained windows to see who was visiting whom, and strained to see what might be in the packages they carried.

The deepest wartime deprivations were still to come, but already, the Netherlands was feeling a squeeze in getting fresh food, new clothing, or parts for their bicycles. Many commuters in Haarlem started to ride on the rims of their bikes because they couldn't get innertubes to replace the already well-patched tubes they'd been using for months.

Physically Haarlem and the Kennemerland, the coastal region of North Holland, had changed as well. The Germans had built and continued to build an array of coastal defenses along the seawall north and west of Haarlem in preparation for an anticipated Allied invasion. Running through the city of Haarlem and elsewhere in the towns and cities just in from the coast, the Reich was building a line of thick walls and checkpoints on city streets and at canal crossings that were called Mauermuurs. The oppressiveness of these barriers, the sense of entrapment and lack of freedom they symbolized, were particularly galling to the Dutch people.

For all the disgust and weariness engendered by the *moffen,* a Dutch nickname for the Germans, there were signs of hopefulness that spring in Haarlem. The war news seeping into the country was encouraging. The Germans had to quit their long siege of Stalingrad in February and slowly began conceding territory back to Soviet forces. At the same time, in North Africa, Rommel was being forced off the continent as the United States entered the conflict in full force. Soon, the Americans and British would be in Sicily, and then it was on to Italy and the European continent itself.

Despite the harsh reprisals inflicted by the Germans in the aftermath of the winter assassinations in The Hague, many Dutch citizens in North Holland were secretly inspired and reassured by the presence of a resistance movement in the area. Even though the number of people actively participating in the movement remained relatively small, there were all the rest who knew of the activity—the fake or stolen identity cards, the housing of *onderduikers*, or the distribution of the underground press—and kept quiet about it.

Every day, the illegal press continued to print newspapers, whether created from basement presses or stencil machines. Every day news of the world arrived from Radio Orange broadcasts from England and picked up on illicit receivers in the Netherlands, where it was talked of between neighbors in whispers and asides. All helped to battle despair.

In North Holland and Kennemerland, scores of men and women risked their lives to spread the news. People read about the war fronts in Russia and North Africa, they got word of the government and royal family in exile in England, and they could read polemics against the Germans and the NSB. News of the latest transgressions of the occupiers were gathered, collected, and published in papers like the *Vrij Nederland* and *Trouw* and disseminated to the citizens of Holland. All over the Netherlands, an underground press continued throughout the war.

This was the world to which Jo Schaft returned from Amsterdam in the spring of 1943, bringing with her to her parents' home on Van Dortstraat her friends Philine and Sonja. This time for the duration of the war. It was hardly an easy thing for Jo's father Pieter or her mother Aafje. They were not naïve, and well knew the consequences if they were caught hiding Jews. Like most everyone else in the Netherlands, they had never anticipated that their lives would take such a turn. But according to Jo's cousin Aaf Dils, "They just thought it was their duty. Sonja and Philine spent the entire day in a room upstairs, and Uncle Piet had also made a very clever hiding place for when there was real trouble." The two had to be quiet because there was a housekeeper or a maid in the house during the day. They were allowed to come down in the evening when the curtains were closed. If any caller came, the girls would immediately fly upstairs and take everything they were busy with. Whether that was a book or a plate with cutlery.[1]

The neighbors were well aware of what was going on too. The row houses on Van Dortstraat shared walls, and the family next door to the Schafts would always remember the sounds of the girls racing upstairs when the doorbell rang in the evening. They never actually spotted Philine or Sonja, but knew they were there from the sounds of scurrying inside the Schaft home, and seeing Jo go out of the house and come back with extra ration coupons, cigarettes, and books.

As happened in Amsterdam, Sonja Frenk had a hard time being confined. She wanted to risk going out with the identity card that Jo had secured for her; she wanted to head back to Amsterdam for a day or two just to see old

1. *Hannie Schaft*, p. 66.

friends and feel a sense of freedom and defiance. Jo Schaft and her parents had to remind her of the consequences of being caught, but of course Sonja knew those quite well and it was still difficult to climb those stairs each night to her shared "cell" with Philine.

Her wanderlust was coming at a bad time. While the crackdown and unrest at Dutch universities had subsided and the universities had essentially been shut down, a new wave of turmoil began to sweep the country that spring after the Wehrmacht general der flieger Friedrich Christiansen issued orders requiring that all former members of the Dutch army would be required to report immediately to German authorities. These same veterans who had been so magnanimously released from POW camps a few months after the German occupation were now going to be rounded up and sent back to Germany to work in the factories aiding the Nazi war effort.

Within hours of the announcement, newspapers in a number of towns across the Netherlands publicized the action. Soon after the headlines, the first strikes began in factories at disparate parts of the country from Twente to Eindhoven to Rotterdam. The day after the announcement several hundred thousand Dutch workers went on strike. Milk truck drivers stopped making deliveries in the agricultural areas of the country, and where they didn't, they were stopped by angry citizens, who dumped the milk in the fields.[2]

As he had been in the first large Dutch strike in Febru-

2. *Dutch Under*, pp. 114–15.

Hoogovens, from a large local family, popular, with quite a few relatives working at the plant with him.

Soon after the strike commenced, the security police began to round up laborers and took them to the police headquarters at Tiberiusplein in IJmuiden. They lined the men up in front of German authorities seated at tables in the front of a large room and quizzed the workers on the kind of jobs they had been doing at Hoogovens and the other plants they were drawn from. The obvious intent was to herd them toward similar work in the German plants where they would soon be bound. Bonekamp was asked if he had a driver's license—a rarity in Dutch workers. He did, and was a very good driver, according to Brasser, but Bonekamp lied to the authorities and was soon released. A few weeks later, when the authorities got wind of his deceit, they came around to Bonekamp's house and quizzed his wife about Jan's whereabouts, but Bonekamp had already gone into hiding—where he remained throughout the rest of his life.

Labor Day, May 1, came that year in the midst of these strikes. In Haarlem, the Oversteegen girls and their friends in the local RVV decided to celebrate with a little rebellious act of defiance. They got their hands on a huge red Communist Party flag, complete with yellow hammer and sickle and debated where they could hang it for maximum effect in taunting the NSB. They first thought of the gargantuan Haarlem cathedral right in the center of town, but were dissuaded by Jan Heusdens, who had

ary 1941, Seyss-Inquart was once again out of the c
which meant that once again, Hanns Rauter steppe
quash the uprising. The revolt had spread in just twc
from Friesland in the north to the heavily populatec
gions to the west. The Germans feared a repeat of
massive February Strike and were concerned that it wou
spread to Belgium as well.

The RVV, as a national organization, was still in its in
fancy and was, at any rate, not set up as a group that could
manage a coordinated political movement. It was designed to give local leaders, like Frans van der Wiel, au-
tonomy and independence: fine for acts of sabotage and
violence, but less helpful in broad political actions like
these. Nonetheless, the RVV announced its support of a
general strike, and around Haarlem and nearby towns,
workers heeded the call. At Van Gelder Papier in Velsen
and at Hoogovens, workers walked out.

At the second of these factories, two leaders of the
strike, Jan Bonekamp and Jan Brasser, encouraged their
comrades to leave. Both had been active for some time in
local resistance movements, and they would soon form a
kind of alliance with the Haarlem RVV, sharing resources
and fellow saboteurs.

Bonekamp, a handsome, curly-haired laborer at Hoogovens, was a bold and confident young man. In IJmuiden, he was a leader in raising money for strike funds and
passing out resistance literature.[3] He was well known at

3. Jan Brasser and Otto Kraan, *Witte Ko*. Netherlands: Pegasus, 1982,
pp. 62–63.

heard that the Germans had placed an observation post in the church.

The second choice was to hang it right in the face of the Blackshirts, at the NSB headquarters in downtown Haarlem. In conjunction with the flag, the girls got the word out through the underground, and among the women of Haarlem, that they should celebrate the day by dressing the kids in red—the color of the Soviet Union—and putting red flowers out in the boxes in their front windows. The girls enlisted a squadron of Haarlem schoolchildren to stand guard for them, and along with Cors and Jan Heusdens on the eve of Labor Day, they proceeded to climb the exterior of the NSB building with the flag in hand.

The next morning, at five o'clock, before any of the Blackshirts arrived at their headquarters, the Haarlem RVVers unfurled the giant flag, and then occupied inconspicuous doorways around the square, waiting to see the reaction from the citizens of Haarlem as well as the NSBers when they arrived for the workday. It was glorious. People stood looking up and grinning at the big red flag flying above. Commuters got off their bicycles to point up at the flag. The resistance in Haarlem was real! There were people fighting back against the oppressors!

By the time the Nazis arrived at the building at seven, the whole town seemed to be awake and buzzing. A carload of furious Blackshirts pulled up to the headquarters and in a matter of minutes pulled down the flag, ripped it up, and stomped on it. But it was too late to shred the sense of encouragement felt in the community. The stunt was the talk of the town, but the girls quickly felt the heat of the authorities searching for its instigators.

To get away from the pressures and make themselves less conspicuous, they were encouraged by others in the resistance to leave Haarlem entirely for a time.[4] Their mother Trijntje had taken Robbie to a town in the eastern part of the Netherlands to visit relatives and lay low herself, and Freddie and Truus soon joined them. They stayed together in a rented room in Enschede.

Enschede was a railroad and waterway hub into Germany, and as a result had been heavily bombed by the Allies. When Truus and Freddie arrived the streets were pockmarked by bomb craters, and the apartment that her mother and Robbie were living in needed much cleaning and repair, including a new front door. One of Trijntje's sisters lived in the town with a husband and two children. The cousins and sisters had a heartfelt reunion, and it felt wonderful to Truus and Freddie to be away from their dangerous existence in Haarlem.

After a few weeks of tending to household duties, the sisters started to look for work and found jobs as "white hats" in a nurse's training unit at a hospital in the city that cared for chronically ill patients from across the region. Though the sisters had no valid IDs or any kind of paper that allowed them to be in Enschede, they ran across a sympathetic nurse who managed the hospital, hired them, and allowed them to stay. She introduced them to

4. *Not Then*, p. 68.

the hospital cook as well, who gave them access to food, which was crucial since without papers, they were not eligible for food stamps.

In truth, it was a much-needed break for the girls, who were still teenagers (Truus was nineteen and Freddie seventeen) when they left Haarlem. And soon enough, they were receiving messages from Frans van der Wiel, encouraging them to resume their resistance work in Enschede, and telling them that, in time, he would send for them to return to Haarlem. Through their aunt Griet, who was herself a member of the local underground, they met some local members of the RVV, including the boilerman at the hospital. With this new crew, they fashioned firebombs out of industrial cleansers and made lead pipe bombs as well.[5] The sisters' urge for resistance was irrepressible: they also found time to map the Twente airport and many of the city's antiaircraft installations.[6]

Meanwhile, the strike itself continued in scattered pockets, particularly in the north. It took another week, in May, before the Germans put a halt to the work stoppage with their typical mix of bloody, brute force and continued oppressions. Rauter decreed that shots would be fired indiscriminately at any public gatherings. Anyone caught distributing or producing leaflets informing workers of strike actions would be rounded up and sent to the camps.

A curfew was set for eight o'clock and a strict enforce-

5. *Not Then*, pp. 91–93.
6. *Hannie Schaft*, p. 73.

ment of a ban on all radios, including the ingenious tiny crystal radios that had become popular within the Dutch population. These radios, which could be easily hidden inside a match box, were capable of picking up the BBC broadcast of Radio Oranje from London, when attached to lengthy antenna.[7]

The Dutch had been living for many months with limitations on household goods and supplies, but the situation was made worse after May 1943. When the borders of the Netherlands were closed to trade after the occupation, the chances of getting a decent cup of coffee or a good cigarette became slim to none. Coffee drinkers made do with what was called "surrogate" coffee; instead of ground coffee beans a variety of grains, and sometimes acorn, were mashed up with hot water to make a weak substitute. Rice, oil, rubber, and soap all became difficult to find; and since Germany itself was beginning to undergo shortages due to the war, any goods or materials to be found in the Netherlands were immediately sent across the border to *Deutchland,* to supply Germans first. Shoe soles were made with cardboard; any scrap of cloth was saved and reused in a dozen different ways because there was no replacement material. To add insult to injury, after the May crackdown, the Seyss-Inquart government began charging extra coupons for the privilege of using the "luxury" surrogate items like coffee.[8]

7. Verzets Resistance Museum, Amsterdam. Online exhibit: WWII, "Handing in Radios."
8. Verzets online exhibit: WWII, "Scarcity, Distribution, and Illicit Trade."

In the process of suppressing the strike, more than one hundred Dutch patriots were executed or killed in random shootings by the German police. Another thousand were shipped to the concentration camp at Vught, in southern Holland. Furthermore, all Dutch men between the ages of eighteen and thirty-five were required to register for work deployment in Germany.

When all was said and done, however, the strike was a great success in at least one respect: it provided the Dutch people with a badly needed morale boost. Unlike the February 1941 action, it was not simply the industrial workers of the country who participated; for the first time, a mix of rural, agricultural workers joined with the laborers against the regime. The Dutch people were now united in their opposition to their German oppressors, moving beyond the actions of the small groups of underground resisters who had thus far led the fight against the Nazis and their NSB collaborators.

Chapter 13

SOMETIME AFTER THE STRIKE, a young college student with bright red hair came to the cigar shop of a member of the local Haarlem resistance named Henk Ypkemeule, who would long remember the red hair and air of confidence Jo Schaft projected. Jo, who would soon adopt the *nom de guerre* Hannie, was probably steered toward Ypkemeule by one of her Gemma sisters in Amsterdam, Erna Kropveld, who had ties to RVV circles and knew the cigar store owner as a liaison officer for the Haarlem Raad.[1,2]

This was Hannie's personal declaration of allegiance to the resistance; this was the moment from which she would not look back. She had done enough swiping of ID cards; she had debated leftist causes and fascist outrages long enough. Hannie was now fully committed to the RVV and she would be bold about it. She told Ypkemeule that she'd

1. Hannie Schaft never fully adopted the name, Hannie, as her own—she continued to be called Jo by her family and old friends—but more and more she started to go by Hannie within the RVV circle as a sort of *nom de guerre*. That is how history remembers her and it will be used through the remainder of the book.
2. *Not Then*, p. 88.

heard of him through a connection in Amsterdam and wondered if perhaps he had something for her to do.

Henk was cool to her offer, but not dismissive despite her college clothes and obvious bourgeois background. He sent her home and soon contacted their mutual acquaintances in Amsterdam to find out if this law student, dressed in neat sweaters and two-toned shoes, was resistance material.[3] When he got a thumbs up from their friends in the RVV, Henk sent Hannie off to the Haarlem group for assignment.

She appeared soon after the Oversteegen girls had gone off to Enschede. Frans van der Wiel and the group were in need of just the sort of assistance that they'd grown accustomed to with the sisters: a freedom from suspicion that was easier for a young woman to achieve than a young man. Van der Wiel liked the look of Hannie and invited her to a meeting at the Wagenweg headquarters, where she quickly became a regular, and was soon taking lessons in shooting and handling a pistol from both van der Wiel and Jan Bonekamp, who was also appearing more and more often at the gatherings at Andriessen's studio.[4]

Hannie and Bonekamp became an unlikely pair. She was a polished college graduate, intellectual, with a middle-class background and stylish ways, still proud of her wavy red hair and careful to brush it out to full effect. She spoke with a level of sophistication and education that was

3. *Hannie Schaft*, p. 71.
4. *Hannie Schaft*, p. 71.

unusual in local RVV circles, and unusual, no doubt, for a working-class man like Jan Bonekamp.

He had a rough appeal. Good-looking. Muscular. Bonekamp exuded intensity and energy, and the few existing photographs of him show a pair of piercing eyes that suggest the seriousness of his purpose. He was not very tall, but had brown, curly hair, an attractive cleft chin, and a bone-crunching handshake.[5]

As the summer unfolded, Bonekamp was still a wanted man by the Germans, both for being a communist and refusing to enlist in the labor camps. He had become part of the *onderduikers*, one moment in IJmuiden, the next in Haarlem, the next visiting his wife and daughter in Velsen.

For all this there was an undeniable chemistry between Hannie and Bonekamp that soon appeared obvious to their comrades in the RVV and would ultimately steer the pair toward a bloody fate.

As a test of her loyalty to the group, Frans van der Wiel gave Hannie a tryout similar to the one he'd given to Truus and Freddie. Hannie was told to hook up with Cor Rusman outside of Henk's cigar shop on a given day. Once they were together and pedaling away from the city center, Cor gave her a pistol and told her that she was about to perform her first serious act of resistance: Hannie and Cor were going to follow an SD officer on bicycles

5. Truus joked that she couldn't play her guitar for weeks after first shaking hands with him. *Not Then*, p. 101.

until the appropriate moment came. Then Hannie was to kill the German with a single shot from the pistol.

They waited along the bicycle path until finally, the officer came by. Hannie quickly pointed her gun and pulled the trigger, but there was no recoil, like she'd felt practicing in the woods at Wagenweg. There was no discharge, no kick from the barrel. It was just a puny click of the trigger. And yet the German on his bike had stopped and was turning back to them with a stupid grin on his face. "Did it go okay?" he called out to Cors, and it was only then that Hannie realized that she had shot an unloaded gun at her new RVV commander, Frans van der Wiel.

Like the Oversteegen sisters, Hannie was enraged by the deception. And despite Frans's explanation—"We have to be sure you are dependable and capable"—she refused to shake his hand.

As with the sisters, Hannie eventually came to understand the importance of the test. The day would come when the pistol would be loaded, the targets would be flesh and bone, your comrades in mortal danger, and it would indeed be necessary to pull the trigger without hesitation. Whether Frans really needed to go to quite these lengths is arguable, but he certainly knew how to make his point.[6]

Hannie Schaft's parents turned a blind eye toward her covert activities, focusing on how much they appreciated

6. *Not Then*, p. 90.

having her in the house and not asking too many questions about what she was doing when she wasn't home. She spent most of her days outside the house, and most of her evenings at home, keeping company with Philine and Sonja. And despite the fact that her university career was on hold, due to the fact that the university itself was on hold, Hannie kept up with her reading, plowing through *Das Kapital* and a dense book on international law.[7]

Hannie openly expressed her internationalist and Marxist opinions to her mother. After the war, she planned to leave the Netherlands and move to Geneva, Switzerland. She wanted to work for the League of Nations and help establish a true and effective international governance based on the principles of communism as outlined by Marx.

But even as she espoused these socialist ideas, she recognized that her idealism would certainly run smack into the realities of the world; that there were other competing points of view out there that would have to be faced and dealt with. Perhaps surprisingly, given what she was doing with the RVV at the time, Hannie was much taken with the non-violent teachings and practices of Mahatma Gandhi.

Hannie never spoke with her parents or her friends about her meetings with the resistance in Haarlem, determined to keep them at arm's length from any of the troubles that might befall the group. She never revealed where she got the pamphlets that she and Philine distrib-

7. *Hannie Schaft,* p. 76.

uted and posted in Haarlem in the evenings, and she kept secret the source of the weapons she occasionally brought home to Van Dortstraat.[8]

Sonja Frenk continued to make trouble in her headstrong, rebellious way. Hannie came home one afternoon to hear the news from her father that Sonja had left for Amsterdam.

Alarmed, Hannie went after her friend. There had been recent raids against Jews in Amsterdam as the Nazis began to scour the city for any Semites who had escaped previous roundups. Hannie visited all the addresses of the women from their Gemma group in Amsterdam but had no luck finding Sonja. She went all the way to Westerbork to inquire whether or not Sonja had been taken to the camp. The guards told her that no Sonja Frenk had been brought there, and Hannie had to turn back.

A few days later, their mutual friend from Amsterdam, Erna Kropveld, received a note from Sonja. She was in the little town of Smilde in the northeast of the country not far from Westerbork. It turned out that she had in fact been picked up in one of the raids in Amsterdam. The Germans put her on a train for the camps, leaving her only one means of escape: to jump from the moving car. Sonja wound up in a dike with her clothes ripped to shreds. Fortunately, she was found by a kind farmer near Smilde, who got her a change of clothes and gave her his daughter's ID.

Everyone at 60 Dortstraat was astonished and relieved

8. *Hannie Schaft,* p. 77.

when Sonja finally made her way back to Haarlem. Unfortunately, her need to escape could not be reined in. Not long after that misadventure, she found a man who was willing to help her escape to Switzerland by a route that would take them through Belgium and France. It cost five thousand guilders, which she paid for by selling family property. In early October, she took off once again. Hannie and her family received a single message from her about a week later from Belgium, telling them that all was well; everything was going as planned. One can imagine the sigh of relief all around. In fact, shortly after she sent the letter, Sonja was captured by the Germans. She was apprehended in Lyon in France and taken to a French transit camp, then deported to Auschwitz. Just four days later in November 1943, she died.

It was a fate about which Hannie never learned.[9]

That fall, Hannie made another trip, this one at the request of Frans. She was to go to the city of Enschede to the east of Haarlem, to contact two young women, sisters, who were working there in a hospital. They were members of the Haarlem RVV and had left town back in the spring when the actions of the group had made things too dangerous for them. Her assignment was to go to the hospital where they had been working, and simply to let them know that they were needed again. It was time to come back to Haarlem.

9. *Hannie Schaft*, pp. 77–78, 80; *Hannie*, p. 44.

Truus and Freddie had no notion that anyone from Haarlem was coming to retrieve them. One afternoon at work, the director of the hospital came to Truus in a ward to let her know that someone was here to see her and Freddie. The director took Truus to an office where she saw Freddie and her aunt Griet waiting. With them was a carefully made-up young woman with bright red hair and rouged cheeks. She wore shoes with heels, stylish glasses, and a nice wool overcoat that looked expensive to Truus. She appeared to be slightly older and was obviously more polished, but Truus detected some nervousness in the woman, and now, looking across at her, felt the same instinct herself. In the pocket of her skirt, Truus had tucked a pistol. A glance at Freddie suggested that her younger sister was as confused by what was happening as she was.

The director left them alone and Aunt Griet tried to take charge. She pulled Hannie toward Truus and introduced the young woman as a friend with a message. She was "Miss De Wit."

The three younger women all sat looking at each other, while Aunt Griet rose, saying she was sure they would all have plenty to talk about, and left the room. Truus surreptitiously reached into her pocket and clicked the safety off of her pistol.

Unbeknownst to Truus, Hannie was reaching for a pistol in her own pocket to do the same thing.

Truus came right to the point. "Who are you and what do you want?"

"Frans sent me," Hannie whispered back.

"Who's Frans?" Truus said, unwilling to be tricked into admitting that she knew Frans, the leader of the Haarlem RVV.

Slowly, Hannie reached into one of her coat pockets and pulled out a scrap of paper. She handed it to Truus, who unfolded and read it. A coded message from Frans. She looked up into the redhead's eyes and a smile slowly spread across her face. That broke the tension in the room, prompting Freddie to smile. Finally, Hannie grinned herself.

"A comrade," Truus said, leaning over to offer Hannie a hug. Next, all three of them were standing, hugging, and laughing like old friends separated by the war, now back together for a reunion.

Soon they were talking as if they were, in fact, old friends. Both Truus and Hannie confessed to having pistols in their pockets, but now the notion that they might have been on the brink of shooting one another seemed like a big joke. Hannie filled the sisters in on what had been happening back in the western part of the country. She had been working with Jan Bonekamp and Jan Brasser (Witte Ko) and had been involved in a botched attempt to pass some weapons through a checkpoint. The girls' old friend, Wim Groenendaal had been wounded by a bullet in the back in the incident and was now recovering, but out of action. Hannie had been told stories about the sisters and their work, and was looking forward to having them back with her in the group. This sentiment helped Truus deal with an unexpected sense of hurt that she felt at the fact that Frans and the group had enlisted another young woman to replace her and Freddie while they were in Enschede.

It helped, too, that Hannie emphasized how much they were needed back in Haarlem, and that Frans wanted them back as quickly as they could come, after finishing their business here at the hospital. They parted ways with hugs and laughter, and promises to see each other soon.[10]

10. *Now Then*, pp. 94–95; *Hannie Schaft*, p. 72.

Chapter 14

A WEEK LATER, TRUUS AND FREDDIE were back at the gang's hideout at Andriessen's studio on Wagenweg in Haarlem, sharing *hallos* and welcome hugs with their old friends in the RVV. After the greetings ebbed, and a sense of familiarity returned, everyone got down to business.

There was much to be done in the city and the workload was increasing.

They needed to make assessments of the occupying forces in the Kennermerland of Holland in order to supply intelligence to Dutch and British forces in London; they needed more personal IDs for the *onderduikers* in hiding; many of them needed to be transported from one safe house to the next; and more weapons were needed as well as more ammunition and explosives. Did anyone have a contact who might be able to supply these necessities? Was it possible that another RVV group could help? Did anyone have a connection?

Nevertheless, the mood was upbeat at the meeting, because of the progress of the war and the fact that the Oversteegen sisters were back at home. They speculated about what a post-war Netherlands might look like. How they could insure a progressive future for the country. And when all the talking was done, they sang the Marseillaise and the Internationale. There was hope for their country. Someday it would be free again and the Nazis would be defeated and gone.[1]

On the practical side, Truus and Freddie needed to find new places to stay. They still were considered "hot" in the city and had to be careful not to be conspicuous.

The RVV found a room for Truus with a couple that was not thrilled to have her staying with them. The husband worked as a laborer for the German Wehrmacht and the wife was frequently ill. Truus spent a few weeks with them until one morning, Frans sent Hannie to the house with a new ID and pistol. It was time for Truus to start working again for the resistance.

Frans teamed Hannie up with the two Oversteegens and over the next several weeks, they got to know one another. The sisters learned about and were much impressed with Hannie's educational achievements and were pleased that she didn't seem too prideful about her schooling. She even taught the girls bits of French, German, and English as they practiced shooting in the woods behind the Wagenweg gathering place, where the trees muffled the sounds of their firing.

Even though she was three years older than Truus, Hannie accepted the fact that Frans gave Truus the leadership role in their little sub-group.[2]

1. *Not Then*, p. 98.
2. *Not Then*, p. 98.

They discussed their reservations about Frans van der Wiel's leadership. As the commander of the group, his occasional recklessness put them all in unnecessary danger. Truus and Freddie knew that Cor Rusman felt the same way, and they passed that knowledge on to Hannie.

Truus and Hannie joined in a small communist cell, which regularly met in addition to their RVV gatherings. They were essentially a study group, discussing the possible organization of a post-war Netherlands. Hannie especially relished these conversations. She was fierce in her opinions, but never damning of those who disagreed. What they all wanted was to improve working conditions in the Netherlands after the war.[3]

Henk Ypkemeule came up with an interesting idea. He knew of a group of Germans who regularly swam at the steam bath in the nearby town of Overveen. The group's leader was a young lieutenant named Willy, who seemed to have no great liking for Adolf Hitler and the war. Henk suggested that if Hannie and Truus were to insinuate themselves into this group, they might pick up on some useful information from Willy.

Both girls were game. Before long, they had shown up at the bath and were getting acquainted with Willy and his friends. Sure enough, they were able to coax out some information about troop dispersal in the area, which they passed back to Henk, who sent it on to the Council of Resistance in Amsterdam. Hannie and Truus were even able to steal two revolvers that had been left unattended in the

3. *Not Then,* pp. 97–98; *Hannie Schaft,* pp. 74–75.

dressing room. Unfortunately after the theft, it was too risky for them to go back.[4]

Late that fall, Hannie was part of a dangerous operation at the Provincial electrical plant in Velsen-Noord, along with Jan Bonekamp and Jan Brasser (Witte Ko, or White Cow, Brasser's nom de guerre). Brasser, who had been Bonekamp's co-worker at Hoogovens and was head of the Zaan RVV, devised the plan after a worker at the plant came to him and suggested that it was a vulnerable target. The plan involved shutting down the power to a large part of North Holland, including train traffic, by attacking the central electrical plant at Velsen-Noord.[5]

A few days before the attack, the worker took Brasser into the plant and showed him the most vulnerable areas of the target. In particular there were two large conveyor belts that transported coal from riverside bins up to a boiler, which fired and powered the plant. If they were incapacitated, the plant would be shut down until they were fixed. A barbed-wire fence surrounded the facility, but there was not much evident surveillance at the site.

Brasser went home and prepared explosives for the job. The bombs were primitive and dangerous to handle. A mix of powdered sugar, hydrogen peroxide, and sulfuric acid would ignite dynamite sticks, which were wrapped in cellophane, with the hydrogen peroxide serving as the trigger to light the fuse.

4. *Not Then*, p. 96.
5. *Witte Ko*, p. 77.

Brasser stored the explosives at the home of a fellow RVV member in Beverwijk and then contacted Bone-kamp, advising him to bring a lookout for the job. Bonekamp told him he had the perfect person in mind. That turned out to be Hannie Schaft.

The two arrived in Velsen on the night of November 27, via canal boat. They met Brasser at an agreed location. He had the explosives and his own lookout, another RVVer name Jan Bak.

Brasser and Bonekamp climbed the fence, with Brasser cradling the dynamite like a newborn baby, while Hannie and the third Jan kept an eye out. Carefully considering their burden, Brasser and Bonekamp sped as quietly and, as safely, as possible to darkened areas beneath the coal el-evators. They set the bombs in place, dropped a bit of acid on each to eat through a cellophane covering wrapped around the plastics before igniting the fuse—the primi-tive bomb trigger—and then raced back to Hannie and Jan Bak.

They sped away from the scene, putting as much dis-tance as possible between themselves and the bomb. Brasser took them to the home of a former work col-league at Hoogovens in Velsen, a safe distance, but not too far from the plant. They barely were inside the door, standing at a window, when they saw a flash in the night sky followed by a dull bang. They waited expectantly for a second explosion, but it never came. The first bomb had apparently rendered the second harmless, and as a conse-quence, just one transport system was damaged.

While not hugely effective as an act of sabotage, the explosion turned out to be a powerful tool of resistance propaganda. The explosion at the electrical plant was the talk of Noord-Holland for days afterward. The mayors of Velsen and another town in the area, Beverwijk, issued a joint proclamation in both Dutch and German announcing that the cities' curfews were to move earlier to 9:00 P.M., while pubs and public entertainment would have to close at 8:00. They warned about potential harsh retribution from the German authorities should there be any further act of sabotage, including the death penalty for the saboteurs. German forces were exempt from the curfew restrictions.

But it had been worth it—if only for the sake of Dutch pride.

Chapter 15

HANNIE RETURNED TO HAARLEM to continue her work with the RVV, while Jan Bonekamp, who was fast becoming one of the most active saboteurs in Noord-Holland, took it upon himself to "liquidate" an inspector of identity cards who worked for the railroad all along the North Sea shore from Holland into Belgium. Hans van de Berg had a reputation for being fanatical in his pursuit of false IDs, and he had exposed a number of individuals from the resistance in the process. To put a stop to this, the RVV sent Bonekamp after van de Berg all the way to Antwerp, where he shot the inspector down.

All of this was transpiring during an escalation of attacks and counterattacks between the resistance and a semi-secret group that had been formed by German SS leader Hanns Rauter in the wake of the assassinations of the Dutch cabinet members the previous February. Rauter enlisted a group of primarily Dutch collaborators within the SS to serve as assassins in what was called Operation Silbertanne (Silver Firs). Every attack against a Dutch NSBer would be countered by an even more violent attack against a suspected member of the resistance. If one collaborator was killed by a resister, ten people assumed to be anti-German would be killed by the Silbertanne squad.

Beginning in September 1943, in response to a resistance attack in the province of Drenthe, three local leaders suspected of anti-German activities were assassinated at the order of the Silbertannes. The papers reported there were no leads in the killings.[1]

In October, just a month before the bombing of the electrical plant, the death squad killed one of its most well-known targets, the Dutch writer A. M. de Jong, in cold blood. In time, the members of the Silbertanne group would become well-known war criminals to all of the Netherlands. In a briefer time, Maarten Kuiper, Klaas Carel Faber, and his brother Pieter Johann Faber would be the personal nemeses of Hannie Schaft and the Oversteegen sisters.

Even as German authorities were tightening the screws on Dutch resisters, they had other pressing concerns. Their roundups of Jews in Holland over the previous year, while extensive, were not as thorough as the Nazi regime would have liked. There remained an estimated twenty-five thousand Semites in the Netherlands unaccounted for, meaning, most likely, they were part of the underground and were being aided and abetted by Dutch sympathizers in the country. In March 1943, Rauter gave a speech to his staff in which he gave a summation of efforts

1. Wikipedia, "Operation Silbertanne."

to date at removing Jews from Holland. Fifty-five thousand had been deported to Germany and an additional
twelve thousand were being held in transit camps. It wasn't
enough: "We hope that in the near future there will be no
more Jews freely walking the streets in the Netherlands.
This is not a pretty task; it is a dirty job. But it is a measure
that will be of great historical significance." He added,
what was taken by his audience as a wry addendum, to his
assessment: "I will gladly . . . do penance in heaven for my
sins against the Jews here [on Earth]."[2]

Earlier in the year, the Zentrastelle fur Judische Aus-
wanderung, or the Central Bureau for Jewish Emigration
in Amsterdam, as the chief authority for rounding up Jews
was euphemistically called, decided to set aside a substan-
tial amount of money to pay for information that would
lead to the capture of individual Jews. Led by Willy Lages,
who also headed the Amsterdam SD, the Zentralstelle
promised a bounty of 7.5 florins for each missing Jew captured with the result of tips from informants. Prices were
doubled if the captured Jew was wanted for any other vio-
lation of the penal code. It was a tempting sum for the police officers, civil servants, and run-of-the-mill informants
who began to let the authorities know of where hiding
Jews might be found.

The program couldn't have been more timely for those
at work toward the "Final Solution." At a meeting in
Poland that October, top Party members heard Heinrich
Himmler give a speech in which he outlined what he

---

2. *Hitler's Bounty Hunters*, p. 168.

called a "difficult decision" up ahead for the Third Reich. Pertaining to the ongoing genocide that was currently being undertaken by the Germans against the Jews, a question remained: "What should be done with the women and children?"

Himmler's answer was unequivocal: "It is not right to eliminate just the men . . . and let the children grow up so that they can later take revenge on our children and grandchildren." What was the Third Reich to do? Himmler answered swiftly: "We have made the difficult decision to wipe this nation off the face of the earth."[3]

Truus was given a terrifying assignment: a group of a dozen Jewish children staying at a polder outside of Haarlem had to be moved quickly. Word from a friendly police officer came to the RVV that the Germans were about to raid the area, and the kids were certain to be swept up in the process.

The plan to guide them to safety had a number of moving parts: Truus was to meet the group at the Central Station in Amsterdam dressed in the uniform of a German Red Cross nurse. She was given official papers certifying that the children were ill with an infectious disease and were being transported to a home in Dordrecht, in the southern part of Holland just beyond Rotterdam, where they were to be isolated from the general populace.

At the station, Truus waited with a young member of the Amsterdam resistance who was dressed in the uniform

3. *Hitler's Bounty Hunters*, p. 18.

of a German officer. As they stood nervously waiting, the "officer" gave passing members of the Wehrmacht "Sieg Heils" while Truus snapped to attention and clicked her heels together. She had to keep reminding herself to be German: act curt, self-assured, peremptory.

The children ranged in age from three years to fourteen. They all had yellow stars and the appropriate transport papers and arrived at the station via an ambulance driven by other members of the resistance. Truus nervously received them, nodding to the "German" soldier and nurse, who escorted them here.

Theirs was an old train, and the car that they were boarding had a sign posted on the door: RESERVED FOR THE WEHRMACHT: TRANSPORT OF PATIENTS. Though Truus sensed the extreme nervousness of the children in her care, in her guise as a German nurse, she could offer no comforting words, no solace to them.

The "German" soldier and the "German" officer from Amsterdam were supposed to accompany Truus to Dordrecht on the train, but soon after the children boarded and found seats, there was a commotion outside the train, and a group of Gestapo agents bustled into the station and whisked by the car. Truus's escorts looked at one another with alarm, then briefly conferred. They decided that they had to follow the SD down the station platform or risk exposure.

Truus watched them disappear with trepidation. In a matter of moments, black smoke began to billow around the car as the train slowly chugged out of the station. As it picked up momentum and her escort failed to come back,

Truus suddenly realized that she would be making the trip with the children by herself. "All the tension, fear, and feigned courage came out. My knees were shaking and the sweat poured down my face," she recalled years later. "My whole body was wet and I started shaking violently. I kept my eyes shut all the while. I wasn't allowed to cry."[4]

Truus calmed herself as the train continued out of Amsterdam. It was just her and the children and she saw terror in their eyes. A dozen kids, already separated from their families—already in a constant state of unrest—heading who knew where in the company of a mean German nurse. Truus had to comfort them somehow and decided the best way to let them know that things would be all right was to give them the truth.

She told them who she was, who she was working with, why she was wearing the German uniform. She said that they had to play along. They were supposed to be ill and contagious. She would take them to a place where they could find safety.

In their eyes, she saw disbelief except, perhaps, in the youngest faces. A little girl named Rosy was holding a doll made of a handkerchief and given to her by one of the older children. She was too small to see out the train window as the landscape passed outside, and Truus decided to put the little girl in her own lap to help her see and show her own good heart and intentions to the others. The moment she touched Rosy, however, she felt the girl stiffen. Truus looked at the other children as she held

4. *Not Then*, p. 79.

Rosy, pleading with her eyes: *Please, believe me! I'm here to help*. But their resistance remained.

The train clicked by the countryside slowly. But eventually the outskirts of Rotterdam began to appear out the window and soon the iron wheels came to a squeaking, grinding, lurching halt. Truus knew that they would have to change trains here to get to Dordrecht. She grabbed the sign outside the car, which explained to other passengers that it carried ill children, and herded the kids out onto the platform and toward their connecting train. Once again, she had to assume the role of the hard-hearted German nurse, so her orders to the kids were punctuated with "*schnells*" and commands barked like a truancy officer. Even little Rosy was not spared. When she stumbled trying to keep up, Truus looked at her with impatience and waved her forward.

When they reached the car reserved for her and her charges, Truus saw an old lady inside, taking too much time exiting. "Get out of here!" she yelled. "*Schnell!*"

Once she had the kids in their places, she sat and again felt herself crumbling. Wishing once more that she had some kind of support for all this. Just then the door of the car opened and in came a German soldier, followed by an officer. "Get up!" she yelled at the children. "Heil Hitler!"

The children all stood and followed her lead, jerking their arms upward in petrified salutes to the soldiers. All except the oldest boy in the group, the fourteen-year-old, who continued to sit with his arms folded and a look of barely contained hatred in his eyes. Hardly realizing what she was doing, Truus leaned toward him and slapped him hard across the face.

The crack of hand on flesh resounded in the car. With tears in his eyes, not quite masking the hatred that still lingered, the boy finally raised his arm in the familiar salute. He was no more than five or six years younger than Truus. He might have been one of the boys in Haarlem who helped out with RVV errands every now and then. But what did it matter now? She was a German Red Cross nurse and he was an insolent Jew.

She handed her transport papers to the German officer, who gave her an approving look and quick, little bow. The papers were all fine. The officer pulled out his cigarette box and as a reward, gave her a smoke before leaving with his escort.

The worst was yet to come.

There was no consoling the fourteen-year-old between Rotterdam and Dordrecht, when she was alone again with her charges. Truus tried to explain, but he was having none of it. He would not even speak to her and who could blame him? Exhausted with the trip only half over, she sat near a window and avoided the eyes of the kids. "Lousy world, rotten life, damn Huns," she thought on that awful leg of the journey.[5]

She got them to Dordrecht and off the train, but there was still the drop-off to negotiate. The children, of course, were not really ill, and were not going to a hospital. The

5. *Not Then*, p. 82.

plan was that they would be picked up by the resistance and delivered to safe houses in the region. But to get them to the next stop on the journey, Truus needed to pick up directions at a photo shop in the city. She risked leaving the kids at the station as she followed instructions that she'd been given on how to get to the store.

Once there, she was told at the counter that she was to guide the children through a minefield to a boat in a nearby canal. Truus was given a detailed map to steer her and the kids through the minefield and was told the route was well marked and that a string of barbed wire would be cut by the local resistance to mark the escape route across the field.

Of course, the cut in the barbed wire turned out not to be as obvious as she'd hoped it would be, and taking a troupe of a dozen kids on a walk through the streets of Dordrecht in a descending darkness made her and them as conspicuous as a tank rumbling down the street. And they hadn't even come to the minefield!

Finally she found the cut, led the kids through it, and gathered them on the other side before they entered a meadow filled with German-planted mines. With all the gravity she could muster, Truus explained to them what they were about to enter. She said that she would take the lead, and the oldest boy, the boy whom she slapped, would be at the end. They would have to crawl, single-file, through the field and must follow directly in Truus's path. Any deviation and they could all be blown up.

Dordrecht was built on an island in the midst of several large rivers that ran into the sea to the west. The boat that

Hannie Schaft at age 2, protected by two cousins.
COURTESY THE IMAGE BANK WW2 NIOD.

Freddie Oversteegen, the youngest of the girls, was just 14 years old when the Germans invaded the Netherlands.
COURTESY THE HANNIE SCHAFT FOUNDATION.

Hannie Schaft, the "Girl with the Red Hair," with a Haarlem windmill in the background.
COURTESY NOORD-HOLLAND ARCHIEF.

Hannie Schaft
(center, above kneeling friend)
with fellow students at university.
She was a leader of a study group
of leftist young women.
COURTESY
THE IMAGE BANK WW2 NIOD.

Arthur Seyss-Inquart,
Austrian appointed by Hitler
to head the occupied government
of the Netherlands.
His nickname was the
vaguely mocking "6¼"
(*zes en een kwart* in Dutch).
COURTESY
THE IMAGE BANK WW2 NIOD.

Truus (*left*) and Hannie (*right*) dressed as a couple
to take part in an action for the resistance.
COURTESY THE IMAGE BANK WW2 NIOD.

Hannie and her partner, the irresistible and reckless resistance fighter, Jan Bonekamp. *Hannie:* COURTESY THE IMAGE BANK WW2 NIOD; *Jan:* COURTESY NOORD-HOLLAND ARCHIEF.

Assassination of Fake Krist. Hannie and Truus were there, but other members of the resistance struck before them. COURTESY THE IMAGE BANK WW2 NIOD.

Hannie after dying her hair
black—no longer the
"Girl with the Red Hair."
COURTESY THE IMAGE BANK WW2 NIOD.

Hannie in prison garb
in Amsterdam detention
prior to her execution.
COURTESY THE IMAGE BANK WW2 NIOD.

The funeral procession at Hannie's burial in November 1945.
COURTESY THE IMAGE BANK WW2 NIOD.

Truus's sculptures *Vrouw in Verzet* (Woman in Resistance),
dedicated to Hannie Schaft in Haarlem, 1982.

COURTESY NOORD-HOLLAND ARCHIEF.

was to be used by her and the children would be tied at one of these rivers; its departure needed to be timed to the tide and current. They weren't supposed to leave until the morning. That was what awaited them on the other side of the minefield.

According to the map that she was clutching in her hand and reading now, by the light of a small flashlight held in her mouth, Truus and the kids would have to negotiate the first field, cross a second meadow that was free of explosives, after which they would have to wait patiently until the tide and currents were appropriate for their escape.

The children had taken the opportunity, when it arose along the way, to pee in the bushes, but none of them had eaten all day. In their eyes, she could see deep exhaustion and fear, yet when she led them on hands and knees into the minefield, they followed silently in a single file without complaint. There were sticks, stones, hillocks, stinging thistles and nettles on the ground crunching against their hands and knees as they crawled along. But they kept their mouths shut.

There was still another test: as the night came on and darkness was complete, a searchlight switched on from the direction of the city behind them, aimed out over the field toward the river somewhere. Truus lay flat on the ground and motioned for the children to do the same until the light arced away from them. Through all of this, the kids didn't whisper, didn't cough, didn't whimper, not even little Rosy.

One knee, one hand, one knee, one hand. She could

feel the abrasions on her flesh as she crawled and knew the kids were feeling the same thing. Still they kept quiet and plodded forward. It seemed to take forever, but she made it safely through the mines and waited there for the others to join her. When they were all in safety, including the boy she'd slapped, Truus felt the tension drain through her body with a rush. She collapsed there, on her back, in the grass, not caring that the kids could see her crying.

They were close, but not out of the woods yet. She allowed herself a moment of self-pity: Why did she have to do this alone? Why was no one there to help her? How had her life come to this moment, with these children, on the edge of this meadow?

Quickly, Truus gathered her wits and again consulted her map. According to the sketch, they were now on the edge of the second meadow before the river. The biggest problem now was time. Looking at her watch, she saw that they would need to kill hours before the currents were right for their escape. The children were at the edge of exhaustion and hunger. They had grown squirrelly almost from the moment they reached the safe side of the mine-field.

To entertain them, Truus started to whisper stories. She thought of all the tales that she and others had told back in her days in the socialist youth clubs. She whispered ghost stories, stories of her childhood, stories that she'd told little cousins as a babysitter. She whispered until she grew hoarse. She whispered until she could think of no more stories to whisper. And still it wasn't quite time.

The children had had enough. Truus could tell that she no longer had any control. They wanted to eat. They wanted to pee. They wanted to shit. They wanted to get up, race around, play, be children again, get out of the awful circumstances of their lives. But, of course, there was a minefield just behind them, and a garrison of German soldiers down the river with an arcing searchlight for movement along the river, just waiting to hear the sounds of a group of a dozen Jewish children trying to flee the clutches of the Third Reich.

"All right, kids," she said. "Let's get serious now, we are going to the boat."[6]

Getting caught in the boat could be no worse than getting caught up here, could it? At least they would be in the water with a chance to row away.

The children immediately became more manageable. She had no trouble leading them across the second meadow, and just as promised it was free of mines. They could hear the rush of the river as they neared the bank; they could smell the water. And the flat-bottomed boat was right where it was supposed to be with four oars and more than large enough for the whole crew.

Shushing everyone to be as still as church mice, Truus guided them aboard. She took a handkerchief that had been supplied in her nurse's uniform and used it to quiet a squeaky oarlock. She had to sacrifice Rosy's homemade handkerchief doll to silence another one. And then stepping out into the cold water up to her waist, she pushed

6. *Not Then*, p. 85.

the boat out into the river and pulled herself onboard. The older boys and girls manning the oars began to pull with as much strength as they could, but they had barely got into the river before the searchlights began sweeping down over the water, arcing this way and that. There were several lights now, and soon one of them fixed on their flat-bottomed boat, lighting up Truus and the children with blinding light.

The oldest boy, the one she'd slapped in the face a lifetime ago, started to stand at his oar. He was through. He had had enough of all of this. "So shoot you goddamned Huns," he yelled, shaking his fist in the direction of the light.[7]

The Germans complied. Automatic fire spattered down on the boy, ripping into his chest and sending him overboard. In falling, he upset the balance of the boat and in a heartbeat it capsized, dumping everyone into the powerful current of the river.

Truus felt children brush her legs as they were swept downstream by the current. At the same time a squad of German soldiers raced to the riverbank and began to spray the water around them with gunfire. Truus swam to the bank from which they'd come with the sounds of crying children ringing in her ears. She pulled herself to safety but then thought that she had to go back in to see if she could save any of the others. The current was just too swift. On a second dive, however, she was able to grab an arm and hold on tight, swimming frantically for the bank.

7. *Not Then*, p. 85.

When she got there and looked behind her, Truus saw that it was Rosy that she'd pulled to safety.

The little girl was gasping for air. Truus pumped her arms and pressed on her stomach and turned her head when a launch of water and effluvia came out. By this time, a covey of Hun boats was speeding on the water and there was no time for going back to see what had become of the others. She no doubt kept their fate in a corner of her mind that she tried never to visit. Rosy was here and they needed to get to safety.

Back through the second meadow, back through the minefield on hands and knees, back through the barbed-wire fence. Back to the road that had brought them here so many hours earlier. She had to carry Rosy down the lane and took a chance that the first farmhouse that they came to would be owned by someone who would take pity on them.

For the first and only time that day, luck was with her. After she knocked on the door, the couple within rushed her and Rosy inside. Truus gave Rosy to the farm wife and collapsed. Both girls were taken to a bed and placed side by side. When Truus woke up to find Rosy missing, she panicked but was soon reassured by the woman and Rosy came in to cuddle with her.

The farmer was a good anti-German. To cover Truus's trail through the meadow from both Germans and their bloodhounds, he took a can of pepper and sprinkled over the tracks.

Truus lingered a few days to get her strength back before she went back to Haarlem. The couple promised to find a good place around Dordrecht for Rosy. After a lingering hug and a final good-bye, Truus took a slice of rye bread offered from the farmwife and climbed inside a van—the owner a friend of the farmer who had agreed to take her to Amsterdam.[8]

8. *Not Then*, p. 87.

Chapter 16

ONE OF HANNIE'S PRINCIPAL CHORES for the RVV was to help locate and map German defenses as they were fast going up on the coast of Holland. As Allied forces continued to advance against the Wehrmacht—by now they were in Italy, moving toward Rome—it was no great secret that eventually they would invade somewhere on the northern coast of the continent. It was an open guess just where that somewhere might be, but with its flatland and ocean-front, and only 250 miles between London and Amsterdam, the Netherlands was a prime possibility for Allied assault.

To prepare for the eventuality, IJmuiden, which was the town that sat at the entrance to the North Sea Canal, just north and west of Haarlem, had been emptied by the Germans. As early as December 1942, bunker defenses were going up everywhere around the port and city, and thousands of homes were demolished to create a wide field of fire for German troops defending this direct sea line into Amsterdam. The population of IJmuiden had shrunk from 9,800 to 1,800 in a matter of weeks. More than six hundred buildings were demolished, and the rubble was hauled to the beach to make piles to serve as defense obstacles to which were attached mines and bunkers.

The port, piers, and canal locks were declared off-limits to the Dutch people. And a huge naval base, protected by tons and tons of concrete, was built to provide shelter for the construction of miniature German submarines as well as E-boats, which were a fast-moving torpedo vessel (like the American Navy's PT boats) designed to attack convoys and invasion fleets in the North Sea.

In addition, the Germans were building launch sites for a new and dreadful weapon that they would begin to employ toward the end of the war: V-1 and V-2 rocket launching sites were being constructed in the region during the early winter of 1943–1944.

It was Hannie and her colleagues in the resistance who were risking life and liberty by pedaling along the Dutch coastline, from IJmuiden all the way to The Hague, to site locations to pass that info on to Allied bombers.[1] All of this traveling around was strictly *verboten*—except for certain pretty, young Dutch women on their bicycles with good counterfeit passes. An ability to chat up German soldiers in their own language, and be smart enough not to give away the deeper intent of their inquisitiveness about just what it was those German boys were doing on the Dutch coast, did not hurt either.[2]

1. *Hannie,* p. 45.
2. *Hannie Schaft,* p. 87.

* * *

Some resentment emerged among Truus, Freddie, and Cor about Frans allowing Hannie to be farmed out with Jan Bonekamp and Jan Brasser to the Zaan RVV and to take on these coastal sojourns on her lonesome. Cor had been a little skeptical anyway about her university background and what he called her "posh" way of talking. He and Truus talked critically about her fierce reactions and know-it-all confidence in political debates, but when Cor wondered out loud how Hannie might respond in real tight circumstances, Freddie jumped in to defend the newcomer and to say that her sister and Cor were going too far with this idle talk. Hannie was as loyal and tough as they. The bad-mouthing needed to end.[3]

Cor apparently wasn't skeptical enough of Hannie's abilities to exclude her from a planned act of sabotage in mid-January. Along with Jan Heusdens, Cor was given an assignment by the RVV to set off firebombs in the Rembrandt Theater on the Grote Markt in Haarlem, and Hannie was picked as his partner. The theater played an endless string of German propaganda movies, which were annoying not only for the obvious reason of limiting entertainment, but also because it was yet another symbol of Nazi control of Dutch culture. As a consequence, the theater drew, almost exclusively, German officers and NSB bootlickers as an audience.

The scheme had Cor and Hannie going to the Rem-

3. *Not Then*, p. 100.

brandt as a couple, sitting in the back of the theater with a firebomb device that they would leave behind after the movie was over. They would set the bomb to explode after the theater was emptied. Jan Heusdens and a fourth RVVer would sit in the front of the theater with a second device, also to be left behind, also to go off after Jan and his friend exited with the crowd.

Trouble began immediately. Instead of a film that night, the theater presented a revue that seemed to go on forever and ended with no denouement to signal its coming conclusion. That gave Jan and his friend no opportunity to prepare and plant the device in the seat cushion, as they had envisioned doing. He simply placed the bomb on a chair, where it was quickly spotted by another theatergoer, who alerted everyone still left in the theater. There was a rush to the exits and the device was never triggered.

As Heusdens and his friend disappeared into the night, Cor and Hannie had no success either. Apparently, they had no good opportunity to set up their device in the theater, either, and were actually leaving the Rembrandt behind when the crowd began rushing for the exit. According to Jan, Cor simply left the second bomb in the lobby. When it finally went off, Cor and Hannie joined in the general commotion outside the theater and he began waving his coat, calling *Fire!* to help cover his and Hannie's escape. [4]

* * *

4. *Hannie Schaft*, p. 89.

Through all of her activities, Hannie was still staying primarily with her parents and Philine at Van Dortstraat. For obvious reasons, she continued to keep her explicit activities from them; nonetheless, they were deeply worried about her work with the resistance.

Philine was kept in the dark about the specifics of her work, just as Hannie's parents were. She remembered the tension in the Schaft home whenever their daughter was around. Contact between Hannie and her parents grew less intimate. There were constant scenes between Hannie and her father. He wanted to know what she was doing and what dangers she was putting herself and her parents in.[5]

Hannie's cousin, Aaf Dils, heard the outbursts within the family as well. She told of a scene where her uncle Piet was so worried about what his daughter was up to that he stood in front of the door and tried to prevent her from going out. Hannie was having none of it: "If you don't let me out, I'll jump through the window," she shouted. Finally, her father let her go; he knew she couldn't be stopped anyway.[6]

The SD was cracking down on resistance activities throughout the city. Collaborators and bounty hunters in Haarlem and Amsterdam were working overtime hunting the *onderduikers* and resisters. Raids were near constant. In February, the well-known watchmaker Casper ten Boom

5. *Hannie Schaft*, p. 90.
6. *Hannie Schaft*, p. 90.

and his two daughters, Corrie and Betsie, were swept up by the police, along with thirty Jews and others in hiding. The Grote Kerk was raided under the suspicion that ammunition was hidden there.

In Amsterdam in the hidden annex attached to her father's old business, where Anne Frank and her family were enduring the occupation, she recorded in her diary that "invasion fever in the country is mounting daily." She wrote that the newspapers were full of talk of a coming Allied invasion and speculation was rampant about what the Germans would do in the eventuality. Speculation was the Huns would most likely flood the land, opening up the dikes and letting the water inundate the lowlands—the same traditional defense scheme of the Dutch themselves. The Franks and their companions in the annex, the van Pels family, argued about just what they ought to do when Amsterdam was attacked and the Germans driven out. The consensus was that they shouldn't allow themselves to be driven into Germany, where they were certain never to escape. But if they stayed, they would need a stockpile of food to survive. What to do?[7]

The general anxiety in the country about the unknowns of invasion rattled both Germans and Netherlanders, and the SD continued to ramp up its activity. Most ominously for the Haarlem RVVers, the Gestapo raided the home and gallery of sculptor Mari Andriessen on the Wagenweg. He was there when they came in and recalled the moment: "They just burst in, led by the notorious

7. *Anne Frank*, p. 147.

policeman, Fake Krist. We were extremely lucky; evidence of the resistance was everywhere in the house. In one laundry basket, there were German uniforms that we used during sabotage. They asked my son what was in the basket. He remained calm and said it was only dirty laundry. In my studio you could find pistols and under one of my sculptures in the garden lay grenades for the taking. It is incomprehensible that they couldn't find anything. But they didn't."[8]

All of the group fled into the woods before the raid so no one was caught, but things had grown too hot for Andriessen. He asked the RVV to quit gathering at his house—a request that was only partially agreed to. A neighbor let him know a short time later that he'd seen men with guns sitting in the window of his studio.

In conjunction with the raids, members of the group felt that Hannie Schaft needed a new identity card. She'd grown too conspicuous, traveling around on her bicycle with her bright red hair, gathering information, transporting weapons, helping to hide the *onderduikers*. A reliable civil servant in Velsen was approached for help, and he was able to secure an ID for her under the name of Johanna Elderkamp. In March, Johanna Schaft became Johanna Elderkamp, a woman born in Zurich, Switzerland; it was a fact that gave Hannie the added benefit of having the identity of a Swiss citizen, a neutral nation.

* * *

8. *Hannie Schaft*, p. 90.

As Hannie was working in Haarlem, Jan Bonekamp had embarked on an escalating string of attacks in the many small towns of Noord-Holland. In the village of Krommenie he was part of a raid on the town hall, looking for government records and documents that might expose members of the resistance. Armed and wearing masks, he and his fellow resisters held guns to the heads of local civil servants while compatriots rifled the files.

Also in Krommenie, he killed a Dutch SS man named Kuipers and then made an unsuccessful attempt on the life of a prominent hairdresser named Ko Langendijk in Velsen-Noord, who was notorious for whispering to the SD about the gossip he heard in his salon.

He shot a turncoat, Jan van Zoelen, in Beverwijk in early March. Van Zoelen had worked with the resistance, but after being hauled into the SD a year earlier, he began informing for the Secret Police. Jan Brasser and, likely, Hannie Schaft were also part of the preparation for van Zoelen's assassination. Prior to becoming an informant, van Zoelen had spent several months working with the resistance, even collecting money for support of the cause. He was also accused by the local RVV in Beverwijk of being a bounty hunter of Jewish *onderduiker* and of personally betraying one of the local resistance leaders, who he volunteered to help with an escape from the Netherlands. Instead, he handed the man over to the SD.

After Bonekamp shot him, van Zoelen was taken to a Beverwijk surgeon named Dr. L. J. (Johannes) Buller, who quickly declared that the wounds were too serious for the doctor to save the victim. German authorities questioned the doctor's decision, claiming that he was quick to declare van Zoelen dead. It was a pronouncement the authorities would not forget.

A month later, in Velsen, Jan Brasser and two colleagues killed a police inspector named Willem Ritman, who was biking home from work. Brasser and his resistance friends fired at the officer from a car driven by Jan Bonekamp, killing him. Ritman was known as a fanatic NSBer, so despised by the rest of the local community—and, apparently, in his own home—that even his widow refused to accept the flowers sent to honor him by his colleagues at the Velsen police department.[9]

In the wake of the March and April liquidations, the Silbertanne group, led by the head of the SS in Amsterdam, Willy Lages, undertook a series of retaliatory measures that began with an assassination of the unfortunate Beverwijk surgeon who had tried unsuccessfully to save the life of the informer van Zoelen. Dr. Johannes Buller was warned in advance that he was on the radar of the Silbertannes, and he consequently closed down his surgery but remained available to needy patients at his home. On April 9, Lages's assistant, an SS officer from Amsterdam named Emil Ruhl, knocked on Buller's door, telling him he was needed immediately. The moment the elderly doctor stepped outside, he was shot dead.

Two other doctors in the region were likewise attacked

9. *Recht op Wraak*, p. 115.

for similar failures to save victims of the RVV: one was killed outright like Buller, another was wounded and survived.[10] It was just the beginning of a purge of suspected resistance members. Before it was through, 486 were arrested and sent to Dutch concentration camps; 149 never returned.[11]

Jan Bonekamp didn't seem to slow down at all in his acts of assassination and sabotage. According to Jan Brasser he would return from his actions with grim, but satisfied, messages: "Another one less" or "Another hundred people saved," he said. In Beverwijk, he and another resister shot down an NSB collaborator while riding by the victim on bicycles, prompting more reprisals from the SS, this time ordered by Hanns Rauter himself.[12]

This killing was followed by an attempt to sabotage a railway line outside of Beverwijk, which was followed by an attempt to bomb a metal-working plant in Amsterdam, followed by a raid of a city hall in Wormerveer in another attempt to destroy civilian census records that gave addresses and information on resistance fighters.

In the midst of this mayhem, the U.S. Ninth Army Air Force sent 350 B-26 bombers in a massive raid on the naval base at IJmuiden, focused primarily on the E-boat pens that were building the German navy's speedy torpedo boats. On March 26, 1944, a daring daytime raid dropped over six hundred tons of bombs on the base in a single hour. It was the single largest bombing raid of the

10. *Hannie Schaft*, p. 94.
11. *Recht op Wraak*, p. 115.
12. *Recht op Wraak*, p. 145.

war for the U.S. Ninth Army Air Force, flattening bunkers, harbor installations, fish markets, and ships. The damage was massive, and Germans fled the compound in a panic. Unfortunately, for all the tonnage dropped and its subsequent destruction, the base itself was not put out of commission. The heavy concrete bunkers surrounding the site withstood the onslaught and E-boats kept being produced from IJmuiden.[13]

There is no documentary evidence that links Hannie's coastal reconnaissance directly to the bombings, but her work certainly found its way to London via radio channels from the resistance. It also, no doubt, impressed Jan Bonekamp and Jan Brasser, the bold leaders of the Zaan RVV. Bonekamp, of course, already had personal knowledge of Hannie, beginning with their pistol practice in the woods behind Wagenweg, and both he and Brasser had witnessed her work at the bombing of the electrical station. They knew as well of her attempted firebombing of the Rembrandt Theater in Haarlem, and had come to fully appreciate her courage and willingness to pursue the most dangerous of assignments.

She started to partner with Bonekamp on a daily basis. They also started to stay together at a farm quite a distance from Haarlem with Jan and Trijntje Bult who ran a small horticultural business in Limmen. The Bults' home was a transit and meeting house for the resistance and *on-*

13. NIOD Institute for War, Genocide, and Holocaust Studies, Amsterdam, imagebase IJmuiden 26/03/1944.

derduikers. Jan was a regular visitor, as was Hannie Schaft from her expeditions checking out the coastal defenses of the Germans. Hannie became friendly with Trijntje, who welcomed her company and appreciated her circumstances.[14]

Hannie and Jan helped with the chores and in the garden and would disappear, sometimes for days. They were constant companions, heading out together by bicycle or train, but also going out to the dunes to practice shooting, perfecting the uniquely Dutch practice of firing pistols while pedaling or riding double on bikes—like American Indians shooting arrows on horseback.

The favorite weapon of the resistance was a 9mm FN military-style pistol, which was flatter than most weapons and therefore fit tightly against the body for best concealment, tucked into a pair of pants, and made for less bulging when carried in a coat pocket. "I have seen Hannie leave from here with a belt of revolvers under her coat. I thought: Child, how risky you are. How daring," Trijntje remembered later. "But she was happy here. She was content."

Trijntje asked her once how she was able to do it, how could she go out and shoot people with Jan? "She said, 'If we don't do it, more people are in danger of being betrayed. It must happen.' "[15]

In all, including the periodic comings and goings, Hannie stayed with the Bults about a month. Hannie helped

14. *Hannie Schaft*, p. 101.
15. *Hannie Schaft*, p. 101.

with the three children in the house, and tried to help with the housekeeping, but was not used to the tasks and, truth be told, was not all that handy around the home. Trijntje had her peel potatoes once, but she left so little of the potato in the process that she was further excused from any similar duty.

Jan, on the other hand, was a constant bundle of energy, always waiting to speed off on some mission. A local police officer came by once to inquire whether or not Jan Bult had sold any asparagus on the black market. When Jan Bonekamp heard about the visit, he immediately offered to shoot the policeman if it was required.[16] Trijntje felt that Hannie's attitude was evolving in that same direction. Whether or not the two were lovers, she could not say for certain. "I didn't see it, but it is possible," she said. "They worked together very intensely. They slept upstairs. I had two rooms there and each had one."

Regarding Bonekamp's wife and daughter, Trijntje once asked him directly what she thought of him being away so much. He said that his wife would have to "'take it. I have suggested to her, come fight with me. But that was impossible. And I couldn't wait around and do nothing.'"[17]

On June 6, 1944, the day history would forever more remember as D-day, the Allies invaded Normandy, and news of that long-awaited attack echoed distantly in the Netherlands. The immediate drama and bloodshed of the great

16. *Hannie Schaft*, p. 102.
17. *Hannie Schaft*, p. 103.

engagement was just too distant to be felt immediately in the land. It did, however, prompt a muted sense of excitement in both the Germans in North Holland, worried about what this might signal for the continued viability of the Third Reich, and within the Dutch population as a whole, aching for relief from the oppressions visited upon them by the occupiers. The initial news from the BBC and Radio Oranje reported heavy Allied losses, as well as success on the beaches and rapid movement into the French interior. There was no call from the Dutch government in exile for any particular actions; no call to prepare to take up arms.

Nonetheless, there was a general sense within the resistance that people ought to be prepared to aid the Allies if and when they should come to the Netherlands. It was in this context that the RVV decided to consolidate a cache of weapons at the Bult farm in Limmen in preparation for any possible Allied action on the Netherlands. If the invasion was to broaden up the Atlantic coast to Holland, the resistance wanted to be ready to stymy German troop movements and defense in any way they could.

Jan Brasser, Hannie Schaft, Jan Bonekamp, and two other resisters volunteered to transfer a weapons depot from one of the Zaan region villages by bike to Limmen. According to Brasser, the number of German road checks had increased in the wake of the invasion, so the group decided to take polder roads through the countryside to avoid major checkpoints. But the route required them to take a couple of ferries and pass over some bridges, all possible areas for the German army to set up checkpoints.

They loaded their bicycle bags with explosives, detonators, and pistols from the stash of weaponry and headed out as a group on the narrow roads, which ran along the dikes above the marshy polders. Everything went smoothly until they came to the final ferry over the canal before Limmen at a town called Akersloot. Jan Bonekamp, who frequently traveled these roads, had said that the ferryman at Akersloot was sympathetic to the cause, but as they rounded the road and looked ahead toward the ferry, they could see a German Kubelwagen (a kind of German jeep made by the Volkswagen company). At least four soldiers of the Reich, in their distinctive turtle-back helmets, a few meters before the ferry, were blocking entrance to the boat.[18]

As they saw the soldiers, it was obvious that the Germans saw them. They would draw attention to themselves if they turned around and headed back toward Zaan and would be easily caught by the soldiers in their Kubelwagen. So the squadron of RVVers slowed their bicycles to a walking pace so they could whisper together as they pondered their next move. Unfortunately, as they quickly determined, there was only one direction in which they could go: toward the ferry and the German troops.

Brasser recognized as they drew nearer that the soldiers they were seeing ahead were members of the Herman

18. *Hannie Schaft,* p. 97.

Goring division, which typically was composed of young, enthusiastic members of the Wehrmacht with a general layer of Nazi zeal. Exactly the wrong type of enemy to run into out here in the hinterlands, carrying bags full of weapons.[19]

But the Dutch resisters stayed calm as they neared. Brasser said that Hannie even attempted a joke. In muted tones, they made a quick determination: if one of the Muffs asked to see what was in the bags slung over the bicycles, the five compatriots would pull out the pistols each carried in a coat pocket and start firing. It would be the Germans or the Dutch resisters who survived.[20]

They heard the familiar cry: Halt! *Ausweisz!* (show us your ID). They did as commanded, pulling out their papers, and waited as each in turn handed over his or her identity card. All were inspected by a German trooper and each was handed back to its owner. No bags were searched, no weapons were revealed, no shoot-out ensued. Hannie and her four friends stepped aboard the ferry with their bicycles.

There was one more breath-holding moment. Just as the ferry was about to leave the shore, another German military *wagen* approached the ferry carrying four officers. It drove right onto the ferry, squeezing the bicycles and riders to the sides of the boat. Soon the ferryman lifted the gate and the vessel slowly motored to the far

19. *Hannie Schaft,* p. 97.
20. *Hannie Schaft,* p. 97.

shore of the canal. Achingly slow, the ferry puttered across the water, but the German officers remained supremely disinterested in the five bicyclists who accompanied them, despite the bulging bags that were draped over the traps above their back tires.[21]

Still holding their breath, the five resisters exited the ferry on the north side of the canal and climbed on their bikes once more. As casually as they were able, they pedaled away on to Limmen and Jan Bult's farm. There in a space Jan had created beneath a haymow, the RVV stashed its new weaponry, ready for use when the Allies landed on the beaches. Which couldn't be much longer, could it?[22]

21. *Hannie Schaft*, p. 98.
22. *Witte Ko*, p. 89.

Chapter 17

JUST TWO DAYS AFTER the June 6 landing at Normandy, Hannie Schaft and Jan Bonekamp were off on their next assignment, this one urged by the Haarlem RVV commander, Frans van der Wiel. The target for the pair was a well-known local pastry chef named Piet Faber, who was the father of two longtime NSBers, Klaas and Pieter, now employed as gunmen by the SS in the Silbertanne group.

Pieter, the son, had offered crucial assistance in the SD's roundup of about fifty Haarlemmers in December 1943 in a sweep aimed at the distribution of a magazine called *Free Netherlands*. Included in the arrests was a well-known bookdealer from Haarlem named Herman de Vries. De Vries was taken to a Dutch transport camp, from which he was soon moved to Dachau, where he died of typhus in April 1945, just weeks before the death camp was liberated.[1] Both boys, Klaas and Pieter, had served in the German army on the Eastern Front and were rabid enthusiasts of the Third Reich.

1. *Hannie*, p. 49.

Faber himself was a solid NSBer, who was well aware of how despised he and his family were by the resistance: his bakery windows had been smashed by locals on more than one occasion; and he had recently taken the precaution of moving out of his home on the Wagenweg in Haarlem and was now living in a rented house in Heemstede, just to the south of Haarlem.[2]

Someone had done reconnaissance on Faber and discovered that he cycled daily from his rented home to his bakery in Haarlem. According to the report, Faber was short and stout, always carried a briefcase on the rack on the back of his bicycle, and had the habit of using one hand to steady the luggage as he pedaled to work.

Given the address and the description, it wasn't hard for Hannie and Jan to find Faber and to hop on their bicycles to trail him. As it happened, there was a witness to what happened on that morning of June 8. A ten-year-old boy named Lex Leffelaar was cutting the grass in his family's front yard, when he saw Pieter Faber pass by, followed quickly by a man and young woman on their own bicycles. There was a loud pop, and another, and the boy watched in shock as Faber fell off his ride while the man and woman pedaled away. Whose bullet hit its target remains unknown, but at least one did.

Lex ran to get his father and they took the mortally wounded baker inside their own home. A neighbor lady, who housed Jews in the underground, brought an orange pillow to place beneath Faber's head. Lex remembered

2. *Hannie*, p. 48.

the moment years later because of the irony that the pillow, which he knew was made by *onderduikers* for other guests of the home, was now being used to comfort Faber.[3]

The authorities quickly took the injured baker to the hospital where he lingered for several days before succumbing to his wounds.

Not everyone in the general public applauded these attacks by the violent wing of the resistance. Not only did they question the necessity of executing Dutch members of the community without any sort of trial or defense of the victim, but the attacks inevitably led to brutal countermeasures from the Germans, which bore heavily on the people. The attack on Faber outraged the local newspaper, the *Haarlemsche Courant*. Though unnamed and unknown, for the first time, Hannie Schaft was exposed as one of the assassins in the editorial. "May the cowardice of the murder of a defenseless man be exposed and [all of us] horrified at the thought that here it is a woman who has taken this life; life, to which God grants women the power to give. Have our people lost their self-reflection so much in the turmoil of these times that they have fallen to this unnatural behavior . . . It is a fruitful time for hatred and lies. They make many of us forget that the time could be very near when, in common need, NSB and non-NSB people will have to rely on each other's assistance."[4]

If any of this registered with Jan Bonekamp or Hannie,

3. *Hannie Schaft*, p. 99.
4. *Hannie Schaft*, p. 99; *Recht op Wraak*, p. 143.

they made no mention of it. There is no recorded comment or defense of what they'd done. Nor did it slow down their work. To Truus Oversteegen, the *liquidation* was just: "After extensive deliberation at the highest levels of the resistance, it was decided that Faber should be eliminated. That man was really dangerous, just like his sons. It was a family business in terror."[5]

Apparently, Jan and Hannie felt the same. Soon after the attack, Bonekamp rode to the Zaandam region to connect with the Council of Resistance there. He saw Jan Brasser, who remembered Bonekamp pedaling up behind Brasser at a bridge over the Zaan, all out of breath. Bonekamp was wearing a heavy coat, which was standard for him, summer or winter, so that he could easily store his pistols in big deep pockets. "Who is next?" Bonekamp wanted to know. Who ought to be his next victim? Everyone who knew Bonekamp commented on how irrepressible he was. A bundle of energy, always looking to do more. So it was now.

Brasser told him he ought to relax for a while, that he'd done all that he could of late. Things might be hot, particularly after the Faber shooting and in light of the fact that the Germans were on edge after the D-day invasion, and subsequent advances made by the Allies in less than two weeks since that early June assault. Maybe he and Hannie should disappear for a time.

But Bonekamp was wired, anxious to get on with the next assignment, and not listening to any sober assess-

5. *Haarlems Dagblad*, August 22, 2009.

ment of his circumstances. Eventually Brasser gave in to
him. In fact, there was someone else on the RVV liquidation list, a police captain from Zaan named Willem Ragut.[6]
The Council of Resistance in Amsterdam had been tracking Ragut's activities for some time. They knew that he
was one of those Dutch police officers who was working in
league with the SD and had collected numerous bounties
for turning in Jews and his fellow Dutchmen. The Amsterdam RVV wanted him gone, and Bonekamp quickly agreed
to the assignment.

Brasser set a meeting time at a café in Zaandam for the
next day, at which Bonekamp would be given the intelligence that had been gathered by the RVV.

Bonekamp brought Hannie to the rendezvous. She
would be part of the plan just as she had been with Piet
Faber. They were clearly now a team.

Brasser, who had a contact in the Zaandam police force,
warned them both that Ragut was a dangerous man. Not
only did he know that he was being watched, but he had
boldly declared to his colleagues at the police station that
any resister looking to gun him down was more likely to
wind up dead than he. In fact, there had been at least one
other unsuccessful attempt on Ragut's life by the RVV in
Beverwijk in December 1943, when he had been attacked
by three people. Ragut was wounded but was said to have
injured at least one of his would-be assassins in his own defense. Hannie and Bonekamp were warned that Ragut

6. *Hannie Schaft*, p. 100; Peter Hammann writing in *Hannie* says the
order came from Frans van der Wiel, p. 49.

now carried two pistols at all times and they should watch out for the second gun, which was holstered on his leg.[7]

Brasser took Hannie and Jan to Ragut's address on the west side of Zaandam and they cycled together to the police station on Vinkenstraat. Jan told Brasser that all would be fine, that he and Hannie could handle things from this point onward. Hannie said that they would accomplish their mission as soon as possible because there was so much work for them to do. Brasser left them to their own devices.[8]

Hannie and Jan continued to reconnoiter Zaandam, which lies just on the northwest corner of Amsterdam. They came back and followed Ragut on several bicycle trips through the city, just as they had with Faber in Haarlem, from the station to his home and back again, discussing moments where it would be opportune to swoop down on him. As well, they mapped escape routes for after the shooting. Then they headed back to the farm of Jan and Trijntje Bult to await the right moment for the attack.

The morning of June 21, 1944, dawned bright and clear as Hannie and Jan took off on their bicycles for Zaandam. Trijntje Bult waved to them as they pedaled away. "See you in a few hours!" Hannie called back.[9]

The plan was to pick up Ragut's trail at his home on the west side of Zaandam, follow at a safe distance, and come swooping down at an opportune moment. Hannie was to

7. *Witte Ko*, p. 108.
8. *Witte Ko*, p. 108.
9. *Hannie Schaft*, p. 104.

take the first shot at the police officer, and Bonekamp would follow to make sure that the job was done.

But there was confusion from the start. Just as they spied Ragut, riding on Bootenmakerstraat, a squadron of RAF bombers appeared overhead. Passersby would later claim that they heard strafing fire coming from the planes, which sent people in the street scurrying for cover, but it was more likely the sound of the ensuing gunfire. Hannie sped toward Ragut, and then took her shot. She missed, but her target fell off his bicycle anyway at the sound of the gun and was now lying in the street. She kept pedaling toward an agreed-upon rendezvous beyond the point of assassination.

When Jan Bonekamp came by to fire what he thought would be a coup de grâce at Ragut, he found the policeman still alive and firing from his second gun. Bonekamp shot several times and hit his target at least once. Unfortunately, he was shot as well. Both men were now off their bikes and continued to shoot until Ragut's gun went silent. Which is probably when Jan realized he had a gruesome wound to his belly.

There was panic on the street. Some passersby still thought the gunfire was coming from the passing squadron of bombers. They watched, frozen in place, as Ragut lay still in the street. Bonekamp managed to get up and stumble a few hundred yards, down an alley and through a narrow gate to a small cottage next to a flower shop. The house was occupied by a pair of old ladies, who were stunned to have a strange man first knocking on their door, then stumbling inside, then putting a pistol on their kitchen table, only to collapse on the floor, where they saw he was bleeding profusely from a gunshot to the stomach. Blood also seeped from the corners of his mouth.

One of the ladies immediately went outside looking for a police officer. Given the commotion, and the fact that a dead man was lying already in the street, one was not hard to find. She brought the officer back to her *kichen*, where he saw that Jan Bonekamp was in bad shape.[10] The assassin needed attention immediately and an ambulance was called to take him to a first aid station within the police department.

Two doctors arrived to tend to Bonekamp and they instantly recognized that his wound was most likely mortal. But the police in Zaandam knew that they were looking at an important member of the resistance and that he didn't have long for this world. He was obviously an assassin and probably an experienced one. They decided to contact the Gestapo in Amsterdam, which rushed to Zaandam.

Bonekamp was given a series of stimulants to keep him breathing as long as possible. When the SD arrived, they immediately wanted to get as much information as they could from him, which required operating on Bonekamp to keep him living, as helpless as his case might be. Through informants at the police station in Zaandam, the local RVV learned of a plan to take Jan to Wilhelmina Hospital in Amsterdam, and the resistance made tentative arrangements to mount an effort to break him out of custody.

10. *Hannie Schaft*, p. 105.

Through all of this a frantic Hannie Schaft had pedaled to a rendezvous point near Limmen, all the while looking back to see if Jan was coming. They had agreed to take separate roads to the meeting place, so in spite of the fact that she'd heard the gunfire behind her, and in spite of her nervousness about Jan's fate, she had been trained to never head back to the scene of a liquidation. And so now she waited, growing more and more panicky with each passing minute.

It didn't surprise her to see Jan Brasser pedaling toward her at the rendezvous site. He had been aware of the action and knew where they were planning to meet. She was actually glad to see him coming. Until the look on his face sent her heart to her shoes. Oh my God, what had happened to Jan!

Brasser had been to Zaandam getting information. He tried to calm her with his voice and manner, but she was having none of it. Where was Jan?

He was still alive, Brasser told her, but Ragut had shot him and he was very seriously injured and being held at the police station. There were plans to take him to the hospital in Amsterdam. This was no time to lose her head, Brasser warned Hannie. The police would certainly be on her tail quickly, and she needed to find a safe hideout. Brasser asked Hannie if she had a good address to go to in Haarlem, and she mentioned the only one she could think of: the Wagenweg studio of Mari Andriessen, which despite being compromised earlier in the year, remained a meeting place for the group. He told her to go there—to go straight there, no stops or detours—and to do it immediately. With her heart thumping and her mind on fire, she started the ride back to Wagenweg in Haarlem.[11]

And that, too, was where Truus Oversteegen was staying—in one of the sculptor's bedrooms. Mari's wife, Nettie, came knocking at Truus's door late that night to say that a young woman had arrived looking for her. Hannie was in tears when the two greeted each other. She was sobbing as the story spilled out: how she and Jan had trailed Ragut, how she had fired and missed, how she kept on pedaling, how Jan was shot and now captured by the SD, how she couldn't go back to save him. Each step in the journey was punctuated with her sobs. Truus got her a glass of water, but her hands were so shaky she splashed much of it over her clothes.

"Will you help me get Jan from the Huns?" she begged Truus. Though Truus wondered how in the world that could be accomplished, she assured her that she would help come morning. Something would come to mind . . . It always did.[12]

That night Hannie told Truus how she felt about Jan. She was in love with him.[13] This would have come as no surprise to Truus or Freddie or anyone else in the group for that matter—anyone could see how the two of them lit up around each other. But Hannie had never talked about it before. She may have been only just then admitting it to herself.

11. *Witte Ko*, p. 111.
12. *Not Then*, p. 102.
13. *Hannie Schaft*, p. 107.

The next morning, Hannie and Truus cycled to Wilhelmina Hospital in Amsterdam, and waited as inconspicuously as possible near the emergency entrance for the ambulance carrying Jan Bonekamp to arrive. Before long, an ambulance pulled up and a pair of heavily armed SS officers climbed out from the front. Two burly male nurses got out from the back and slid Bonekamp out on a stretcher. Jan was instantly recognizable to the girls by the curls of his hair. Hannie whispered, "Oh, Jan. Oh, Jan."[14]

Truus nudged her back toward their bicycles. There was no possible way to rescue him. And what would they do between the two of them with a mortally wounded man on a stretcher? Run him back to Wagenweg?

As they rode home to Haarlem, Truus thought about the dangers they'd placed themselves in by going to the hospital that morning: Hannie with her bright red hair pedaling to the hospital after an assassination just the previous night, which would certainly have been the talk of Haarlem and probably Amsterdam as well. As she rode, she urged both on faster, and faster. Hannie was wearing a scarf, but Truus made sure that every strand of her red hair was tucked out of sight.

There was one checkpoint on the way back to Haarlem. Thankfully they made it through with no questions, despite the fact that both were carrying FN pistols in their overcoats.

14. *Not Then*, p. 103.

* * *

By the time they arrived at Wagenweg, Hannie was inconsolable, to the point of disorientation. It was obvious that they would have to think for her, and everyone in the RVV Council agreed that she could not return to her parents' home on Van Dortstraat; furthermore, it was no longer safe for her friend Philine to stay there. Everyone would need to lie low for a while, including Truus. Frans immediately whisked Hannie away to the safe home of Lien and Harm Elsinga, where she collapsed from exhaustion and was soon discovered to be sick with the mumps. She hadn't even had the opportunity to say goodbye to her parents.

In Amsterdam at the Wilhelmina Hospital, Jan Bonekamp had died. But not before he was interrogated by a German Gestapo agent. Truus suspected that it was the burly nurses who got him to give up names and addresses by playing on his terribly weakened condition. But perhaps she couldn't bear to think anything else. In addition to the stomach wound, he'd suffered a spinal injury and was in terrible pain. In his delirious state, he gave the SD the address of his own wife in IJmuiden, as well as Cor Rusman's in Haarlem, and, finally, the name of Hannie and her parents' address on Van Dortstraat.

The next day, the police raided the Schaft home in Haarlem. Thankfully, Philine had already left for a new hiding place in Amsterdam. Pieter and Aafje were not so lucky.

According to Emil Ruhl, the Gestapo agent who led the

raid and would re-enter Hannie's life at a later time, the SD had been looking for her for a long while. He recalled many instances of reports of sabotage and liquidation mentioning a woman with long red hair. "For us this girl was a terrorist. That is why we followed every trail, until we found her parents' address."[15]

After bursting into the house, Ruhl demanded that Hannie's father tell him where his daughter was. Pieter Schaft responded bitterly that she had long since disappeared and that he actually had no daughter anymore.

The Gestapo took both Schafts to Vught, the concentration camp in the south-central part of the Netherlands, which was built to supplement Westerbork as a transit camp in 1943. The hope was that Hannie would be enticed to come visit her parents and be immediately captured for her efforts.

Meanwhile back in Haarlem, a poulterer named Cor Koelman, whose name had also been given up by Jan Bonekamp in his death throes, was visited by the SD and shown a picture of Hannie. In fact, he had never seen her and truthfully told the Gestapo as much. Jan Bonekamp, on the other hand, had frequently come to his house to help with the chickens, he said. It seemed ridiculous to lie about that actuality. Afterward, they asked an endless string of questions, but surprisingly kept Cor Koelman out of their snare.

At the Elsinga house, Hannie was sinking into a depres-

15. *Hannie Schaft,* p. 108.

sion in the aftermath of Jan's death and the imprison-ment of her parents. Lien Elsinga remembered that Han-nie had very little to say right after she arrived. Gradually, her story came out, but in the beginning, the Elsingas, who hadn't known her previously, had trouble coaxing anything from her. "She just sat there a little bit. In the first few weeks, she practically did not leave the house."[16]

Aside from her depression, she was sick from the mumps, an illness that made her oddly embarrassed be-cause it was such a disease of children. She was also con-cerned because the Elsingas had small children of their own, and she didn't want to infect them.

One of the few trips that Hannie made was to her par-ents' home to pick up some clothes. The house had been locked up by the authorities, forcing her to climb through an upstairs window to gain access. She was spotted by a friendly neighbor with her arms full of clothes, as well as the family mail. The neighbor advised her not to come back. An NSB family living on the same street knew that Hannie was wanted, and they had a pair of snooping boys who would give her up in a minute. Hannie gave the neighbor a kiss and never went back.

The Elsingas soon discovered that Hannie was the daughter of Piet Schaft, a respected teacher in the com-munity. They learned this from a colleague of Harm Elsinga's, who had been gossiping about the fact that the Schafts had been arrested and transported to Vught, and that the police were looking for their daughter. Harm

16. *Hannie Schaft*, p. 111.

asked his friend if the daughter had long red hair and when he got a yes, he realized who was staying with his family.

An appointment was quickly made with a hairdresser. Hannie's red locks were dyed a deep black. Between that and a pair of glasses borrowed from a college friend in Amsterdam, she was largely unrecognizable.

Chapter 18

ON A WARM DAY in the first week of August that year, a cluster of police officers from the SD in Amsterdam, acting on a tip from a Dutch informer whose identity remains uncertain to this day, burst into the office building at 263 Prinsengracht in Amsterdam and began a search of the structure. On the first floor was the business warehouse; on the second floor, the company offices. Above the offices, there was another floor that was used for storage. Tucked away on the landing between was a revolving bookcase, which led to a hidden annex behind the business. For the last two years, it had been the hiding place for the eight members of the Frank and van Pels families, all of whom were quickly rounded up by the police, including Otto Frank's fifteen-year-old daughter, Anne. In a matter of two hours, the SD had finished its business.[1]

The families were sent to Westerbork for a few weeks, and then were sent on to Auschwitz, on one of the last

1. www.AnneFrank.org, Reconstruction: the arrest of the people in hiding.

shipments of Dutch Jews taken from the country. For three nights and days, the trains rumbled across Germany toward Poland—seventy-five people packed inside each windowless car.

At Auschwitz, men and women were separated as they were herded off the train. This was the last moment Otto Frank would ever see his wife and daughters. New arrivals had their heads shaved and were immediately put to work digging sod. At the end of their days, they would be prodded back to crowded barracks, built in the shadows of the constantly smoking crematoriums in the center of the camp.[2]

Slowly, Hannie became more responsive to what was happening around her, and in the world at large, and returned to the Haarlem RVV Council. Once again, Truus, Freddie, and Hannie began to head out on assignments. They traveled frequently along the coast between Leiden and The Hague, disguised as German girls, where they would flirt with soldiers of the Wehrmacht with the intention of learning about the V-2 missile movements in the area.

Public transportation had become more dangerous because of frequent checks conducted by the Wehrmacht. They rode bikes from Haarlem to the village of Wassenaar, their usual destination on the coast, even though the distance (almost thirty miles) was taxing.

Everyday life in the Netherlands grew more difficult as

2. *Anne Frank*, p. 278.

the Allies advanced nearer the country. Food was becoming scarce and raids to pick up Dutch citizens for work assignments in Germany became frequent. At the end of July, Hitler imposed a new set of orders that stipulated there would no longer be criminal proceedings against political opponents of the Nazi regime. Instead, the Gestapo was given license to take measures into their own hands. In other words, they could simply kill suspected saboteurs and terrorists without going through the trouble of first hauling them in to a Dutch detention center for deportation to the camps.[3]

As German defenses in Normandy began to melt and the Allies neared the outskirts of Paris, the Reich became alarmed about the possibility of losing everything to the British, Canadian, and American attacks. To help slow the progress of the Allies and turn the momentum in the war, Hitler decided to step up his missile program: the V-2 rockets.

The V-2 was a top-secret weapons system that the Nazis developed with the aid of pioneering rocket scientist Wernher von Braun. It was the world's first long-range guided ballistic missile, and it was hoped that it would be a monumental difference-maker in the war. No longer would Germany have to rely on its devastated Luftwaffe in air battles over England and Europe. They could simply rain down death and destruction from the continent, including from the Netherlands, with the push of a button from one of the mobile launchers they were developing.

3. *Hannie*, p. 52.

Initially the Germans had planned to employ these devices from fixed, bunkered sites, but the efficacy of mobility—keeping Allied bombers guessing where they might be—prompted the creation of movable units. These terrifying devices, which would be used for the first time in just a few weeks, would ultimately deliver destruction to multiple locations in England, France, and even at The Hague in the Netherlands. But in early August 1944, their power was still theoretical, and Hannie, Truus, and Freddie were sent out searching for evidence of where the Germans might be deploying them.

Hannie was still prone to bouts of melancholy about Jan, but she played her role well. She spoke German like a native and she and Truus, who hardly knew the language, acted the part of old friends. Hannie would explain that Truus's German was limited by the fact that she'd been raised her entire life in Holland by German parents who had moved to the country when she was very young. The soldiers always seemed to buy the lie, perhaps because it was delivered by such a charming young woman.[4]

The girls were fast becoming the principal eyes and ears of the RVV in Haarlem. Unlike the men in the group, they were in little danger of being picked up suddenly and sent to the work camps in Germany. Without raising suspicions, they could spend exorbitant amounts of time just hanging on a street corner or at a café, pretending to chat and gossip as they spied on houses, or trailed collaborators or NSBers. They could travel between Amsterdam

4. *Hannie Schaft*, p. 116.

and Haarlem with full bicycle bags without raising eyebrows because it was assumed that a woman's bicycle bag would be full of food rather than weapons.

They could also move children more easily than men. It was a task that could be difficult due to the simple heartache involved. Truus remembered seeing what she called "stumpers," little Jewish kids four and five years old, who had gone completely gray while in hiding. One boy had been literally underground for a full year, in the cellar of a home. He had nothing to play with, no toys, only a jar to pee in and three books. "Hannie couldn't stand that. It was so awful. She would wind up crying every time. I prefer to fight, she said."[5]

According to Truus, Hannie in her down moods considered turning herself in to the Germans, thinking that if she did so, they might release her parents. She and Freddie spent hours talking her out of the idea. Not only was it unlikely that the Nazis would make that sort of arrangement, but she would also jeopardize the whole Haarlem RVV if she were subject to questioning by the Gestapo.

She and Freddie were given the assignment of keeping an eye out for Hannie when she was in these moods. They tried to distract her by making fanciful conversations about what they would do in the future. What they would do after the war. Truus and Freddie talked of getting married and getting better educated. But Hannie had a hard time responding to this. "I just don't see an end," she responded morbidly. "When I try to imagine

5. *Hannie Schaft*, p. 118.

what lies ahead, what I see is like a big curtain falling over everything."[6]

Hannie followed the progress of the Allied advance through the BBC's Radio Oranje broadcasts that she heard on the Elsingas' radio. There was excitement in the house when Paris was liberated, joy when the Allies moved into Belgium. Hannie's response, though, was muted; her depression lingered despite getting out and working with Truus and Freddie.

Even a note from Philine in Amsterdam failed to lift her out of her despondency, though she responded with a letter of her own. To her old friend, she explained her circumstances and her state of mind: "My mental condition is deplorable: I cannot read a book, nor a novel, nor a study book. In my spare time I knit (sic!) A stocking!! . . . I am considerably less hard than I was: getting acquainted with death was not easy."[7]

Later in the letter she wrote about the town's reaction to news about the Allies coming soon: "The people are in such a festive mood. I am sitting here like a smiling Buddha and I am also expected to be in a festive mood. I'd rather curse."[8]

"When will it all be over? Maybe on my birthday. Now I am becoming melodramatic. If I don't see you at all any-

6. *Hannie*, p. 52.
7. Verzets Resistance Museum, Amsterdam. Three Girls in Resisance [museum's translation].
8. *Hannie Schaft* (translation of letter by Google Translate with edits by the author).

more, I will give you some guidelines for the future, a. Solidarity, b. continuation of all of our work . . . c. Don't think anything cowardly about my friend. He behaved beautifully. There should be more such people. He was one of the nicest guys I have ever met. Remember this, it is very important. Philine, see you soon. Kind regards, Jo. P.S. I catch fleas almost daily!"[9]

Philine later explained the cryptic reference to knitting the stocking. Before she went into hiding in Haarlem, Hannie came to Philine's apartment to tell Philine that her father had been taken to Westerbork. He would later die in Sobibor. For a full week following the news, Philine could do nothing but knit. It was Hannie's way of showing both her state of mind about losing the war and losing Jan, as well as her bond with Philine.[10]

Lien Elsinga also remembered Hannie knitting a pair of socks, a thing she'd never done before. After the war, Lien found them in her home and sent them to Hannie's mother, Aafje. "She was very moved by the gesture."[11]

9. *Hannie Schaft,* pp. 118–20 (Google Translate with edits).
10. *Hannie Schaft,* p. 120.
11. *Hannie Schaft,* p. 121.

Chapter 19

TOWARD THE END OF AUGUST and into early September in the south of Holland, something strange was happening. In village after village could be heard the unmistakable rumblings of German heavy vehicles, tanks, trucks, armored cars, along with the whir of hundreds of bicycles and a mix of the clacking noise of wagon axles and a variety of other vehicles. All signaled the beginning of a large-scale movement of German troops out of the regions of the Netherlands that bordered Belgium. From Roosendaal in the west, to Eindhoven in the east, the Wehrmacht was packing up and moving north and east to escape the Allied advance, which was now herding a rout of German forces out of France and Belgium.

German troops were using every conveyance possible as they headed toward roads leading back to Germany. They carried with them what loot they could, with an emphasis on all the wine and cognac they could haul. At first the Dutch villagers who came out to see them pass were skeptical about what their eyes were telling them. Could it be after four long years of occupation, they were finally leaving? But the whispers they heard—that Brussels had fallen to the Allies; that the Allies were knocking at the gates of Antwerp—all seemed to confirm the possibility that the Germans were done in France, Belgium, and now Holland.

More news was similarly affirming: on September 1, Seyss-Inquart ordered German civilians to move to the east of Holland, as to be closer to the German border. NSB head Anton Mussert quickly became weak-kneed as well, ordering members of the Dutch Nazi Party to the eastern realms of the Netherlands. Both of these stalwart leaders were among the first to hightail it toward safety. They quickly moved from The Hague to Apeldoorn, where Seyss-Inquart took to a concrete and brick bunker that he'd had built earlier during his regime for just such emergencies. Here he nestled as British tanks rousted the Germans from Antwerp, just a handful of miles beneath the Dutch border.[1]

Railway stations were overrun by terrified NSBers and their families, trying to get transport out of the country. There was a run on banks as fascists tried to liquidate their savings accounts. Dutch Nazis appointed to office by the Germans tried to squeeze salaries, advances, and back payments out of the municipalities they had just been governing.

To hasten their flight, they only needed to listen to Radio Oranje out of the BBC in London. On September 4, Queen Wilhelmina came on to broadcast to the

---

1. *A Bridge Too Far*, p. 20.

Dutch people that liberation was imminent. Her son-in-law, Prince Bernhard, who had been named Commander-in-Chief of the Netherlands Armed Forces, followed by announcing that he would first begin his command by ordering the unification of Dutch resistance forces, including the LO (the organization that principally led efforts to hide the *onkerduikers*), the OD, which was the group of former Dutch officers and officials, who were preparing to step into the governmental breach when the Nazis were eradicated from the Netherlands, and, finally, groups like the RVV, which practiced direct and sometimes violent actions against the Nazis and their Dutch collaborators. Another group known as the KP (for Knokploegen) which was an action arm of the LO, also engaged in a variety of direct measures against the fascists, including, robberies, sabotage, and assassinations. These separate organizations were to be collected into a single unit under Bernhard's command to be called The Forces of the Interior.

There was more exciting news to come. General Dwight D. Eisenhower, Supreme Commander of Allied Forces, spoke next on the radio to announce that "The hour of liberation the Netherlands have awaited so long is now very near." Finally, Dutch prime minister in exile, Pieter Gerbrandy, announced to the people of the Netherlands that "the Allied armies, in their irresistible advance, have crossed the Netherlands frontier." He encouraged his citizenry to "bid our Allies a hearty welcome to our native soil."[2]

2. *A Bridge Too Far*, p. 21.

Not surprisingly, all of this news, along with the obvious fact of German soldiers exiting the country posthaste, set off a wave of excitement that has since been immortalized in Dutch lore as Dolle Dinsdag, or Crazy Tuesday, September 5, 1944. The Dutch poured out into the streets suddenly emboldened, waving flags and strips of orange ribbon, which were freshly cut from bolts of fabric, flying out of shops across the country. Schools closed and factories shut down. The evacuating NSB families were jeered as were the straggling German forces plodding their way through the towns and villages of the Netherlands.

That it was all premature was a realization that would come pretty quickly; in just a matter of days really, when German forces halted in the northeastern part of the country and began re-organizing under the leadership of a newly re-appointed Commander in Chief of the Western Front. Field Marshal Gerd von Rundstedt, a legendary German general, had held the same post just months earlier at the time of the Normandy invasion. His failures then had led Hitler to can him; the failures of his successor led Hitler to take a second look at von Rundstedt. Now the general was tasked with putting the spine back into a German army that had been pushed around and through France.

In Haarlem, it was still Dolle Dinsdag, and the local Council of Resistance decided to take advantage of the chaos by attacking a target they had long sought to silence: Fake Krist, the head of the Haarlem police, and two of his henchmen, fellow officers Harm Smit and Franciscus Willemse.

Krist had a reputation for cruelty that included torturing resistance figures that he'd arrested. In one case, it was said that he brought in a son of one of his detainees and tortured the boy in front of the father until Krist got the information that he wanted.[3] He was long an officer in the Haarlem police and also an early member of the NSB. Krist had been involved in the February 1943 reprisals for the assassination of the German officer Alois Bamberger. He'd also overseen the arrest of a group of twenty-six Haarlemmers plotting an attack on the camp in Westerbork just that past summer. The Haarlem cop also led the search of Mari Andriessen's home earlier that year.

The plot was devised by Frans van der Wiel and at its heart was the familiar core of his group, Truus, Cor Rusman, Jan Heusdens, and Freddie with the addition of Henk de Ronde, a young student from Amsterdam, just nineteen years old, who had joined the group at about the same time as Hannie. He was the son of a captain in the Dutch Navy and an ardent anti-fascist, according to Truus, who said that he shyly told her once that he thought his father would be proud of him for defending his country against the Nazis. The young man had been "at odds" with his dad growing up. "'But I think he would understand me now,'" he told Truus.[4]

Truus and Jan Heusdens were assigned to liquidate Harm Smit who lived along the Spaarndamweg. Hannie

3. *Not Then*, p. 128.
4. *Not Then*, p. 127.

Schaft and Cor Rusman were to assassinate Franciscus Willemse, an NSBer and officer in Zaandam, who had been notorious in police efforts to clean up the illegal press in the area. Freddie was given her familiar role as the scout and lookout of the various teams.

Henk de Ronde had trailed the movements of Fake Krist for some time and was given the task of taking him out. Krist had recently given up being driven to work and back, and instead had been commuting by bicycle from his home near the Cathedral on Leidsevaart. This was where de Ronde was lurking on the morning of September 5.

The city of Haarlem, fresh from hearing the Radio Oranje broadcasts from the night before, was in a state of high excitement, as was everyone else in the country. Additionally, morning rumors were flying around that the Allies were currently in the city of Breda, within the Dutch borders, and that Canadian forces would be arriving in Haarlem via the Wagenweg by sometime late that afternoon. The railway station was already bustling with NSB families packed and ready to board trains heading east toward the German border. Like Seyss-Inquart and Anton Mussert, the mayor of Haarlem, a man named S.L.A. Plekker had packed up his office and was leaving town for safety in the country to the east of Amsterdam.

In this climate, bright and early that morning, the assassins headed out to their targets. Heusdens and Truus lingered by a bridge on the Sparne River, outside the home of Harm Smit, playing lovers as they had on past assignments. Truus was a head taller than Jan, which meant their "makeout" sessions were a little awkward, making them giggle as they kissed, occasionally peeking up at the front door, looking for Smit to exit. It wasn't long. Five minutes. Ten minutes. And there he was, big as a dairy cow, at the door wearing a tan jacket and wishing his wife a good-bye.

Smit got on his bike and they followed on theirs, holding hands as they pedaled, still playing the lovers. Jan whispered for Truus to go ahead and take the first shots as they'd planned. She did, with sharp-eyed success, leaving two black holes in the tan coat, which Jan saw as he pedaled behind. Smit fell off his bicycle, but was not yet dead. He began screaming for help as Jan stopped to return to finish the job. Smit suddenly had his pistol in hand and was now firing back; he hit Heusdens with a bullet that tore straight through the resister's leg.[5] From a distance, Jan aimed and fired, hitting the policeman in the head, stopping him permanently.

Truus got off her bike as well. Both went up to Smit's body, Jan limping all the way. They emptied the police officer's pockets and grabbed his pistol. Truus asked Jan if he could still ride and he proved it by hopping on his bike and pedaling off to a doctor who did work for the resistance.[6]

One cop was down.

Henk de Ronde was posted near the cathedral at a site that had grown familiar to him during his reconnaissance

5. *Not Then,* p. 110.
6. *Hannie Schaft,* p. 123.

of Krist. Unfortunately, Krist saw him lurking around and immediately suspected what was up. He raced ahead of young de Ronde and then ducked into a side alley as Henk passed. Quickly, the hunted and the prey switched posts and now it was Krist on the tail of de Ronde. De Ronde was able to cycle away, but any opportunity of taking Krist out that morning was gone.[7]

That left the final team of Hannie and Cor Rusman looking to gun down Franciscus Willemse.[8] They were staking out an area near the cemetery on Schoterstraat when they spotted their target. As with Truus and Jan, the plan was to attack in succession, with Hannie going in first, shooting as she biked past the policeman. She did just that, hitting Willemse in the arm with her first shot. Unfortunately, when she squeezed the trigger on a second round, her gun jammed, and as she tried to fix it, working the slide to eject her spent shell while continuing to ride by, Hannie lost her balance and fell.

Willemse was not finished. He remained on his bicycle, wobbling as he pedaled near her, aiming and firing. His bullet went into and through Hannie's thigh, sending her to the ground as a crowd began to gather at the sound of the shoot-out. Now it was Cor Rusman's turn to jump into action. He swooped in toward Hannie and quickly scooped her up, setting her on top of the basket at the front of her bike. They sped away as the citizens of Haarlem gaped.

7. *Hannie Schaft*, p. 123.
8. *Recht op Wraak*, p. 126.

She told him to take her to the only place she could think of at the moment: her family doctor, a man named Lancee who worked on Duinoordstraat. The doctor knew her from previous visits and knew that she was in the resistance, but had no idea, until this moment, what she did for the cause. Looking at the wound now, he also knew that she was lucky. The bullet hit no bone. He bandaged the wound and sent her on her way, satisfied that he had all the information that he wanted about Hannie Schaft.[9]

In the wake of the assassination and attempted killings (Willemse survived the ambush), it was once again necessary to find a good hiding place for Hannie. The feeling was that the Elsinga place was getting overused and Hannie should find a new spot. She wound up staying for a week with a teacher from Haarlem, who offered her a pleasant room overlooking his garden. There she rested and read and received visits from her RVV comrades, including Jan Heusdens who was recuperating from his wound as well. Both were in pain; both were glad to see one another alive.[10]

The Haarlem Council had missed its principal target and was certain to feel the heat once again in the city, especially when Dolle Dinsdag proved an illusory end to the miseries in the Netherlands. The conclusion to the occupation was far from at hand. In fact, not only was the battle for the Netherlands just beginning, but the hardships for the Dutch people were about to escalate.

9. *Hannie Schaft*, p. 124.
10. *Hannie Schaft*, p. 125.

Chapter 20

LESS THAN TWO WEEKS after Dolle Dinsdag, the Allies initiated a battle plan that they hoped would not only liberate the Netherlands but allow the Allies to drive into the heart of Germany's industrial belt in the Ruhr.

On the morning of September 17, a massive wave of British and American planes flew over the Dutch countryside toward the eastern part of the nation. Their cargo was a seemingly endless string of paratroopers leaping into the sky above the green and gold landscape of the Netherlands from Eindhoven in the southeastern part of the nation, up to Arnhem near the German border in the north. Rocking down beneath their white parachutes, looking like a field of daisies in the sky, forty thousand troopers floated toward landings on Dutch fields and dykes below, constituting the largest airborne assault of the war.

Called Operation Market Garden, the attack's intent was to catch German forces in chaotic retreat, secure a series of bridges running from Eindhoven to the most crucial bridge in the attack, the one over the Rhine in

Arnhem, thereby cutting off German forces in the Netherlands and leaving Germany itself open to attack.[1]

Bypassed in the attempt was the coastal region of the
Netherlands. North Holland, where Germany had flat-
tened IJmuiden and built its coastal defenses, was to see
no giant invasion fleet out beyond its dune-covered
shores; no mass of Allied troops wading onto the beaches
to liberate the people. While thunderous war was deci-
mating the cities of Nijmegen and Arnhem in the interior
of the nation, to the west—in Amsterdam, Haarlem, Rotterdam, and The Hague—an unsettled period arose in
which Germany and its fascist collaborators in Holland remained the chief power in the country, but the resistance
had added strength and organization. Prince Bernhard
and the Dutch government in exile were now more inti-
mately involved in the resistance than they'd ever been,
and a new centralized organization was placed over the di-
vergent resistance groups in Holland, including the Resistance Council in Haarlem.

To aid Allied forces fighting in Arnhem, the resistance
called for a strike of railway workers across the country to
coincide with the Allied attack at Arnhem. The hope was
that without the railroads, German defenses and commu-
nication would be handicapped at the height of the battle. Reinforcements moving from the west to the east
would be slowed and the German supply chain would be
disrupted. The resistance was also prepared to join in the

1. See *A Bridge Too Far*, pp. 112–14.

fight against the Germans once the bridgehead was established.

Unfortunately, the battle for Arnhem was lost by the Allies in a matter of days. British, American, and Polish troops who fought bitterly on the streets of Arnhem were beaten back by the Germans at that bridge over the Rhine and were forced to retreat back toward the Belgium border, leaving behind hundreds of dead, hundreds of POWs, and a lovely medieval city leveled by the brute destructiveness of twentieth-century armaments. The railway strike had limited effect on its outcome.

In the aftermath of the battle and the supporting strike, Seyss-Inquart came out of his hidey-hole to impose a food embargo on the Dutch people in an attempt to force workers back to the rails. The Germans, as well, began to squeeze tighter on the citizenry as supplies in the Reich began to dwindle. The homeland needed more of everything, and the Netherlands were turned upside down and shaken for every last coin and turnip.

Even before Market-Garden fuels for running power stations and manufactories were almost gone, likewise finding gas for stoves and other home consumption was apportioned to next to nothing. The government limited the hours that gas could be supplied. Bakeries were similarly limited, which meant that in all of Haarlem only twenty bakeries remained open that fall. Finding a loaf of bread could be a day's long task.

Before the railway strike, trains were running on limited schedules. Local tram traffic was limited as well. Coal rations were reduced to a quarter. The electric power was cut off for family use on October 9; only companies deemed vital by the Nazis would continue to be supplied with power.

The cinemas were shuttered. Schools, which had been closed during the battle for Arnhem, were not reopened because they could no longer be sufficiently heated for children. As food supplies dwindled, a central soup kitchen was established; in its first week it served sixty thousand people in the North Holland region.[2]

On top of all of this, the Germans were once again nervous about an attack by sea. Having beaten back the paratroop invasion, they assumed the Allies would try again, this time, by direct assault in Kennermerland. They began a massive forced evacuation of the towns on the coast. What was left of IJmuiden after it was already largely leveled in earlier preparations was now torn down. With it went parts of Bloemendaal, Santpoort, Driehuis, Beverwijk, and Haarlem. Evacuation agencies in each of the towns tried to help, but families were forced to empty their lifelong belongings onto the street and haul them away as their houses were demolished before their eyes to make way for ever more German bunkers and impediments to an Allied attack.[3]

As the miseries set in, and the Allied forces backed out of their quick strike at Germany, the people in the west of

---

2. *Hannie Schaft*, p. 128.
3. *Hannie Schaft*, p. 129.

Holland began to realize that the liberation was not coming anytime soon. As a consequence, the resistance groups in Haarlem became more active than ever.

Hannie, her leg healed and her spirits somewhat rekindled, joined Truus and Freddie in a continued pursuit of the Haarlem police chief, Fake Krist. Since he was such a dangerous target, they also looked for other opportunities, including the possibility of liquidating one of the chief contractors used by the Nazis to demolish buildings in IJmuiden. His name was Christiaansen and word was that he had a posh villa in Bloemendaal.

The girls located the house and sat watching it for three days, studying the contractor's movements. Ultimately, they decided not to assassinate the target; instead they decided to simply frighten him with a few shots over the head and let justice be carried out after the war, by whatever tribunal was established to mete out a proper retribution.

"For days we hung around the villa," Truus remembered. "The man just didn't want to come out. And we did not dare to climb over the wall into his garden, because he had a bitch of a bloodhound there. That beast was so trained that he didn't even want to eat meat that we had given him."[4]

One consequence of the fighting at Arnhem was that the Wehrmacht was suddenly in desperate need of more bicycles. As it had early in the occupation, the German

4. *Hannie Schaft*, p. 130.

armed forces began confiscating bikes from the Dutch with an even more thorough eye than they'd used before.

Bicycles were an essential component of resistance work, of course, and when supplies ran low, Henk de Ronde took it upon himself to steal one back for the resistance. Unfortunately, he was caught in the act by Fake Krist himself, who recognized de Ronde as his attempted assassin from Dolle Dinsdag. De Ronde was immediately taken to Gestapo headquarters in Amsterdam, where somehow he broke free temporarily from his guards. It was only a matter of seconds before the young student, who had so wanted to please his Navy captain father, was gunned down outside the Sicherheitspolizei station on Euterprestraat in Amsterdam.

"We were unashamed by our tears," Truus remembered.[5]

It was yet another reason for the Haarlem RVV to hate Fake Krist.

More than a few people in the resistance at large had similar feelings toward Krist. In fact, he had been the subject of three additional attacks by area fighters since Frans's group had tried to liquidate him on Dolle Dinsdag.

Freddie was sent to gather information on Krist's schedule and routine. It was her particular skill. Not only was she young and inconspicuous, but she was quick, agile, and particularly thorough in her observations. She tended not to overlook the small details. She mapped out his route for them; each morning he passed near the cathe-

5. *Not Then*, p. 128.

dral on Westergracht with a bodyguard in tow, a meaty man who Freddie had nicknamed Oink. The cathedral might be the place to pick up his trail.

On the morning of October 25, 1944, Hannie Schaft and Truus Oversteegen were standing on the Leidsevaart, right in the heart of Haarlem just as they had been directed by Freddie and Frans. Around a quarter past eight they saw Krist approach the bridge at Westergracht. The girls climbed on their bicycles and pulled in behind him, pedaling fast to catch up. But even before they could pull their pistols from their coat pockets, a shot rang out, followed quickly by another, and two more. The guard, Oink, had kept pedaling, but now he came to a quick halt and pulled a rifle slung around his back into shooting range and looked around for an attacker as he moved toward Krist. He saw Hannie and Truus and told them to get a doctor.

Truus said, "Yes, sir, right away," as she and Hannie took off in the direction of a screaming, crying woman, who appeared on the scene. They would later discover she was Krist's lover. The hysterical woman looked at Hannie and Truus and also asked them to get a doctor. The girls again said they would and sped off past Krist, lying wounded on the pavement, pausing for Truus to lean toward him and say, "You filthy piece of shit."[6]

As it turned out, a second resistance group in Haarlem had been tracking Krist's movement with the same intent as Hannie and Truus. A man working with the KP, an ex-

6. *Not Then*, p. 130.

pert marksman named Gomert Krijger, with assistance from Jan Overzet,[7] had stationed himself in a first-floor window of a primary school catty-corner from the cathedral also at the Westergracht Bridge. They waited there to ambush Krist, having no idea that the two girls from the Haarlem RVV would be biking behind with the same intention.

All hell broke loose afterward. A squad from the police department came rushing onto the scene with sirens blaring. A half-dozen blocks around the site were cordoned off and a search begun. Men loitering near the school were grabbed indiscriminately and placed in the back of police vans. The rifle used by the assassin in the school was discovered hidden in a piano in the gym room. Even before that, eight houses surrounding the school on the corner of Westergracht and Leidsevaart were emptied, with occupants given only a few minutes to gather their belongings. People were running every which way, frantically hauling anything they could from their homes as the police screamed at them. In a matter of minutes, the houses were put to the flame by the authorities.[8]

The next day, the resistance asked Hannie, Freddie, and Truus to go back to the Westergracht neighborhood dressed in nurses' Red Cross outfits. There was to be a commemoration of Krist at the site of the shooting. The

7. *Hannie*, p. 56.
8. This incident will become one of the central moments in a famous 1982 novel *De Aanslag* (The Assault) by Haarlem-born writer Harry Mulisch. The book was subsequently turned into an Academy Award–winning foreign language film of the same name (1986).

girls were sent to get images of the officers congregating in the aftermath, as well as to get license plate numbers of the vehicles. The girls managed to get their hands on a camera and some film, and Freddie was able to secure a lookout post in a house on Leidsevaart, from where she could take photos of what was going on. Truus would try to sketch some of the faces.

What they failed to notice in the middle of all the activity was that two police vans had pulled up to the scene. Hannie and Truus wandered around, even dropping some flowers where Krist had fallen, pretending to mourn the police officer's death.[9] Then from the back of the wagons, the SD pulled nine Haarlemmers in leg chains. They had been arrested the day before on suspicion that they were involved in the shooting of Krist. Now they were lined up along the street in front of the crowd, which slowly began to understand that there was to be no investigation of what happened the day before, there would be no trials. The girls tried to drift away, but with the exception of Hannie, who managed to flee, the Gestapo corralled dozens of others in the crowd. Truus and Freddie and the other Haarlemmers would be forced to witness what was about to happen.

The nine prisoners were taken to a strip of grass near the intersection of Leidsevaart and Westergracht, adjacent to the bridge where the *liquidatie* had occurred. A black-capped officer issued a command; weapons were raised and poised to fire. Then in the deadly silence that

9. *Hannie Schaft*, p. 134.

followed, an old man in the crowd softly began to sing the national anthem of the Netherlands, "The Wilhelmus."

He didn't get far in the singing. A second command rang out, and a horrible cascade of gunfire cracked loudly across the city and echoed seemingly forever against the solid brick walls of the ancient Grote Kerk.

The horrified crowd was forced to watch as the dead martyrs were then picked up and put back into the vans that had brought them. They sped away as quickly as they'd come, only leaving the ghostly recollection of the victims.

Etched now in Haarlem beneath a statue memorializing their sacrifice near the cathedral in Haarlem are the names of those executed that day: Willem Buhler, Ferdinand Maaswinke, Jacob de Vries, Johannes Wutrich, Cornelis Vlot, Wilhemus de Boer, Dornelis Erends, Kalei Tempelman, and Robert Loggers.[10]

10. *Hannie*, p. 56.

Chapter 21

THERE WOULD BE REPERCUSSIONS within the resistance over the screwup that had sent two teams of assassins after Krist on the same October morning. The new central command, the Forces of the Interior, was ostensibly under the leadership of the queen's son-in-law, Prince Bernhard, who had returned from London and was now back on the continent but attached to Allied forces in Belgium. In the Netherlands itself, the organization was led by regional commanders, who needed to control disparate groups, like Frans van der Wiel, which had long been accustomed to acting autonomously. It would be no easy task to rein them in.

In Haarlem, the new leadership was headed by a former Dutch prosecutor named N. G. Sikkel, a brother-in-law of Pieter Gerbrandy, the Prime Minister of the Dutch Government-in-Exile. Sikkel appointed a second tier of commanders based out of the city of Velsen, bordering Haarlem to the north. These were commanded by a pair of Velsen police officers named J. P. Engels and Arend Kuntkes. All had been a part of the OD, the resistance group whose members were drawn primarily from elements of the Dutch military, government and civil service supplanted during the occupation. Some had been functioning as a sort of government-in-waiting, some had continued to work with the occupation regime as part of the constabulary, but with a foot in the resistance, as well, serving as informants to the movement.

Not surprising that between the new leadership and the RVV in Haarlem, there were almost immediate suspicions. To the Velsen crew, van der Wiel and the trio of young women in his cell were loose cannons and had been for some time. There were basic political and class differences between the two; Sikkel, Engels, and Kuntkes were members of the Dutch civil service and bourgeoisie, who were supposedly secretly aligned with the resistance.[1] Van der Wiel and his cohort had begun as a communist resistance organization with working-class ties. They still maintained links to leftist politics and felt a deep unease about allying now with a group of cops and prosecutors who maintained ties to the collaborationist regime still in place in the Netherlands.

In addition, there was obvious sexism among the new leadership: the fact that the heart and soul of the Haarlem RVV was a pack of three young women meant that their expertise and merit could be all too easily dismissed by the new all-male power structure within the command.

---

1. In fact, there were accusations to come in long and bitter political and cultural battles in North Holland, that they collaborated with the fascists against communist elements in the resistance. See *De Velser Affaire* for details.

For van der Wiel, the girls, and everyone else associated
with the Haarlem RVV, it was hard to fathom that they
were now to be allied with a group of Dutch cops who had
worked at times with some of the same men the RVV had
actively sought to assassinate. These new commanders
were so cocksure of their safety within the current regime
that they neglected even the most basic cautions, like having the group gather in safe houses for meetings and assignments. A former Velsen police commissioner who was
part of the new order, an old comrade of Sikkel's and Engels's in the Velsen police, invited local leaders of LO, the
KP, and the RVV over to his house for a discussion over
how to overcome their differences. He lived in a nice villa
in Heemstede and not surprisingly, the leaders of the
"underground" resistance, thought it was crazy to have
such talks in one's own house. These guys were living in a
different world.[2]

Hannie, Truus, and Freddie began to have doubts
about some of the assignments that they were given by the
new leadership. They were asked to make multiple trips to
The Hague to deliver small packages to contacts in that
city. As the weather turned wintry, they were forced to
ride into prevailing coastal winds the fifty-five kilometers
(about thirty-five miles) from Haarlem to the capital.
Hannie wrote a note to Philine Polack about one of these
trips. "In the morning at six o'clock out the door, head-
wind, and smashing waves [on the nearby coast]. 9:15 I
was at the final destination. I was best compared to a soak-

2. *Hannie Schaft*, p. 135.

ing mop." On the way back, she was pushed so hard by a storm at her back that she got lost and wound up heading into Schipol.[3]

Truus remembered another trip to the home of Mr. Engels, who made them wait in the entryway while he fetched them a quarter [of a guilder] and four cigarettes for the trouble of their journey, like he was tipping a messenger.[4]

With all the trouble and work involved in delivering these parcels, it was hard not to wonder what was in them that was so crucial to the cause. "We thought we were delivering important messages," remembered Freddie Oversteegen. By the fourth or fifth trip, they couldn't resist opening a package. Inside, they found jewelry and four packs of cigarettes. This was what was so important?

They rode to Sikkel's home after their discovery to complain. He couldn't believe that they were being taken advantage of by his colleagues—in fact, he *wouldn't* believe them. Sikkel sent the girls back to the Velsen officials to straighten things out with them on their own. The Velsen cops were more shocked that Freddie, Truus, and Hannie had dared to open the packages than remorseful that they'd sent the young women all the way to The Hague to deliver jewelry and cigarettes intended for their wives or girlfriends.[5]

3. *Hannie Schaft*, p. 153.
4. *Not Then*, p. 108.
5. To a man, the Velsen contingent denied to Ton Kors that any of them would be so thoughtless as to put the girls in jeopardy to deliver jewelry and cigarettes. *Hannie Schaft*, p. 154.

The trio immediately stopped making the trips to The Hague.

There were other, lengthy bike trips that needed to be made that winter. The hunger had set in across the country with a vengeance, and in dire straits, people across North Holland, including Hannie, Truus, and Freddie, made long, wandering trips out to the polders—the lowlands reclaimed for planting out in the countryside—asking farmers for any sort of sustenance, including the nation's most famous export: tulips. The idea of eating these flowers, rather than admiring them and selling them to the world, was so unusual that recipes on how best to prepare the bulbs were printed in local papers.[6] Grocers and bakers were getting robbed for their goods; a loaf of bread was a prized commodity. There was so little fuel to heat meals, the woods around Haarlem were being cut down to provide firewood. Because it was against the command of the authorities, much of the chopping was taking place in the dead of night.

The war had bypassed the Netherlands. At least the war of liberation was gone: after the failure of the battle at Arnhem, the Allied front had reverted to the southeast, back toward Belgium and southwestern Germany, where General George Patton's army continued its push toward the Rhine. Holland, for the most part, was left to its own devices, just as its circumstances were growing more and more dire. A certain desperation began to filter into the

6. *Hannie Schaft,* p. 156.

behavior of everyone living through what was sensed to be the final days of the war.

The girls and the resistance were not immune to these pressures. Nor were the Germans, who in early December had issued yet another demand for more Dutch workers to fill needs for their desperately shrinking workforce in the homeland. They also needed parts for their industrial factories and had started shipping entire manufactories from North Holland to Germany on freight cars.

Though the trips to The Hague ended, there were other questionable requests from the new Velsen-led resistance. On Christmas Eve, the girls were asked to go to the bombed-out submarine bunker in IJmuiden, where a German soldier, with whom the resistance had made contact, was offering several boxes of explosives for the resistance. The Germans at the base would be partying that night because of the holidays; similarly, the new leadership was spending Christmas Eve partying with their own families. Hannie, Truus, and Freddie, the unmarried women in the group without families of their own, and unable to connect with their own parents (each was staying with different families, rotating through safe houses through the final stages of the occupation), were assumed to be available for a particularly inconvenient action.

It was a freezing cold night and a full moon illuminated their trek from the bicycle path to the bunker, where they were supposed to be assisted by two men who knew the lay of the land. But after cutting the barbed wire to allow the trio access to the grounds, the men ghosted, apparently feeling their work was done, leaving Hannie, Truus, and Freddie to their own devices.

Along with the glaring moon, a searchlight scanned the field they needed to cross to reach the bunker. To avoid its sweep, the women had to crawl on hands and knees through the swampy land by the canal. This put them in face-to-face contact with a variety of scurrying rats, who inhabited the brackish water and industrial wastes down by the canal.

When they finally reached the bunker, the girls waited an interminable length of time for their German connection to show, all the while listening to the partying of the German soldiers within the concrete structure. When he finally arrived, the collaborator simply showed them where the ammunition was—five boxes of it—and then immediately went back to the party, fearing that his absence would cause alarm among his fellow soldiers.

"Have you ever felt the weight of five boxes of ammunition?" Truus asked rhetorically many years later.[7] Not just feeling the weight but dragging those boxes back across a field beneath sweeping searchlights was the task faced by her, her sister, and Hannie Schaft on that moonlit night. The three of them, living that winter on a diet of root vegetables and tulip bulbs, were down to skin and bones.

Somehow they did it. Strapping the boxes to their backs, they crawled and inched their way over the field, through the rats, up to the path, heaved the ammunition

7. *Hannie Schaft*, p. 158.

onto their bicycles, and hauled them to their Velsen leaders, who were less than appreciative. "They were pissed because they had to feed us," Truus remembered.[8]

The girls had been on another "tulip run" in the polders outside the city—trying to collect any food they could from farmers they knew outside of Haarlem and the city—a prospect no one could ever remember happening before. They were pedaling home along the Spaarne River when they ran into Frans, who steered them to a fancy house near Keanu Park. It was his new meeting place, he said—he'd been set up by a wealthy patron of the resistance—and the interior was sumptuous. Freddie curled up in a luxurious leather chair near the fireplace, Hannie quickly became absorbed in a wall full of books, while Truus browsed through the artwork gracing the walls.

Frans called them away from their reverie toward a blueprint that he'd spread across a table. It showed a familiar bridge, one that they soon recognized as the bridge over the Spaarne that linked downtown Haarlem with the industrial areas north of the city. It didn't take long for them to get the gist of where he was going with this. "You want us to blow that up?" Freddie asked.[9]

Yes, that was precisely what Frans wanted, and they had much to do and only a few days to do it. They needed to check out the bridge itself, find a way to get close enough to plant explosives, and study the movement of guards

8. *Hannie Schaft*, p. 158.
9. *Not Then*, p. 145.

around the structure; but first and perhaps most impor-
tantly, they needed to pick up the materials for the bomb
and learn how to use them.

The last of these matters took them once more out into
the polders, where they were directed to the farm of a man
named Gerrit, who had been trained by British special
forces in the use of explosives. He took them inside a potato
shed out in the middle of his fields, a location chosen so
that he could see any trouble coming from a safe distance.

His first words inside the shed were, "No cigarettes!"[10]
After which he pulled out a package from under a table. It
had a fuse attached to a chunk of dense clay-like material.
"Let's call this putty," he said. Then he pulled out a metal
box, which he very carefully set on the table. It had several
tiny glass tubes filled with colored liquids. Agents and
reagents. "This is picric acid," he said of one. "You have to
be very careful with this, otherwise you'll get to heaven
before you know it."[11]

Gerrit carefully explained how to set up the explosives
and how to detonate them. He was concise and clear in
his lecture, and by the time he'd finished, the girls were
willing to believe anything he told them.

After eating a dinner of carrots and German *kuch*
(cake) back in Haarlem, they headed out into a chill winter night. They needed to arrive at the bridge after eight
o'clock to avoid the first patrol that marched over its span.

10. *Not Then*, p. 147.
11. *Not Then*, p. 147.

They were to wait inside a barbed-wire perimeter by the bridge until they heard an all-clear whistle from Frans, who would be stationed on the other side of the canal watching the movements of the patrol. Freddie was to remain on their side of the bridge as a second lookout. She carried two pistols in her pockets; Truus and Hannie had the explosives in their own deep pockets and had no room for the 9mm FN. Another comrade from the RVV had come by earlier to cut the barbed wire.

The two older young women snuck through the cut wire and pressed themselves against a damp bank beneath the girders and trestles of the bridge. Suddenly, right over their heads, they could hear the crunch of German boots marching on the gravel leading toward the bed of the bridge. Hannie was wearing a wristwatch with luminous, radium-painted hands. She flashed it toward Truus who read the time: 8:05. They continued to stay pressed against the embankment, waiting for the patrol to come back to their side of the bridge. According to Hannie's watch, only ten minutes passed, but it seemed like half the length of the occupation before they saw the bobbing light of the leader of the patrol coming back across the bridge.

Now they waited impatiently for Frans's signal from the other side, indicating everything was all clear on the north side of the Spaarne. Again, the illuminated watch hands moved at a snail's pace and they waited. Finally, they heard Frans's whistle and knew it was time to set the putty on the railroad bridge itself.

As they walked down the railroad tracks to the bridge

they recognized an immediate problem; there was no walking space on the structure between the tracks and the steel guards on the side of the bridge. Beneath the rails that they were walking on flowed the Spaarne at a daunting distance beneath their feet.

Steeling their courage once again, they stepped onto the rails and carefully inched forward. Luckily the span of the bridge was not long, and they were able to reach its middle quickly. Once there, Hannie and Truus pulled out the putty and packed it onto a span beneath their feet. Truus was trying to set the fuse in place when both saw the bobbing light of a patrolman coming right at them from the end of the bridge.

There was no place to hide except over the side, clinging behind the beam that served as the guide rail for the bridge. They left their would-be bomb where it was, climbed up and carefully backed over the edge, where they clung desperately to the top of the steel panels with their fingertips, while their toes rested precariously on the bottom ledge of the beam. With the rushing Spaarne flowing what seemed like hundreds of feet below, they hung there, with aching hands and bloodless fingers. "The steps came near, as did the light," Truus remembered. "I couldn't see a thing, except for the rivets of the bridge that lit up in the torchlight. My hands were burning, my heart was pounding. The metal was mercilessly cutting my fingers."[12]

When the footsteps and the flashlight finally reached

12. *Not Then*, p. 152.

the end of the bridge, Truus and Hannie were just able to pull themselves back up over the side, but their exertions had taken a toll; they were barely able to stand, and when they did, they realized they no longer had enough time to set the fuse on the bomb. They limped and struggled to get back to their hiding place on the embankment, rubbing and squeezing their hands to get the blood circulating again.

Freddie found them there and dived into their huddle. She had had her own terror: there was a dog with one of the soldiers on the first pass over the bridge and he came over to sniff Freddie, who had to nudge him away before he alerted his master.

The girls had to duck and take cover one more time as the patrolman with the flashlight made another circuit over the bridge, but finally this peril passed as well and they were able to get on their bicycles and leave the attempted sabotage behind.

Their disappointment at failing to blow up the bridge in Haarlem was quickly subsumed by another action at another railway, between IJmuiden and Velsen. This time the girls were teamed with a group of young men from Velsen and Santpoort, which included a pair of teenage boys, a trio of brothers, some experienced resistance fighters who had served in the Dutch navy, and the son of a vicar. Frans brought the group together at a tobacco shop in Santpoort, near to which the local RVV had fashioned a hiding place dubbed "The Bunker."

The Bunker had its own water system, toilet, food supply, and a stash of weapons. It had been dug underground in the woods not far from the cigar store, for the purpose it was now being used. Ventilation came by way of a shaft formed by a hollow tree. The entrance was covered with moss and branches. To Truus, Hannie, and Freddie it was as collegial a setting as they had ever found during the war. In the bunker, "I felt like a partisan," Hannie said.[13]

The night of the sabotage the group gathered first in the cigar store, waiting for an all clear from one of the Velsen resistance members who was out scouting the site. They smoked cigarettes while waiting, a fact that perturbed one of the three brothers, who thought it was crazy to do so with the plastic explosives, fuse, and percussion cap sitting exposed on a table nearby. There was a squabble between him and Frans over this carelessness, but it was settled by the time the scout returned with the word that all was clear.

The group headed out toward the railway, looking for all the world like a military platoon. Frans's Haarlem group was better armed than it had ever been before, with sten guns [a British made submachine gun] slung over their shoulders as they made their way through the streets of Santpoort. "We look just like Huns," Hannie whispered to Truus.[14]

When they got near their destination, Frans divided the group, sending the scout and Piet, the brother who had chided him about the cigarettes back at the cigar shop, to

13. *Not Then*, p. 170.
14. *Not Then*, p. 171.

set the explosives on the track, while dividing the remainder of the group into two sections posted on either side of the track.

There was one breath-holding moment when a German patrol of about half a dozen infantrymen appeared and marched down the track. But the two groups had adequate time to slip into the ditches. When they had passed, Truus, Hannie, and the others stayed behind and kept watch, while Piet and the scout set the timer and fuse for the explosives. After that, Frans again broke up the group and sent them back to the bunker in two smaller packs to await the outcome.

They had tea and lounged quietly on straw mattresses, intently listening in the still night. They not only heard a thunderous explosion, but there was also a blue flash of light that flickered down to the bunker. Then came a terrible screeching of steel train wheels fighting to stay linked to steel tracks, and finally a thudding shake of the ground as a derailed train came to a grinding, ripping halt in the Dutch countryside.

Frans popped the corks on several bottles of wine and they all toasted the success of the enterprise. That night they stayed together in the bunker, surrounded by an arsenal of weapons including the sten guns, some rifles, carbines, and a machine gun. Truus remembered it well: "Being together with comrades without feeling ill at ease was a wonderful thing. I'd never experienced anything like it." She also offered an aside to Hannie about their company. "These boys from Velsen are quite different from the Velsen gentlemen [the Velsen police officers] we sometimes have to deal with."[15]

As it turned out, in months to come, Truus would take a special interest in one of the boys from Velsen: Piet, the calm leader of the group, whose last name was Menger.

15. *Not Then*, p. 173.

Chapter 22

THAT WINTER, HANNIE had her good moments and her bad. Her friends noticed a kind of carelessness about her behavior that was unlike the Hannie they had known before. She made a couple of trips to Amsterdam to do work for the resistance and take shelter away from Haarlem. Erna Kropveld, Hannie's old Gemma friend, recalled her coming to the door to see if Erna had a bed for the night. The next morning, as she was handing Hannie's coat to her, Erna realized from its heft that Hannie was carrying a pistol. Kropveld chided her friend for bringing a gun into the house without letting anyone know. Erna kept counterfeiting machinery and instruments in the home that were always hidden away. But if any police had knocked on the door and found Hannie's pistol, they would have turned the rest of the house upside down and discovered what Erna was doing there. It was a surprising bit of carelessness from someone who'd always been so thorough to cover her tracks and the tracks of others.

Another friend, Annie van Calsem, also recalled Hannie coming by and asking to spend a night with Annie and

Annie's parents. Hannie, who was meticulous about her dress, looked untidy that night. She said that she had been drinking with some German soldiers earlier in the evening in order to get information out of the Hun boys. Later they were walking along the canal, and whether true or not, Hannie said that she bumped one of the *moffs* into the cold water, an extremely risky bit of playfulness, Annie thought.[1]

Her cousin Aaf Dils saw her that winter, too, and also commented on Hannie's shabby clothing. In addition, her hair was unkempt and unsightly. The black dye job needed refreshing; it was about half-black/half-red now and looked cheap. She looked tired and worn. Of course, this was all happening in that awful last winter of the war when everyone was hungry and exhausted. But it seemed clear to Aaf that Hannie had seen one too many comrades fall. She no longer valued life in the way that she once had.[2]

Truus had the same thought. Gone was the fierce and stylish young woman they had first known. What was left was just a shell of the vibrant person she had been. After the war Truus would look back and wonder whether Hannie had a death wish. "It was such a stupid horrible time, with that winter, that cold, no food, the Germans who picked up almost every man from the street, the resistance work that went on day and night, the comrades who fell, the blow of the death of Jan Bonekamp."

1. *Hannie Schaft*, p. 139.
2. *Hannie Schaft*, p. 139.

The one thing that still meant anything to Hannie was her resistance work, and she threw herself into it to a reckless degree, taking on the most dangerous assignments.

All Truus and the others could do was try to slow her down.

Slowing her down, along with everyone else in the Haarlem RVV, soon became the intent of a whole number of forces after a confusing action in January involving a group of new recruits to the Haarlem RVV and the Velsen leadership.

Sander van der Wiel, brother to Frans, had become an active member of the cell. He brought with him a handful of others who were joining to add potential resistance fighters to what was anticipated to be a bloody end to the war. Not all of these newcomers were reliable recruits; in fact, some proved to be more interested in causing general mayhem than fighting Germans or NSB collaborators.

In the middle of January, the new members headed out to the polders to confront and rob a farmer who they suspected of profiteering off the famine. In the process, they executed the man, whose name was Willem van de Zon. As it turned out, however, not only was Zon innocent of making profits off the Hunger Winter, but he had long and solid ties to the resistance. He had hidden a number of Jewish people through the course of the war and was actually giving food away during that hard winter.

Regional Commander of the Interior Forces Sikkel was

furious at the tragic screwup, as were a number of others in the Velsen group, including an officer named Cees van der Voort. Van der Voort asked Freddie Oversteegen to draw up a list of people who might have been involved in the attack. She asked Sander van der Wiel, who gave her a list, including his own name. Many years later, Freddie remained tortured by her involvement. She said that she had been assured by van der Voort that no one on the list was going to be hurt. She thought that the men whose names she offered would simply be arrested as black marketers and tried after the end of the war. (That turned out not to be the case, as would be revealed in just a few weeks in a Haarlem square.)[3]

Van der Voort would later deny any involvement in the Zon incident.[4] The fact that he and others in the Velsen group would continue to play a shadowy, sometimes shady role in upcoming resistance activities of Freddie, Truus, and Hannie Schaft also suggests that their concerns had at least as much to do with the fact that the attack was carried on outside their immediate control as it did with concern over Zon's killing.[5]

The upshot for the Haarlem RVV was that unless ordered by the Forces of the Interior, their duties were limited to nonviolent acts, like acting as couriers or delivering papers around the city.

It was not a proscription that went down easy with Hannie, Truus, and Freddie.

3. *Hannie Schaft*, p. 161.
4. *Hannie Schaft*, p. 162.
5. *De Velser Affaire*, pp. 169–72.

* * *

"No more liquidations," remembered Truus. "No more armed resistance. We were no longer allowed to wear guns." It felt like a dire threat to their own safety. The girls, who had begun their resistance as teenagers who'd never even hefted a pistol, let alone fire one at another human being, were now so dependent on having a weapon in their coat pocket that they felt unsafe and vulnerable without one. The Germans were still in the streets, armed to the teeth; hunger reigned in Holland and people were starving to death, yet their hands were tied? It made no sense.

In late January, the Germans arrested one of the most famous figures of the Dutch resistance, a banker from a well-to-do Amsterdam family named Walraven van Hall, who was called the financier of the resistance. Early in the occupation, he had set up an illicit fund called the National Assistance Fund (NSF) within the bank at which he served as a director. Through fraud and illegal loans, he was able to siphon millions of guilders from the bank to the resistance . . . right up until the day of his arrest. At first the Germans didn't know who it was they had captured. When they learned their arrest had netted the principal source of funds of the Dutch resistance, they drove him and several other prisoners to Haarlem and executed them on Jan Gijzenkade, a street near the Spaarne River.

In light of the executions and the continuing roundup of Hollanders to be shipped off to German labor camps, the RVV in general, and the three girls in particular, continued to clamor for the go-ahead to take concrete, violent action. They visited Gerben Wagenaar, a communist leader in Amsterdam, who went to Sikkel on their behalf. Wagenaar subsequently told them that Sikkel was inclined to follow the lead of his OD colleagues—the Velsen group—more than the Council of the Resistance—in keeping the trio sidelined.[6]

But there seemed to be gaping contradictions in every order and direction from the Interior Forces. Hannie, Truus, and Freddie remained in contact with these same Velsen police officers—Joop Engels, Arend Kuntkes, Cees van der Voort—who were supposed to be holding them back. And the assignments they were about to receive from the group did nothing to suggest they were supposed to rein in their work. Of course, these were men who existed as one author says in "a twilight zone between collaboration and resistance."[7] They had been living with contradictions for years now, and they would soon direct Hannie, Truus, and Freddie toward violence against subjects who were sometimes solidly guilty of crimes of betrayal and collaboration. And sometimes not so solidly guilty. While Sikkel might have been skeptical about the effectiveness of liquidations, he would ultimately countenance a number of them. Evidence of his involvement, however, was twice removed from his fingerprints: first, by

6. *Hannie Schaft*, p. 165.
7. *De Velser Affaire*, p. 168.

the fact that the assassinations were ordered by the Velsen cops; and second, by the fact that they were carried out by a trio of ordinary young women.[8]

For their part, Hannie, Truus, and Freddie had grown resigned to their role in the resistance by this time—even as their anger and hatred toward Germans and their collaborators continued to fester. They considered themselves soldiers, for good reason, in the cause of the resistance. As Truus would say years later, "Especially after the war the question was always asked whether it was necessary to keep shooting those people. You should try to view that in the light of the occupation." There were policemen and Gestapo everywhere, she remembered. There were Dutchmen ready and willing to betray their fellow countrymen. It was impossible for the resistance to pick up those traitors and put them under lock and key. The prisons belonged to the Germans. And how would they feed them anyway when members of the resistance couldn't feed themselves. "There was really only one solution: shooting."[9]

In contrast to what her Amsterdam friends had suggested about Hannie's growing carelessness, Harm Elsinga, who still hosted Hannie on occasion that winter, recalled a very controlled young woman: "She was always very careful not to leave any traces . . . when she left for a dangerous assignment, she said we had to go through the whole house to see if there was anything to be found of

8. There are conflicting points of view about exactly who ordered who to do what between *Hannie Schaft* and *De Velser Affaire*.
9. *Hannie Schaft*, p. 169.

her in case of a house search. When people from the resistance came here, they went upstairs to talk. Never
downstairs in the room. Cees van der Voort was here and
we have seen Kuntkes. Van der Voort has often been here.
She sat very still and thoughtfully in the chair. Like she
saw everything in advance. Every step she would take was
considered. Risks had to be avoided."[10]

On March 1, Haarlem police inspector Willem Zirkzee
was gunned down one bright morning on the Leidse-
plein, a square near one of the oldest canals in Holland,
built to link Haarlem and Leiden in the seventeenth century. Zirkzee was an NSB officer and had worked frequently with the SD out of Amsterdam. He was also
rumored to have turned in a number of Jewish family
members to the Gestapo. Zirkzee was going off to work
when two young women, Hannie and Truus, disguised in
workmen's clothes, shot him at point blank range on the
square under the orders of the Velsen group. An eye witness at the scene said that everything was so fast that he
hardly saw it. He heard shots, saw the man fall, and
watched as two young women pedaled away. Panic immediately arose in the area. Some people who lived close by
started dragging things out of their house because they
thought that the Germans, just like the Krist case, would
set the nearby houses on fire.[11]

Another Haarlemmer, who lived right near where the

10. *Hannie Schaft*, p. 168.
11. *Hannie Schaft*, p. 169.

shooting occurred, grew immediately concerned about what had happened after the assassination of Fake Krist the October before as well. "Last time something like this happened was on the Westergracht diagonally behind [her family's home on the square]," said Lizzy Krelage. "Now people feared that the Germans would do what happened before."[12]

It took almost a full week before the Germans exacted their retribution. Just as in the Krist matter, two trucks drove into the city to a market square on a street in Haarlem called The Dreef. They came straight from an Amsterdam prison and pulled up in the midst of a crowd of shoppers with utter disregard for the people milling about. Fifteen young men were hauled out from the back of the trucks, handcuffed in pairs. Among them were several of the young men from Velsen who were arrested after the killing of the farmer Zon back in January. Some of the names were from the list that Freddie had passed on to the Velsen commanders.

Unlike the executions following the Fake Krist shooting, there were no preliminaries, no observances for Willem Zirkzee. Eight of the hostages were lined up and an SS lieutenant barked a single command. The machine-gun fire sputtered and echoed in the square. In a matter of seconds, all eight prisoners were mowed down in a pile, while the remaining seven victims-to-be looked on.

The lieutenant noticed some movement in the heap of

12. *Hannie*, p. 64.

bodies and ordered his troops to fire another round into the mass. More sputtering fire, more echoing. Then the second group was lined up beside the first. Again, the lieutenant gave the order and again the bodies fell in a heap. There was silence. It was as if there was no breath left in the city. The bodies were tossed without ceremony into the beds of the trucks that had brought them. When one prisoner from the second group showed signs of life, he was pulled from the back of the truck, put on the ground, and his body was riddled with another dose of machine-gun fire.[13,14]

13. *Hannie,* p. 62.
14. In 1949, sculptor Mari Andriessen, whose studio was the hiding and gathering place for the Haarlem RVV, would create one of Haarlem's most well-known artworks in honor of the fallen. Four years after the executions, on March 7, his work, *Man in Front of the Firing Squad,* was unveiled near the Houtplein.

Chapter 23

HANNIE AND TRUUS WERE UNDAUNTED. This was war and they were soldiers.

Freddie's guilt over the executions would grow and fester over time. It would be the sort of war memory that would linger and hurt deep into old age. But for now, she, too, was just a soldier seeking retribution for the murder of her comrades.

She was biking in downtown Haarlem on March 15, when she happened upon Ko Langendijk and his fiancée shopping in the market. Langendijk was a fashionable hairdresser in IJmuiden, who at some point during the occupation began passing along to the NSB the gossip and anti-German remarks he heard about the underground in his parlor. Soon enough, he became an informer, a particularly well-paid one judging by his ostentation. He had been a target of the resistance for a long time. Even Jan Bonekamp made an attempt on his life in days gone by.

Freddie raced back to find her sister and Hannie. After telling them about seeing Ko and his girlfriend, she then led them to Grote Houtstraat in the heart of the city, where Ko and the woman were still walking their bicycles in the square.

Truus and Hannie sent Freddie to check for any police in the area and made sure their 9mm FNs were ready for action. Riding together on a single bike, Truus at the pedals and Hannie in back, they began to slowly trail their target as the lovers neared the viaduct.

On the bridge in front of the Labor Council building, Truus started to pick up speed. *Shoot!* she said to Hannie, but Hannie's pistol jammed and she cursed. Truus shot as well, but with just one hand on the handlebar the wobbliness of the bicycle jerked her aim and she missed. *Shoot again*, she shouted to Hannie, who did just that. This time there was no misfire, and Langendijk crumpled to the pavement with his fiancée, a woman named Fransie Kleijn-Dalhause, screaming beside him.

Kleijn-Dalhause remembered the bridge the rest of her life, being on her own bike next to Ko and seeing two girls pass them: "The girl on the back was wearing a gray jacket and a headscarf. She looked a bit mouse-like and had her hand in her coat, like Napoleon. As I got in the left lane, I suddenly saw that she took her hand out of her coat and it held a gun, which she shot. A couple of times."[1]

After the first pass, Truus stopped the bicycle, turned it around to face Ko, taking aim herself.

Ko Langendijk had seen the two girls riding behind him on a bicycle. He had seen one firing her pistol and knew that he'd been hit when his nose exploded with

1. *Hannie Schaft*, p. 170.

blood. Several more shots hit their target, and he fell in the street. Still Langendijk hadn't lost consciousness. In fact, though he was seriously wounded, he wasn't dead.[2]

For the girls, there was no time to go back to make sure they'd killed him. They got back on the bike and took off. They could see people coming out of the Council of Labor building and knew that police would be arriving shortly afterward to seal off the area. There was a station right around the corner on Kenaupark, which would be quickly alerted if the shots hadn't been heard there already. Hannie and Truus had little time before the barriers went up and the neighborhood would be cordoned off, making escape extremely difficult. Just as they were deciding what to do, one of the bicycle tires went flat. They ditched the two-wheeler and looked around for a spot to hide out.[3]

They saw a café in a nearby hotel, and Hannie and Truus made a quick decision to step inside. Truus took off the newsboy cap that she typically wore when they went out together; Hannie took off her scarf and shook her hair out. There were four men inside playing cards and a bartender. Truus speculated that the cardplayers must have been black marketers because "who else could afford a drink in those days?"[4]

Outside, the police had already arrived and were herding witnesses and suspects in the square. Hannie and Truus knew that they would be soon going door-to-door,

2. *Hannie Schaft*, p. 170.
3. *Not Then*, p. 137.
4. *Hannie Schaft*, p. 171.

and it was only a matter of time before they came into the café.

They knew the bartender by reputation—in the underground, he was thought to be a profiteer and unreliable—which is why Truus made sure he saw her gun when she ordered drinks for her and Hannie. "When the Huns come in here," she warned him, "you make sure you tell them that we've been here at least an hour. Understood?"[5]

The girls then went into the restroom and Hannie took out her makeup bag. They each quickly applied a heavy swipe of lipstick and a liberal dose of powder, combed their hair, and returned to the bar to take their posts by their gin and tonics. Just another pair of loose young women hanging out at the hotel bar in the middle of the Hunger Winter. They each took gulps of gin to both settle their nerves and make sure that they had the smell of liquor on their breath. Then they noticed the cardplayers eyeballing them. "The best thing for you gentlemen to do is continue your game and act normal," Truus said. "I already told this man [the bartender] that we've been sitting here drinking for at least an hour. If we catch one of you trying to betray us, that'll be the end of all of you! If we have to die, we'll take you with us."[6]

Outside, there was shouting, running here and there, barked commands. A pod of helmeted Germans and menacing machine guns. When the *moffen* burst into the café, it was a pair of infantrymen and a single officer. One

5. *Not Then*, p. 138.
6. *Not Then*, p. 138.

of the troopers headed toward the girls at the bar, while
the officer lingered over the cardplayers. "Hi there,
Heinzie," Truus said boldly, falling against the soldier,
pretending to be a drunken young lush, roaring with
laughter. He pushed her away but not too forcefully and
he caught the eye of both Hannie and Truus. They responded by hanging on his neck, flirting, until he brushed
them off.

The officer made the rounds, checking everyone's ID,
while outside in the square, police and soldiers kept arriving, including a truck full of helmeted green sleeves and
motorcycles with sidecars, continuing to seal off the area.
As the officer made his way over to the bartender, the
hub-bub outside prevented Truus from hearing their discussion. She only saw the bartender shaking his head,
which could mean any number of things. Truus took another gulp of gin and held her breath.

Whatever was said apparently satisfied the SS officer.
With the constant German clicking-of-the-heels habit, he
turned and led his troops out the door. As it shut behind
them, the air went out of Truus's lungs like a burst bicycle
tire.

They lingered in the café through their drinks, occasionally peeking outside to see if there was a means to
safely exit through the throng of soldiers outside. The opportunity came when they saw Heinz, the young soldier
that Truus had pressed against in the bar. He was now
manning the corner in the direction they needed to go.
They stepped outside and boldly headed straight in his direction, sashaying and giggling as they approached. Could

he please be a nice Heinzie and let them by? Please, Heinzie? They had to get home to *die mutti*—the mom. Wouldn't he pretty please let them pass?[7]

He ignored them for a brief moment, but then, just wanting them gone, he let Hannie and Truus go.

Just four days after the attempt on the hairdresser's life, Hannie and Truus stood at the door of a man named Gerdo Bakker in Haarlem on a weekday evening, ringing the bell. When a woman answered the door, Hannie asked to see Gerdo, who was an auto and motorcycle dealer in the city.

According to the Velsen police, who had ordered this liquidation, he also had been part of a kickback scheme with Velsen and IJmuiden contractors hired by the Wehrmacht to demolish homes in the towns. Like the Velsen police themselves, he existed in a gray area that involved some black-market work, some criminality, and some work for the resistance. Though as a post-war investigation would ultimately suggest, he was not involved in traitorous practices or even serious collaboration. As best as anyone knows, Hannie and Truus were being employed to provide payback for particular officers in the Velsen group (Van der Voort, Kuntkes, and Engels, according to one account).[8,9]

Regardless, when Gerdo Bakker was called to the door by the woman who answered (his mother-in-law, as it

7. *Not Then,* p. 140.
8. *De Velser Affaire,* p. 174.
9. *Recht op Wraak,* p. 168.

turned out), Truus and Hannie shot him at the same time. Both hit him in the chest and were triumphant at the deed.

"Murderer!" Truus called out at his prone body.[10]

Bakker's widow said that she saw two women ride away, both wearing headscarves. She was surprised to know her husband had been done in by the resistance; she had thought that Gerdo had been a member of the same.[11]

At around the same time as their attack on Bakker, the girls—including Freddie—were plotting against a Haarlem woman named Madame Sieval (variously called Cheval), a woman of French heritage who lived near the Elsingas on Twijnderslaan. Again the order for the liquidation came from the Velsen regional command, who said the woman had close ties to the SD and that German officers were frequent visitors, along with the notorious police inspector Fake Krist, who was said to have been a beau.

Freddie staked out Madame Sieval's home for a time, but became frustrated by the fact that the woman, who had a nanny and a young child, rarely came outside. They asked the Elsingas if they knew of anyone in a nearby house who might let them spy on the target's home from theirs. They got lucky and were able to occupy a room in a place right across the street. The only problem was that the house was owned by three elderly sisters, one of whom was suffering from dementia.

10. *Not Then*, p. 120.
11. *Recht op Wraak*, p. 168.

For three freezing days, they sat in the front room of the sisters' home, with snow piled outside and temperatures below zero. They had to breathe on the windows to be able to spy on Madame Sieval's activities across the street. The sisters were kind, bringing a blanket to share and tea, but there was nothing with which to heat the house.

They passed the time talking about the future. Aside from the task at hand, the girls were obsessed by the coming end to the war. The forces of the Soviet Union were nearing Berlin. Auschwitz had been liberated by the Russians at the end of January. Hitler was trapped in his bunker. Yet control of Holland remained in the hands of the Nazis and their collaborators. And perversely for the trio of resistors, the end seemed to be coming too quickly now.

"We talked all the time about liberation," Truus recalled. "It could have happened any day, but we still didn't want to stop our work. We often talked about the Netherlands and about the whole of Europe after the liberation. There were all sorts of cries for revenge and justice.

"Hannie thought that was all a side issue. She was much more worried about Germany and the Hitler Youth, the way they had been completely indoctrinated. She predicted disillusionment in the future. And as far as the Netherlands was concerned, she worried that here, as well, children had been too deeply influenced by NSB members. Of course, she wanted the liberation, but she was always worried about the future."

About what they were doing—all the stalking, all the

sabotage, all the killing—the girls were unequivocal and would remain so the rest of their days. "We had to do it," Freddie would say years later. "It was a necessary evil, killing those who betrayed the good people. I felt no pity." One does not shoot a human being, she said. A soldier shoots the enemy.[12]

Out of the house, finally, came Madame Sieval.

"She's coming! She's coming!" cried the demented sister. She had been watching, too, from an upstairs room. Her excitement threatened to be heard in the street outdoors, where Madame Sieval—wearing a fur coat—was standing there in the street with her nanny. Between them was the woman's little boy in a snow suit and sitting on a sled. Truus went to calm down and shush the sister, but at any rate, with the little boy right there, it was no time to be gunning down a mother.

The next day offered a better opportunity. The sun was out and the snow had stopped, when the woman in the fur coat stepped outside. Despite the fact that there was still snow on the road, she had her bicycle with her and started to ride away.[13,14]

In an instant, agile little Freddie was out the door and following the fur coat on her own bike. By the time Hannie and Truus were outside to join in the chase themselves, Freddie was poised on a corner down the street, frantically waving them on. They quickly caught up and

12. *Under Fire*, p. 146.
13. *Not Then*, p. 167.
14. *Hannie Schaft*, p. 173.

saw the fur coat ahead, "like a beautiful specimen of a new breed of bear," Truus remembered, outside a café called Het Groene Woud (The Green Forest). Both she and Hannie fired their pistols before noticing a group of schoolchildren just meters away. ·

Madame Sieval screamed, but to the amazement of the girls, she ran away. In an instant Truus, Hannie, and Freddie were steering through the endless alleys and backstreets of Haarlem in a frantic escape to a friend's place, where they hung out until night fell and they could safely go home to their respective safe houses.

Word came the next day: Madame Sieval had been saved by her thick fur coat, which had either trapped the bullets or exaggerated the width of her body, throwing off the aim of the shooters.[15]

15. *Not Then*, p. 168.

Chapter 24

IT WAS A CLEAR AND LOVELY EVENING on the first day of spring 1945, when Hannie Schaft packed up a load of illegal underground newspapers—*De Waarheid* and *Vrij Nederland*—and several sandwiches given to her by Lien Elsinga, with whom she was once again staying, and headed off for IJmuiden for delivery. She wasn't planning to return that evening, which is why she took all of the extra food.[1]

The snow, which had inhibited her and the Oversteegen sisters' attempts on Madame Sieval, was fast melting and the streets were clear and damp. She biked off toward Haarlem-Noord along the Jan Gijzenkade (a canal in the city) intending to cross at Rijksstraatweg, where the Germans had constructed one of their ugly Mauerwalls and built an intimidating checkpoint. It was the sort of routine stop that Hannie had charmed her way through on countless occasions in her journeys through the city, but this time her bag was searched and the newspapers she was carrying were quickly discovered. Given all the violent

---

1. *Hannie Schaft*, p. 174.

measures she had undertaken over the past two years and the fact that even now she was carrying a pistol in a hidden compartment of her bag, it was more than a little ironic that it was the relatively innocuous illegal papers that prompted her detainment.[2]

Two sisters of Frans van der Wiel happened to be nearby and saw her apprehension. They tried to get in touch with Frans to alert him and the RVV of Hannie's situation, but they couldn't find him in time to make a difference. Meanwhile, Hannie was taken first to a Wehrmacht barracks nearby, and then to a detention house, a villa near the Haarlemmerhout—the Haarlem wooded park—where she was placed in a cell. In the process of being moved from one location to the next, her pistol fell out of the compartment in her bag, which alerted her initial jailers that they had grabbed someone of particular interest. No one carried a pistol if they didn't intend to use it.

Her guards demanded to know who she was, but Hannie wouldn't talk. At 11:00 P.M., they took her to yet another detention center in Haarlem, where a Dutch prison guard, who was sympathetic to the resistance, got to see her, but he was unable to do anything to help before she was put under lock and key for the night with a guard posted at the door.

By coincidence, Emil Ruhl, one of the more notorious and high-ranking Gestapo agents in Amsterdam, was visiting Haarlem that night, dropping off a prisoner. He knew

2. *Hannie*, p. 66.

well the work and deeds of Hannie Schaft, the "Girl with the Red Hair," all the way back to her days roaming Noord-Holland with Jan Bonekamp. She knew of Ruhl and his reputation as well. When he learned that a girl had been arrested with newspapers and a gun, he had the prison guards bring her to him. With her dark hair she remained unrecognizable to him, but on a hunch he took her in his car on the drive back to Amsterdam. About halfway home it dawned on him who he had as his passenger. "In my mind, I was going through all sorts of files, trying to figure out who she was," he recalled. "Then suddenly, I knew. 'You're Hannie Schaft.' It was quiet for a moment. Then she turned to me and said, 'Yes.'"[3]

In Amsterdam, Hannie's interrogation brought excitement to the SD. The Gestapo finally had its "Girl with the Red Hair," and even the head of the secret police in Amsterdam, Willy Lages, came to look in on her as if she were some rare creature from an exotic land.

Ruhl took the lead in the interrogation. "We knew at the Sicherheitspolizei that she had committed the attack on Ragut and the baker Faber from Haarlem together with Bonekamp," Ruhl said in testimony after the war. "After her arrest, I was charged with the investigation."

Ruhl got Hannie to admit to the attacks on Ragut and Faber. She also confessed to the attacks on Smit and Willemse on Dolle Dinsdag. She was also suspected in the

3. *Hannie Schaft*, p. 177.

assault against Langendijk, but for unknown reasons she wouldn't confess to it.[4]

Hannie did not give up any names of her resistance comrades or any of the addresses of their hideouts or safe houses, but the Elsingas' address was printed on Hannie's fake ID card, which meant that they were soon visited by the Gestapo. Knowing that she was captured and knowing that their address would be on her papers, the Elsingas had quickly taken measures to "clean" the house of any evidence and were spared arrest.

Between her interrogation sessions with Ruhl, Hannie was kept in a claustrophobic cell measuring only a few square feet. She was given a straw mattress on an iron bed, as well as a table, a chair, and a jug of water. A small barrel was her chamber pot. Hannie was kept isolated from other prisoners and was not allowed to talk even to the German prison guards. There she languished for days at a time, paraded out for midnight interrogations and then sent back to the bleakness of her cell.

The black dye in her hair was washed out, revealing its original red color. She was hauled out of her cell and into the prison courtyard to be photographed detainee-style: a profile shot with her arms at her side; a second photo, staring straight at the camera.

In the shot where she is facing the camera, her eyes look worn down and tired. Her fists are clenched with the thumbs tucked into the fingers. She wears a dark sweater

4. *Hannie Schaft*, pp. 178–79.

and skirt, with a handkerchief tucked in at her waist and plain black shoes. In the profile shot her hands are in the same clenched position, but her head is tilted back a little, as if she were trying to gaze out over the prison wall. Perhaps hoping by some miracle she could catch a glimpse of the Swiss Alps in the far distance, where she had once dreamed of working for world peace with the League of Nations.

A Dutch woman, a doctor named Ada van Rossem, was imprisoned at the same time as Hannie. She remembered seeing Hannie in the prison cells and heard talk of her. The word was that as the weeks passed and the war wound down, with still no Allies arriving to liberate the country, Hannie was reaching the end of her rope. She didn't want to eat anymore and the German woman who served as prison guard didn't know exactly what to do with her.

Her jailers began to leave her for days at a time, and the isolation no doubt was as bad as the interrogations. But she refused to give up any of her comrades. Lages came to speak with her; Ruhl continued to interrogate her, trying to get her to confess to the shooting of Langendijk. The Gestapo agent even brought in the victim's fiancée, who, of course, had been there at the shooting, to see if she would identify Hannie. They tried some ham-handed trickery—asking Hannie to take a cup of tea to the fiancée in an interrogation room in the hopes that there would be an immediate spark of recognition between the two—but the fiancée failed to recognize Hannie.

In the end it made no difference to Hannie; she was

worn down by it all and ultimately confessed to the attempted assassination.[5]

As it turned out, her admission spared five Haarlem women who had been arbitrarily rounded up from the resistance to be executed in retaliation for the attack.[6]

As Hannie languished in the prison, efforts to release her were being made both by the Forces of the Interior and her colleagues within the RVV. A police inspector in The Hague, with solid connections to both the Velsen officers and the SD in Amsterdam, was approached by the Haarlem RVV to work on Hannie's release. The exchange suggested was pretty straightforward: if the resistance quit its campaign of liquidations, the Germans would refrain from any more executions of prisoners.

There remained, however, within the Sicherheitsdienst, powerful voices who wanted their revenge against the Girl with the Red Hair, despite the fact that the war was winding down, despite the fact that she was a woman, and despite the fact that the Germans were losing and it was looking increasingly like there would be a price to pay for the horror that they'd inflicted on the citizens of the Netherlands and Europe.

---

5. A great deal of confusion surrounds the visit from the fiancée and Hannie's "confession." The fiancée offered a variety of different accounts of what happened in post-war testimony, saying at one point that she identified Hannie, at another that she couldn't. Ruhl's account of what happened offers yet another layer of confusion.
6. *Hannie Schaft*, p. 189.

"To us, she was a *Morderin*," said Emil Ruhl, using the German feminine case for "murderer." "She was a terrorist who shot our people; someone who hunted us as we hunted her. In the Euterpestraat there was a special office that was only concerned with combating communism, and she was one of the members of the resistance we had been looking for for a very long time. She was dangerous to us, inhumane, because she shot without mercy. For her at the end of the war: *Kein Gerechtigkeit aber Vergeltung* [Not Justice but Retribution] and that is why she was executed."[7]

Truus did not give up on Hannie. In the days after her arrest, she pleaded with the Forces of the Interior to find a way to free her or at least spare her life. She pedaled to The Hague to talk with one commander about the agreement the Forces were supposed to have reached with the SD about refraining from liquidations in exchange for the Germans agreeing not to execute prisoners. He was not very helpful. He told her that it was thought that Hannie was no longer in Holland, and Truus could detect no sense of urgency in his voice in discussing where she might be.[8]

She went back to the more familiar surroundings of the Velsen group in Haarlem. They seemed to lack any sense of urgency either. In fact, she arrived in the midst of a party, where Arend Kuntkes and Kees de Roover were

7. *Hannie Schaft*, p. 190.
8. *Not Then*, p. 192.

toasting the upcoming liberation of Holland. They tried to reassure her by telling her that Hannie had not left the country; she was in prison in Amsterdam. Holland would soon be free. They offered her champagne, told her to relax, it would all be taken care of. But Truus was in no mood. "In this circle of people, whom I never quite trusted, where I would never find the understanding and friendship I found with Cor and the others of the early days, I couldn't express my feelings. I disappeared into the room our hostess had prepared for me."[9]

In mid-April, Truus decided to take matters into her own hands and go to Amsterdam to see if there was anything she could do to free Hannie. She ran into the group of guys who had helped her and Hannie blow up the train tracks in Santpoort and dropped a suggestion on them. With the German forces in such disarray now that the war was ending, did they think it was possible that with combined RVV resources between their group and the group in Haarlem, the resistance could actually storm the prison in Amsterdam and release Hannie and any other fighters inside?

The Santpoort group, composed mainly of boys and young men, was always enthusiastic for action. They were immediately interested when she told them about her plans. She noticed, however, that the older guys in the group kept their own counsel. In fact, the one named Piet—the most down-to-earth, matter-of-fact member of

9. *Not Then*, p. 192.

the group; the one who had warned against smoking near the bomb back when they were planning the railroad sabotage—was conspicuously silent. They all shook hands when they broke up, but Truus had a sinking sense that her plan was not feasible.[10]

Finally, she decided to go off on her own to the Weteringschans prison in Amsterdam. She wore a familiar costume: a nurse's uniform with a Red Cross cap. She brought along a bag of underwear that she planned to use as a ruse; she would say that she was bringing it at the request of the woman she was looking for. She and Freddie had even taken the time to write encouraging notes to Hannie on cigarette papers that they had sewn into the hems of the garments.

Truus rode her bike right up to the wall outside the detention center and rang a bell to enter. A peephole slid open at the door and she used the bit of German that Hannie had taught her to ask to see the duty officer. She could hear the chains and bolts being opened and the door swung open to reveal a Dutch SS officer. He allowed her in and listened as she spilled forth a long and elaborate tale about a poor girlfriend of a German hero, mistakenly imprisoned. The man was now on his deathbed, wounded in a sea battle just off the coast, would it be possible to release the woman to see him? Or if not, to at least allow Truus to see her, tell her the news, and bring her a change of undergarments?

---

10. Piet Menger, the man with the down-to-earth, matter-of-fact look, would marry Truus in a few months.

The Dutch officer let her tell the full story before stopping her with the sad news that there were no women at Weteringschans. But he could offer her a ride to the detention center on Amstelveense Road. Truus held her disappointment within and agreed to the ride to the second prison.

Once there, she found herself shuffled off to a waiting room where others sat clutching their own little bags for the prisoners, waiting for the attention of a supervisor, who marched into the room carrying a book and saluting "Heil, Hitler" to those waiting.

Truus waited forever to be called. When finally she was ordered up to the woman with the book and asked who she was looking for she announced, "Jannetje Johanna Schaft." The woman's book came open so that Truus could see the page with Hannie's name.

"*Ist nicht mehr da,*" the woman said, closing her book and marching away.[11]

She is not here anymore.

11. *Not Then,* pp. 198–200.

Chapter 25

LIBERATION FINALLY CAME to the Netherlands on May 5, 1945, not quite five years from the day the Germans first streamed over the Dutch border. Truus would remember waking up at an early hour to hear people outside singing, "Oranje Boven," a patriotic salute to the Dutch queen and her ties to the people. She guessed what it meant.

"Up and out!" she yelled to Freddie, waking up the whole family at the safe house where they were staying. "The British are coming!"

Everyone was in the street talking excitedly, wondering which direction the Allied troops would be coming from. It turned out that the Canadians would be their liberators, not the British, and they would eventually be coming by way of the city of Wageningin in the central Netherlands, where German forces agreed to capitulate to the Canadian forces.

Wending their way through excited and joyous crowds of Haarlemmers, Truus and Freddie went to the local headquarters of the Forces of the Interior to see if anything needed to be done in conjunction with the liberation. There they saw Kees de Roover and Arend Kuntkes who invited them to stay and have something to eat and drink, but the day and the sudden sense of freedom had made the girls full of energy. They decided to simply ride their bicycles around Haarlem for a time, until Freddie ran into a friend from the *De Waarheid* and went off to help deliver newspapers announcing the grand news.

Truus kept pedaling. Before she realized where she was, or what she was doing, she found herself halfway to Amsterdam. There were flags of red, white, and blue everywhere. A little boy stood in the street waving a flag several sizes too big for his little arms. Someone had written on a sign in English: WE ARE FREE!

When she got tired, a total stranger on the street gave her a cup of tea. They clapped each other on the shoulders and yelled "We are free!" in each other's faces. Truus kept pedaling. It was only when she was at the doorstep of the safe house at which Philine was staying that she realized where she wanted to go.

They hugged when they saw one another and then stepped out into the street together. "I realized that this was now possible," Truus remembered. "Philine could be out in the world again. She was allowed to be human again. Is that possible?"[1]

They decided to go together to the prison on Amstelveenseweg, to check once more on Hannie. Word had

1. *Not Then*, p. 203.

spread that the prisoners would be freed because of the liberation. Maybe there had been some kind of mistake. Maybe she had been there all along.

For Philine, the idea of walking out on the street all the way to the detention center, without worrying about being arrested, seemed strange. They passed people waving flags, people putting flowers on sites where there had been roundups and executions.

At the prison a large crowd had assembled. The doors would soon be opened and the detainees released to their friends and families. Everyone had flowers, and so Truus went looking for some and came back to Philine holding a bouquet of red tulips. There was a huge shout of joy and welcome when the gates on the Amstelveenseweg center creaked open. An official from the Forces of the Interior read out the names of the detainees. It turned out to be filled with women only: young, old, in good health and poor. One at a time, they stepped out into freedom to huge shouts of appreciation and welcome. Truus and Philine waited through a long list of detainees, but none were Hannie. When the last woman was called, she had no one to greet her, so Philine stepped forward with their tulips and gave them to the woman.[2]

They walked back to Philine's safe house, through the ongoing celebrations in the city. They hugged. Truus got on her bike and pedaled through the dark night, home to Haarlem.

2. *Not Then*, p. 205.

Chapter 26

THREE DAYS PRIOR to Truus's first visit to the Amsterdam prison, Hannie Schaft was taken from her cell by a German guard named Mattheus Schmitz and a Dutch SD detective named Maarten Kuiper, who had been part of the notorious Silbertanne hit squad. Ada van Rossem, the Dutch doctor imprisoned in a cell in the same detention center, heard a scream outside her cell in the halls of the prison and knew intuitively it was Hannie Schaft. Hearing the shuffle of resistant feet moving down the prison corridor, van Rossem guessed what was happening, and assumed, from the scream, that Hannie had come to understand her fate too.[1]

Hannie was taken to a waiting car outside, where two German soldiers, Korbs and Kluting, sat waiting with machine guns in their laps. Schmitz drove off toward Haarlem, where the car stopped at the local command center to pick up another soldier, who brought a shovel that he

1. *Hannie Schaft*, p. 201.

threw, ominously, in the car before entering. The new-comer guided Schmitz toward Overeen, just beyond Bloe-mendaal and toward the dunes out by the ocean.

On a dirt road in scruffy terrain marked by tufts of windswept grasses and rolling sand dunes, the car halted and all of the occupants climbed outside. Hannie was placed between Kuiper and Schmitz; the machine-gunners, Korbs and Kluting, marched behind, with the local gendarme and his shovel bringing up the rear.

Schmitz and Kuiper let her walk a few paces ahead of them. The wind whistled around them, kicking up bits of sand, and whipping Hannie's hair across her face. Without warning, Schmitz pulled a pistol from his holster, aimed at Hannie's head, and fired. He missed, only grazing her. Hannie put a hand to her head, felt the blood there, and said simply, "Oh!"

In subsequent reports, written by Kuiper's boss Ruhl, it was claimed that Hannie turned to her executioners after the bullet missed her and said, "I was a better shot." That turned out to be dramatic license: Ruhl was not in the dunes.

What happened instead was that Kuiper took his own revolver, aimed, and fired. There was no glancing blow this time; the bullet hit Hannie square in the back of her head. Another shot to the head finished the job. She died quickly.

The local gendarme from Haarlem, dragging along with the group, came up and hastily dug a grave in the sandy soil. He and Kuiper subsequently rolled Johanna

Schaft into the shallow hole and swiftly covered her up. It was all done with such disregard that strands of her red hair poked through the dune, marking her grave with the signature of her notoriety.[2]

After liberation, Willy Lages, the head of the SD in Amsterdam, was soon captured by the Canadians and quickly became the definitive source for what happened to Hannie. Though he and another Gestapo officer would bicker in post-war testimony at war trials about just who ordered the murder of Hannie, the undeniable fact was that she was taken to the dunes outside of Bloemendaal and executed by Maarten Kuiper under the orders of the Amsterdam SD.

In the third week of May, her friend and boarder Harm Elsinga went to Amsterdam and tracked down the Canadian officer who had interrogated Lages. He asked the man what Lages had said happened to her. The Canadian told him that Lages gave a one-word response to Harm's question: *Erschossen*. Shot. Just like that.

Elsinga informed the Forces of the Interior leader, Sikkel, of what transpired. Sikkel passed word on to the Haarlem RVV, as well as to the parents of Hannie Schaft. Their daughter had not been spared. Like so many countless others, she had been killed by the Germans. *Erschossen*.

---

2. *Hannie Schaft*, p. 202. That Hannie's red hair stuck out from her grave was subsequently refuted.

On May 22, 1945, Pieter Schaft wrote to members of Hannie's family with the sad but simple truth: "Dear all, what we feared has turned out to be reality: our only treasure, our dear Joop, was killed by the Gestapobeulen at the very last moment (probably April 17). We are stunned and dismayed and I can no longer write."[3]

3. *Hannie Schaft*, p. 205.

Epilogue

THERE WERE ONGOING RUMORS throughout the latter stages of the war that the dunes beyond Bloemendaal, the area where Hannie Schaft was executed and buried, held secrets beyond the whereabouts of her body. Poachers, out in the nature preserve trapping rabbits and foxes, claimed to have seen German vehicles traveling on the Zeeweg, the road that led out through the dunes to Zaandpoort and the North Sea, during the war. They heard shots being fired out in the scruffy land, saw the mounded evidence of what appeared to be fresh graves in the sand.

Toward the end of May 1945, a group of Haarlemmers trekked out into the dunes with an Amsterdam funeral director named Bleekemolen, who had recently been arrested by the newly established Political Investigation Service to follow up on these rumors. Since the previous November, when the services of a local crematorium were no longer available because there was no gas at hand for its purpose, Bleekemolen had been assigned by the SD and local police in Haarlem with the task of burying people executed by the Germans in the dunes. He was an ef-

ficient choice. In his interrogation, he not only remembered where he buried the bodies, he revealed that he actually kept notes on his work. Out on the dunes with the
group of Haarlem citizens searching for evidence of executions, he quickly led them in the right direction.[1]

Searching on the north side of the Zeeweg on the first
day, he pointed out three large grave sites. In the next
four weeks, three more pits were found. In all 311 bodies
were uncovered in just a month's time. In July, looking on
the south side of the Zeeweg, an additional ten sites were
located, in which 91 more bodies were buried.

Exhuming the corpses was a gruesome and laborious
task. The bodies lay in the fashion in which they were dis-
posed, without coffins, in pits with lime sprinkled around
the remains. Shoes and jewelry were removed from the
dead by their executioners and taken back to the Amsterdam Weteringschans, the detention center from which
many of the victims were hauled. Along with the citizens
of Haarlem searching for the bodies, a trio of forensic
pathologists looked for evidence of maltreatment and
causes of death.

After eliciting directions under interrogation from
W.H.M. Schmitz, one of Hannie Schaft's executioners, authorities found Hannie Schaft's body in the dunes on
June 1. She was wearing the same prison garb that she had
been photographed in a few days before her death—a
dark sweater and skirt, with a white-green handkerchief
tucked into the skirt band. According to the careful and

1. *Hannie*, p. 76.

precise notes of the pathologists, her legs were sheathed in beige stockings and she wore a pair of loafers on her feet. They found no injuries to her torso and internal organs, but two bullets of differing caliber entered the back of her head. The first shot struck the back of her cranium on the right side. The heavier caliber shot, the second bullet, entered her head on the left side, went through the brain, and exited above her right eye. It was likely the fatal round.

The body was buried just seventy-five centimeters deep, but there was no evidence to suggest that her red hair marked the grave as was previously reported. Hannie's body was removed from its temporary grave and placed in a coffin for reburial, along with the hundreds of other victims. Of all the remains uncovered, Hannie was the sole woman found in the dunes.

Even as the bodies of the resistance martyrs were being discovered, there was talk among civic leaders from the various communities involved of creating a cemetery for those found on the dunes that would serve as a memorial to their sacrifice. By the end of July, forty-five tombs had been uncovered containing 421 men and Hannie. Forensic research, along with records uncovered by investigators, suggested that 105 people were executed among the Zeeweg dunes, while another 317 were killed in Amsterdam and the various communities of Noord-Holland and taken out beyond Bloemendaal for burial.[2]

A Comite Eeregrafhof (Honorary Cemetery Commit-

2. *Hannie*, pp. 81–82.

tee) was formed and met for the first time in Amsterdam at the end of July. One of the group's first decisions after pounding the gavel was to determine that there should be a solemn and special service to mark the reburial and creation of the cemetery. Because it would be technically impossible to bury all 422 coffins at once on the occasion, a single body would be chosen to symbolize all of the martyrs found in the dunes. It didn't take long for the committee to decide that person was to be the lone woman in the group: Hannie Schaft.[3]

Exactly where to put the cemetery became an argument between the Bloemendaal municipal council, the Cemetery Committee, regional commissioners, and the National Service of the Netherlands, which maintained the dunes area north and west of Bloemendaal as a natural reserve. Considerations included the heavy summer beach traffic to the ocean along the Zeeweg and future municipal expansion of Bloemendaal toward the ocean. Intervention of Queen Wilhelmina herself in the project alleviated some bickering, primarily having to do with the architectural design for the cemetery.

By mid-September the major disagreements had been settled and work began on the cemetery. The memorial would be established in the nature preserve far enough off the Zeeweg to protect its somber setting from the busy summer beach traffic. It was to be erected a few kilometers outside of Bloemendaal, on high land in the dune

3. *Hannie*, p. 82.

area, which would afford visitors a wide view of the setting, particularly mindful of its relationship to the rising sun in the east. Uniform plots with uniform stone markers were to be laid out in parallel rows in rectangular fashion within the cemetery acreage. While final architectural details and memorials continued to be added for the next several years, an opening ceremony of the cemetery was set for November 27, at which the royal family, headed by Queen Wilhelmina herself, would be in attendance.[4]

There was some confusion over Hannie Schaft's name. The committee maintained her position of honor as the single body representing all of the martyrs of the resistance killed in the dunes, but they referred to her as "Anneke" Schaft, rather than her given name of Jannetje Johanna Schaft. It was a problem that would not be cleared up in time for the memorial.

On November 26, the general public was allowed to say good-bye to Hannie in the Grote Kerk in Haarlem, with several thousand streaming past her coffin beneath the vaulted arches in the church nave.

The next day, the queen arrived for a memorial service, also held at the Grote Kerk. Afterward, she received a handful of widows of the more well-heeled martyrs of the resistance, including the financier of the movement, Walraven van Hall; and the sculptor, Gerrit van der Veen. She opted not to meet with Hannie's parents, a slight that was rectified (the royal family hoped) by the fact that the

4. *Hannie*, p. 83.

queen offered to have Hannie's bier encased by the
Dutch flag that Wilhelmina had flown over her home outside of London on Dolle Dinsdag (September 5, 1944),
the day when she and all of the Netherlands thought that
their country had been liberated.[5]

After the service and after the brief reception, a huge
throng marched solemnly to the cemetery, carrying Han-
nie's coffin. There were dignitaries by the hundreds.
Packed trains from Amsterdam pulled into the station at
Haarlem adding to the crowds. In addition to the queen,
Prince Bernhard and Princess Juliana were also there.
Most walked the five-kilometer distance from Haarlem to
the cemetery, but the royals took a car.

Her coffin was carried by civic leaders followed by other
dignitaries, as well as the Boy Scouts and other youth
groups from Haarlem, Bloemendaal, and Heemstede.
Though he and his wife didn't get to meet with the queen,
Pieter Schaft was deeply moved by the gift of her flag, and
the overall service left an indelible impression on him,
"which while not dampening the sea of personal distress,
will nevertheless bring some comfort and peace to those
left behind."[6]

The one sour note in the whole proceedings was the
status of Hannie's living comrades from the resistance. In
the procession, they were relegated to a position behind
all of the dignitaries, civic leaders, and youth groups. The
fact of the matter was that the organizers had little or no

5. *Hannie*, p. 84.
6. *Hannie*, pp. 84–85.

interest in reminding the solemn visitors of the violent nature of the Dutch resistance.

In the aftermath of the liberation, Truus and Freddie Oversteegen began to work for the Political Investigation Service, an organization created to search out and punish Dutch traitors, collaborationists, and bounty hunters. The sisters quickly became disenchanted with the group. It was headed by many of the same figures from Velsen and the Forces of the Interior, who had come to dominate the resistance in the last months of the occupation. In the estimation of Freddie and Truus, the organization continued to walk a fine line between justice and appeasement. Furthermore, they showed little or no interest in the ideological warfare that the sisters, Hannie Schaft, and the RVV had waged throughout their struggles.[7] In fact, there were ongoing whispers that the leaders of the Velsen group may have been complicit in some of the detainments and subsequent executions of leftist leaders within the resistance.[8]

The stark post-war divisions that would create the Cold War between the Soviet Union and the West were already in evidence, and the Dutch government, in general, showed little interest in celebrating or even remembering the contributions of the Communist Party and other leftist groups involved in the resistance. Needless to say, it was an oversight and neglect that more than rankled those in

7. Verzets Resistance Museum, Amsterdam. WWII: Dre Meiden in Verzet.
8. *Hannie*, p. 98.

the resistance who had given so much in the fight against the Nazis. Hannie Schaft's gravesite became a symbol of the acrimony between leftists and Dutch authorities.

Beginning a half year after the burial, on the anniversary of the Liberation, Hannie's grave became the site of a gathering of former resistance figures to celebrate her life and the contribution she and other leftists had made to the resistance. In the succeeding years of the 1940s the cemetery and Hannie's burial ground became the center of commemorations of resistance activities. Truus and Freddie were active participants in the Hannie Schaft Committee, which had been formed to organize these gatherings.

In November 1948, a large group at Hannie's gravesite heard speeches from leftist leaders hailing ideological causes that did not sit well with the Honorary Cemetery Committee. In 1950, a Dutch Communist Party leader again drew the condemnation of the committee, which declared that any future commemorations at the burial grounds must honor the entirety of the Dutch population since those saluted at the site represented the whole of the Netherlands and not simply its leftist martyrs.[9]

Matters came to a head the following year. In the fall of 1951, the Honorary Cemetery Committee informed the Hannie Schaft group that they would not be given a permit to hold a ceremony honoring Hannie on the anniversary of her burial in November. At the same time the

9. *Hannie,* p. 96.

mayors of Haarlem and Bloemendaal denied the group permission to march through their cities. The committee said it would close and lock the gates to the cemetery and no one from the commemorative group would be allowed to enter.

Leftist newspapers like *De Warrheid* along with leaders of the Hannie Schaft Committee and socialist and communist youth groups called for a large rally in response. Almost five thousand people gathered on the Zeeweg that Sunday late in November to march to the cemetery. Many carried placards with Hannie Schaft's portrait pasted to the boards.

Truus Oversteegen was now Truus Menger-Oversteegen. She'd married Piet Menger, her Velsen comrade from the railroad bombing in the last months of the war. He was also the young man who had cautioned her about trying to attack the detention center in Amsterdam to free Hannie. They married in November 1945, just before Hannie's reburial. Together they had a young daughter named for her old friend. Little Hannie was a toddler at that time and Truus asked her mother to babysit so that she could be at the march. Truus and Jan Brasser (Witte Ko) were given the honor of leading the parade out to the burial ground.[10]

They didn't get that far. There to greet them in the road was an overwhelming force of police joined by two armored vehicles and a contingent of armed Dutch sol-

10. *Not Then*, p. 207.

diers. Fire trucks had also been hauled to the town outskirts to spray recalcitrant demonstrators with pressurized
hoses.

Despite the blockade, the marchers moved forward
until they were face-to-face with the police. Enraged by
this treatment from local and national authorities, Truus
stepped forward near to one young soldier. "I fought for
liberation for five years," she screamed. "Would you really
shoot at me? At us?"[11] As the boy turned white, an older
cop took Truus by the arm and dragged her away.

There was really little to do in the face of this power.
The marchers called the police fascists and cowards and
collaborators but were ultimately turned back and regath-
ered at the Bloemendaal town hall where Truus, for one,
gave the mayor a piece of her mind. A few of the demonstrators snuck past the roadblock to lay wreaths on Hannie's grave, but in the process, they were caught and
wound up being fined for their trouble.

To the small band of resisters who'd fought so hard for
Dutch freedom, the war seemed like ancient history. They
still tasted the bitterness of the years of fighting, not just
against the Nazis, but the Dutch collaborators as well.
Their fear was that many of the same people who had sat
by silently watching as Jews were rounded up and sent to
Westerbork, or actively helped the Gestapo and NSB by
discreetly pointing toward those involved in the resistance, or accepted bounties for the task, were not only es-

11. *Not Then,* p. 207.

caping punishment but actually reassuming the powers that they'd held prior to the war.

Like her sister, Freddie Oversteegen got married after the war. Her husband, Jan Dekker, worked for many years at the steel company, Hoogovens in IJmuiden, where Jan Bonekamp and Jan Brasser had labored prior to joining the resistance. Freddie raised three children and led a relatively quiet life out of the limelight until her later years. She suffered from periodic bouts of depression, troubled by her memories of the war, and the post-war direction that the Netherlands took. She told an interviewer late in life that she felt as if the war had robbed her of her childhood. "One could not be a child, that time. We missed our mother very much, to feel her arm around us or have her stroke our hair. There were none of those things back then."[12]

In the years after the war, Truus began to study sculpture with Mari Andriessen, whose home and studio had been the center of RVV gatherings during the war. In time she would become one of the most accomplished artists in the Netherlands, with some of her most well-known pieces depicting and dedicated to Hannie; her sister, Freddie; her fellow resisters; and one in an Amsterdam school, a sculpture dedicated to Jewish children lost to the Holocaust. In 1967, Truus and Hannie were recognized in the scrolls of the *Righteous Among Nations* by the Yad Vashem,

12. *Under Fire*, p. 146.

Israel's monument to the memory of those who died in the Holocaust, and those who served the cause of Jews in countries around the world. She traveled to Israel to be honored with others in a large and formal ceremony.

Truus became an active speaker, more than willing to share stories of the resistance to students and young people all over Holland. During the 1950s and '60s, when the nation and its government showed little interest in rehashing the war, and less interest in acknowledging the contribution made to the resistance by leftist fighters, Truus was one of a handful of speakers to step up and remind people of the contributions made by her and her friends in the resistance.

Both she and Freddie sat for a number of interviews with journalists, especially beginning in the 1970s and '80s, when a younger generation of Netherlanders began to take a closer look at what had happened during the war and to honor the leftists, whose resistance had been neglected by the nation. Journalists re-examined the postwar interpretations of the occupation, which had typically saluted the heroic resistance—downplaying some disturbing facts. One of the principal ones being that no occupied country in Europe lost a higher rate of its Jewish population to the Holocaust than did the Netherlands. Of the 80,000 Jews living in Amsterdam at the start of the occupation, only 5,000 remained when liberation came. An estimated 75 percent of the Jewish population in the Netherlands was lost to the Holocaust.[13] In all, 100,000

13. Wikipedia, "History of the Jews in the Netherlands."

Jews were taken on trains from the country headed for camps in Germany and elsewhere.[14]

In 1976 Haarlem journalist Ton Kors published an account of Hannie Schaft's life (*Hannie Schaft*, Amsterdam: Van Gennep, 1976), after interviewing many of her contemporaries from the war years, including Truus, Freddie, and surviving friends, family, and resistance members. The book helped prompt Truus to write her own memoir of the war years called *Not Then, Not Now, Not Ever* in 1982 (an English translation of Truus's work by Rita Gircour was published in 1998).

The life of Hannie Schaft had been an ongoing interest of Netherlanders from the war forward. Along with a handful of other well-known Dutch figures like van Hall and Corrie ten Boom, her life and sacrifice came to represent the story of the Dutch resistance. Dutch author Theun de Vries published a popular fictional account of Hannie's story titled *The Girl with the Red Hair* in the mid-1950s. In 1981, film director Ben Verbong turned that book into a very successful Dutch movie of the same name.

There was renewed interest in what had happened toward the end of the war when the Velsen group came to dominate the resistance movement as well. Rumors persisted that its leaders, headed by Nico Sikkel, had betrayed a number of communists in the movement at the

14. Geert Mak, *Amsterdam: A Brief Life of the City* (English trans, Philipp Blom). New York: Vintage Books, 2001, p. 264.

behest of the government, in order to quash their post-war influence in the rebuilding of the nation. It was suggested that among those who might have been betrayed was Hannie Schaft.

There had been one post-war investigation conducted about the matter in the 1950s, but since many of the same officers who were a part of the Velsen group served on the committee doing the investigation (at which both Truus and Freddie were witnesses), it was given little credence on the left.

Periodic calls for more investigation through the last quarter of the twentieth century culminated in a book by Dutch writer Conny Braam, the title of which, *Het Schaandal* (The Scandal, 2004), suggests the conclusion she reached about the people involved in what came to be known as the Velser Affaire. Braam's book prompted a number of foundations and governmental agencies to call for a full study of what had happened. Independent researcher Bas von Benda-Beckman began an exhaustive work that ultimately produced another book titled *De Velser Affaire* that concluded that while there was ample evidence to show that the Velsen officials were working many different angles in the war, working with both the resistance and Dutch government officials, there was no evidence of a conspiracy headed by the Dutch government-in-exile to eliminate communists in the resistance. And there was no evidence of a betrayal of Hannie Schaft.

It is not likely to be the last word on the subject in the Netherlands.

* * *

Meanwhile Truus and Freddie aged gracefully, living well into the twenty-first century as white-haired ladies residing in senior living facilities. Both still kept abreast of leftist politics and supported progressive causes. "If I were sixteen now," Truus told one interviewer, "I suppose I would join Greenpeace or work with Amnesty [International]. I never lost my ideals."[15]

Freddie became more willing to discuss her past as the years went by, even admitting to one journalist that she had grown a little bit jealous of all the attention her sister had been given, saying, "You know I was in the resistance as well."[16]

The sisters appeared jointly in a number of Dutch and European television documentaries about the resistance during the war and sat for several interviews for magazines and newspapers. The documentaries are especially enlightening as they offer a vivid sense of the character of the two sisters. *Twee Zussen in Verzet* (Two Sisters in Resistance) filmed in the last year of Truus's life is particularly compelling, featuring lengthy interviews with the sisters in their Haarlem surroundings, as well as interviews with some of their children and in-laws. The sisters appear as well in the lengthy German documentary series, *Schattenkampf: Europas Resistance gegen die Nazis 1941–1942* (Shadow Fight: Europe's Resistance against the Nazis),

15. *Under Fire*, p. 146.
16. *Vice* interview, May 11, 2016.

where some scenes of their war experiences are re-enacted. While confessing the difficulties of what they had to do during the war ("I never got used to it," Truus said), they remained unrepentant about their work. "We had to do it," said Freddie. "It was a necessary evil, killing those who betrayed the good people. I never felt pity. One does not shoot a human but the enemy, a traitor."[17]

In April 2014, Truus and Freddie Oversteegen were jointly honored by the Dutch government in a ceremony led by Prime Minister Mark Rutte with the War Mobilization Cross, honoring their work during World War II. Just a couple of months later, the city of Haarlem likewise honored the sisters with a ceremony that included naming a street in the city after each of them: Truus Oversteegenstraat and Freddie Oversteegenstraat both intersect with Hannie Schaftstraat on the south side of the city. Finally, in November 2015, on the seventieth anniversary of Hannie's reburial, Truus and Freddie were guests of honor at a memorial honoring Hannie at the Grote Kerk in Haarlem.

Truus died the next summer in 2016 at the age of ninety-two. Freddie died two years later in September 2018. She was ninety-two as well.

17. *Under Fire*, p. 146.

ACKNOWLEDGMENTS

This book owes its deepest gratitude to the remarkable lives of its three protagonists: Hannie Schaft and sisters Truus Menger-Oversteegen and Freddie Dekker-Oversteegen. It is an honor and privilege to tell their story, and I hope I have done them justice. I hope, too, that I have done justice to the story of the Dutch resistance in World War II, especially as it was fought in the city of Haarlem. Truus Oversteegen's memoir of her years fighting with Hannie, Freddie, and the others in their resistance cell has been an enormous aid to the writing of this book, and I owe a particular debt of gratitude to her. Her frank and unadorned writing style (as translated by Rita Gircour) created a narrative of the Haarlem resistance that was, as it needed to be, both horrific and human. Her voice rang in my head as I was writing.

I'm indebted as well to journalist Ton Kors, who, writing in the mid-1970s, not only did the first extensive biography of Hannie Schaft but collected interviews of many of the principals, almost all of whom are now long gone. His papers, which can be found in the Noord-Holland

Archief in Haarlem, include interviews with relatives, college friends, remaining members of the RVV, and even members of Haarlem and Amsterdam SD, who spent the war hunting for her.

Historian Peter Hammann, who grew up just down the street from Hannie's house on van Dorstraat in Haarlem, has provided much needed insight into Hannie's life, as well as the life of Haarlem and the resistance during the war. His 2017 biography, *Hannie*, has been a terrific source for this project. Along with sending me a copy of his book, Peter has sent me his own translation of *Hannie* which has been enormously helpful given my serious deficiencies with the Dutch language. In particular, he has helped me better understand the conflicting political narratives of the Dutch resistance that emerged after the war and animated the controversies surrounding Hannie's memorial grounds.

Visits to the Netherlands to research this book were aided by staff at the Verzet Museum in Amsterdam, at the National Institute for War, Holocaust and Genocide Studies (NIOD) in Amsterdam, the Noor-Holland Archief in Haarlem, and the Anne Frank House in Amsterdam. A number of online resources have been very helpful as well for the many long-distance aspects of the research for this book. The Hannie Schaft Foundation (hannieschaft.nl), which Truus and Freddie helped found, is an active group that continues to commemorate the lives of Hannie, Truus, and Freddie. Similarly, Jan Bonekamp's life and sacrifice are celebrated by an organization with strong communist leanings found at janbonekamp.nl.

I want to thank Rob Muns of the Netherlands-American Association of Minnesota (NAAM), who was very helpful in the early stages of the project, offering advice about my visit to the Netherlands and inviting me to my first Koningsdag celebration at the Dutch Club in Minneapolis.

I want to thank Wendy McCurdy, my editor at Citadel, who has been a pleasure to work with in addition to being an insightful editor of the manuscript. Wendy actually was the first to suggest to my agent that the story of these three girls in Holland would make a compelling book. A colleague of hers at Citadel saw the obituary of Freddie Oversteegen in September 2018, passed it along to Wendy, who contacted Farley Chase, who contacted me—a very fortuitous string of events. Farley has represented my work for more than a dozen years now. This is our fourth book together and from the very first he has never been anything but the most stalwart advocate of my writing. I deeply appreciate his help, guidance, and all-around good-guy-ed-ness.

Thanks to my wife, Susan, to whom this book is dedicated. And thanks to my children, Sam and Hannah. Double thanks to Hannah, who not only served (along with Susan) as my research assistant on our trip to Haarlem and Amsterdam but more than once saved her gawking old man from bicycles whizzing past in the two-wheeled traffic lanes of Amsterdam's busy *straats*. Endless love and thanks to all of you.

INDEX

AJC (Arbeiders Jeugd Central), 4
Akersloot, 23, 175
Allied forces, 113, 119, 161, 194–95,
    200–201, 223–24
  liberation of Paris, 198
  Normandy landings, 173–74, 181
  Operation Market Garden, 209–
    13
Amsterdam Jewish Council, 43–44,
    45, 48–50, 79–80
Amsterdam Raad van Verzet (RVV),
    110–11, 182
Amsterdam Weteringschans, 262–63,
    265–66, 272
Andriessen, Mari, 243n, 281
  Gestapo studio raid, 166–67, 204
  studio as hiding and gathering
      place for RVV, 89, 92, 113–
      14, 131, 186–87
Andriessen, Nettie, 187
Annie, 111–12, 114–16
Anschluss, 8, 33–34, 35
Anti-Semitism, 38, 39, 42–43, 46, 47–
    51
Apeldoorn, 201
Arbeitseinsatz, 101–2, 104, 105–6
Armed forces of the Netherlands, 9,
    14–15, 17, 140, 202, 219,
    279–80
Attack on Pearl Harbor, 69
Auschwitz concentration camp, 38,
    80, 136, 193–94, 251

Bakker, Gerdo, 249–50
Bamberger, Alois, 107–10, 204
Bannink, Hendrik, 110, 111
Battle of Arnhem, 209–13
Battle of the Netherlands, 12–19,
    70–72
  in Amsterdam, 15, 17–19
  bombing of Rotterdam, 16–17,
    18, 29–30
Bavo, Saint, 20–21

Bernhard, Prince, 7, 15, 202, 210,
    219, 276
Beverwijk, 23, 144, 145, 168–70, 182,
    212
Bicycle infantry, 10, 14
Bicycles, 40–51, 69–70, 71–72, 107–
    8, 119, 213–14
Blitz, the, 18–18 113
Blockade of Germany, 9
Bloemendaal, 5–6, 23, 24, 107, 212
Bloemendaal dunes
  execution of Hannie, 268–69,
    271–72
  exhumation of Hannie's body,
    272–73
Bonekamp, Jan, 281
  death of, 189–90
  Hannie and, 131–32, 171–73
  resistance activities of, 73, 123–
    24, 138, 146, 163, 170, 171,
    181–82
    Faber assassination, 178–81
    Ragut assassination, 182–87
    transfer of weapons depot,
      174–77
    van Zoelen assassination, 168–
      69
    Velsen-Noord plant bombing
      attempt, 143–45
  shooting of, 184–88
Braam, Conny, 284
Brasser, Jan ("Witte Ko"), 73, 279,
    281
  resistance activities of, 73, 123–
    24, 138, 163, 170, 171
    Ragut assassination, 181–83,
      186–87
    transfer of weapons depot,
      174–77
    van Zoelen assassination, 168–
      69
    Velsen-Noord plant bombing
      attempt, 143–45

Brinker, Hans, 24
Britain
    the Blitz, 18–18 113
    declaration of war, 9
    Munich Agreement, 28–29
British Military Intelligence, 88
Broekman, Kees, 39–40, 53, 114,
    260–61
Buchenwald concentration camp, 38
Buhler, Willem, 218
Buller, L. J. "Johannes," 168–70
Bult, Jan, 171–73, 174–75
Bult, Trijntje, 171–73, 174–75, 183

Central Intelligence Agency (CIA),
    71
Christiansen, Friedrich, 108, 122
Coffee, 128
Cold War, 277–78
Comite Eeregrafhof (Honorary
    Cemetery Committee),
    273–74, 278–79
Communist Party (CP) of the
    Netherlands, 7–8, 39–40,
    44–45, 97, 98, 107, 124–25,
    278
CS-6, 102–4
Czechoslovakia, 8, 28–29

Dachau concentration camp, 38,
    178
Das Kapital (Marx), 134
Davids, Louis, 13
D-Day. *See* Normandy landings
De Aanslag (The Assault) (Mulisch),
    216*n*
De Boer, Wilhemus, 218
De Geuzen (the Beggars), 45–46
De Jong, A. M., 147
De Jong, Loe, 16, 17
Dekker, Jan, 281
De Koevoet, 39–40
De Ronde, Henk, 204–8, 214
De Roover, Kees, 260–61, 265
De Velser Affaire (von Benda-
    Beckman), 284
De Vonk (The Spark), 39–40, 53–54,
    68, 96
De Vries, Herman, 178
De Vries, Jacob, 218
De Vries, Theun, 283

De Waarheid (The Truth), 39–40, 53–
    54, 68, 73–74, 96, 254, 265,
    279
De Wit farm, 31–32
Dils, Aaf, 26, 27, 99, 121, 165, 235
Directorate of Military Intelligence,
    88
Dolle Dinsdag, 203, 208, 214
Dordrecht, 10, 20, 149, 152, 153–55
Dreef, The, 242
Dutch East Indies, 15, 76
Dutch famine of 1944–45 (Hunger
    Winter), 223–24, 236–37,
    247
Dutch government-in-exile, 15–16,
    101, 120, 174, 201–2, 210,
    219–20
Dutch Jews. *See* Jews in the
    Netherlands
Dutch Reformed Church, 81–82
Dutch resistance, 39–47, 71–72, 88,
    95–98. *See also specific figures
    and groups*
    conflicts among groups, 96–98
    executions (liquidations), 97–98,
        102–4, 120, 146, 168–69,
        178–87, 213–18, 236–53
    hiding *onderduikers*. See
        Onderduikers
    press, 39–40, 43–54, 59, 68–69,
        73–74, 96, 120–21
    radio. *See* Radio Oranje
    reprisals against, 103–9, 127–28,
        146–48, 169–70, 178, 204
    strikes, 44–45, 47, 52–53, 68, 122–
        24, 127–29
Dutch universities. *See also* University
    of Amsterdam
    anti-Jewish measures, 38–39
    crackdown on, 104–6, 122
    labor draft, 101–2, 104, 105–6
    loyalty pledge, 104–6
Dutch Volunteer Legion, 102
Dutch Youth Federation, 31–32

Eastern Front, 69–70, 102, 113, 120,
    178
E-boats, 162, 170–71
Eisenhower, Dwight D., 202
Elsinga, Harm, 189, 190–92, 198,
    208, 240–41, 250, 257, 269

Elsinga, Lien, 189, 190–92, 198, 199, 208, 254, 257
Engels, J. P., 219–22, 239, 249
Enschede, 126–27, 136
Erends, Dornelis, 218

Faber, Klaas Carel, 147, 178–79
Faber, Piet, 178–81
Faber, Pieter Johann, 147, 178–79
Falsificatie Centrale (FC), 82–83
February strike, 44–45, 47, 52–53, 68, 122–23
"Final Solution," 81, 148–49
Food embargo, 211
Food rations, 82, 128
Forced labor, 70, 79–80, 101–2, 104, 105–6, 122–23, 129
Fortress Holland, 16
France
    declaration of war, 9
    Munich Agreement, 28–29
Frank, Anne, 50–51, 80–81, 166, 193–94
Frank, Margot, 50–51, 166
Frank, Otto, 50–51, 80–81, 166, 193–94
Freddie Oversteegen. See Oversteegen, Freddy Nanda "Freddie"
Free Netherlands, 178
Frenk, Sonja
    befriending of Hannie, 29, 30
    capture and death of, 136
    in hiding, 99–100, 106, 121–22, 134–36
    identity card for, 51, 79, 99, 121–22
    at University of Amsterdam, 39, 47, 48, 51
Fritz, 84–86

Gandhi, Mahatma, 28, 134
Gemma, 29, 46–47
Gerbrandy, Pieter, 202, 219
German occupation. See Nazi occupation of the Netherlands
Gerritsen, Joseph M., 97–98
Gestapo, 35–36, 61, 115, 150, 185, 195, 197, 214
    Andriessen studio raid, 166–67
    Shaft home raid, 189–90

Geuzen, 62
Gircour, Rita, 283
Girl with the Red Hair, The (de Vries), 283
Goring, Herman, 175–76
"Granny," 112–13, 114–17
Great Depression, 1–2, 4, 26
Green Police. See Ordnungspolizei
Griet, Aunt, 127, 137
Groenendaal, Wim, 40–41, 52–53, 73–74, 77, 138
Gutenberg, Johannes, 19

Haarlem
    geography of, 22–24
    German defenses, 119, 161–62
    history of, 20–22
Haarlem City Council, 4
Haarlem Grote Kerk, 20–21, 166, 275–76, 286
Haarlem Grote Markt, 9, 19, 20, 52, 163
Haarlemmerhout, 23–24, 40, 255
Haarlemmertrekvaart, 22–23
Haarlem Raad van Verzet (Council of Resistance; RVV), 74–78, 113–14, 127, 130–32, 140–41, 189, 194, 238–39. See also specific members
    sexism in, 220–21
    strikes, 123–24
    Velsen leadership, 219–24, 236–37, 239, 249, 259, 283–84
Haarlemsche Courant, 108–9, 180
Hague, The
    Battle of the Netherlands, 15–16
    parcel deliveries, 221–23
    winter assassinations, 102–4, 108, 120
Hals, Frans, 21
Hannie Schaft. See Schaft, Jannetje Johanna "Jo" "Joop"
Hannie Schaft (Kors), 283
Hannie Schaft Committee, 278–79
Heemskerk, 23
Heemstede, 59, 221
Heerenhek, 88–90
Het Parool (The Motto), 68–69
Het Schaandal (The Scandal) (Braam), 284

Heusdens, Jan
    February strike, 52–53
    resistance activities of, 73–74,
        110, 124–25
        Rembrandt Theater bombing
            attempt, 163–64, 171
        Smit assassination, 204–8
Hiding Place, The (ten Boom), 84
Hillegom, 85
Himmler, Heinrich, 35, 43, 44, 45
    "Final Solution," 148–49
Hitler, Adolf, 195, 203, 251
    Battle of the Netherlands, 13–14
    early rise of, 8, 33
    invasion of Poland, 9
    occupation of the Netherlands,
        37, 96, 101, 103, 142, 195
Hitler Youth, 251
Hoebeke, Rinus, 52–53, 63, 65
Holocaust, 281–83
Hoogovens, 53, 73, 123–24, 143,
    144, 281
Hunger Winter, 223–24, 236–37, 247

Identity cards, 51, 72, 79, 82–83, 99–
    100, 140, 146–47, 167
IJmuiden, 123–24, 161–62, 189, 210,
    212, 224–26
IJmuiden Power Plant, 170–71
IJssel, Lake, 10
IJzerdraat, Bernardus, 45–46
Invasion of Poland, 9, 11, 29
Italian campaign, 119, 161
Italo-Ethiopian War, 27

"Jewish problem," 38, 51, 148–49
Jews in the Netherlands, 42–44, 48–
    51, 79–87, 99–100, 108,
    118, 135
    anti-Jewish measures and
        roundups, 37–39, 42–43,
        86–87, 147–49, 193–94, 280
    Battle of the Netherlands and
        suicides, 17–18
    "Final Solution," 81, 148–49
    forced labor, 70, 79–80
    hiding onderduikers. See
        Onderduikers
    Holocaust, 281–83
    Pillar System, 49–50

transporting of Jewish children
    by resistance, 84–86, 149–
    60
John Frost Bridge, 209–13
Juliana, Princess, 7, 15, 276

Kastein, Gerrit, 102–4
Kaufman, Hannah, 54–55, 58
Kaufman, Jerrit, 54–55, 58
Kenaupark, 73, 226, 246
Kennemerland dunes, 5–6, 119
Kennermerland, 140, 212
Kleijn-Dalhause, Fransie, 219–24,
    236–37, 239, 249, 259
Kleverpark, 24, 25
Koot, H., 43–44, 47
Kors, Ton, 222n, 283
Koster, Laurens Janszoon, 19
KP (Knokploegen), 202, 215–16,
    221
Krelage, Lizzy, 242
Krijger, Gomert, 216, 216n
Krist, Fake, 167, 203–8, 213–18
Kristallnacht, 38
Krommenie, 23, 96, 168
Kropveld, Erna, 79, 130, 135–36, 234
Kuiper, Maarten, 147, 267–69
Kuipers-Rietberg, Helena, 81–82
Kuntkes, Arend, 219–20, 239, 241,
    249, 260–61, 265

Labor. See Forced labor
Lages, Willy, 148, 169–70, 256, 258–
    59, 259n, 269
Landelijke Organisatie voor Hulp
    aan Oderduikers (LO), 81–
    82, 95, 96, 109, 202
Langendijk, Ko, 168, 244–49, 256–
    57, 258–59, 259n
League of Nations, 27, 134
Leffelaar, Lex, 179–80
Liberation Day, 264–66
Liberation of Paris, 198
Limmen, 23, 171–72, 174–75, 177,
    186
Loggers, Robert, 218
Louise, 84–86
Loyalty pledge, 104–6
Luftwaffe, 18, 195
Luyting, Nellie, 29, 30–31, 46–48,
    100

Maaswinke, Ferdinand, 218
Madame Sieval, 250–53
Man in Front of the Firing Squad
      (Andriessen), 243*n*
Martin B-26 Marauders, 170–71
Marx, Karl, 134
Menger, Hannie, 279
Menger, Piet, 231–32, 233, 261–62,
      262*n*, 279
Menger-Oversteegen, Truus. *See*
      Oversteegen, Truus
Moffen, 119, 247
Mok, Karel, 64–65
Mulisch, Harry, 216*n*
Munich Agreement, 28–29
Mussert, Anton, 42
   "Leader of the Dutch People,"
      101, 103
   NSB and, 7, 18, 29, 96, 101, 201,
      205
   resistance activities against, 40–
      41, 42
Mussolini, Benito, 27

"Naar de bollen" (song), 13, 13n
National Assistance Fund (NSF),
      238
National Socialist Movement (NSB),
      201–2
   founding and rise of, 7, 27, 29
   Nazi occupation of Netherlands,
      29, 30, 40–41, 43–44, 71,
      96, 101, 146–47
   release of members, 18, 19
   resistance activities against, 40–
      41, 124–26
Nazi occupation of the Netherlands,
      30–43, 108–9
   anti-Jewish measures and
      roundups, 37–39, 42–43,
      86–87, 147–49, 193–94, 280
   Dolle Dinsdag, 203, 208, 214
   Dutch collaboration. *See* National
      Socialist Movement
   forced labor and resistance, 70,
      79–80, 101–2, 104, 105–6,
      122–23, 129
   German retreat, 200–203
   Hunger Winter, 223–24, 236–37,
      247

Liberation Day, 264–66
   police system, 35–36
   press and propaganda, 36–37
   war children, 34–35
Netherlands Journalists Association,
      36–37
Ninth Army Air Force, U.S., 170–71
Noordwijkerhout, 31–32
Normandy landings, 173–74, 181,
      203
North Africa campaign, 113, 120,
      129
North Sea Canal, 22, 24, 161
Not Then, Not Now, Not Ever
      (Menger), 283

Occupation. *See* Nazi occupation of
      the Netherlands
Office of Strategic Services (OSS),
      71–72
Onderduikers, 11–12, 54–58, 80–84,
      95, 96, 99–100, 120–22, 140
   Landelijke Organisatie voor Hulp
      aan Oderduikers, 81–82,
      95, 96, 109, 202
Operation Barbarossa, 47–48, 59, 60
Operation Market Garden, 209–12
Operation Silbertanne, 103–4, 146–
      47, 169–70, 178
Ordnungspolizei (Order Police;
      OD), 35–36, 44, 76, 86, 95,
      202, 219–20, 239
Overeen, 23, 108
Oversteegen, Freddy Nanda
"Freddie"
   Battle of the Netherlands, 12–14,
      15–16
   death of, 286
   early life of, 1–2, 4–8, 26
   in Enschede, 126–27
   February strike, 52–53
   hiding *onderduikers*, 11–12, 54–58
   Liberation Day, 264–66
   loyalty test of Frans, 63–67
   meeting Frans, 59–67
   meeting Hannie, 136–39
   Noordwijkerhout camping trip,
      31–32
   post-war life of, 277–78, 281–83,
      285–86

relationship with sister, 58–59
resistance activities of, 39–41, 52–
54, 60–67, 73–78, 111–12,
113–14, 127, 163
The Bunker sabotage, 230–33
Gerritsen assassination, 97–98
guilt over executions, 244
Haarlem bridge bombing attempt, 226–30
hanging of flag, 124–26
IJmuiden bunker, 224–26
Krist assassination, 213–18
Langendijk assassination attempt, 244–49
luring of SS officer, 88–94
Madame Sieval assassination
attempt, 250–53
Mussert and bicycle bells, 40–
41
parcel deliveries, 221–23
sidelining by Velsen group,
237–40
tracking V-2 missile
movements, 194–97
"tulip run," 223, 226
Oversteegen, George, 3–4, 91
Oversteegen, Jacob, 1–3
Oversteegen, Robbie, 6, 13, 26, 52–
58, 94, 126
birth and paternity of, 4, 4n
Oversteegen, Trijntje van der Molen
Battle of the Netherlands, 12–14,
15–16
early life of daughters, 2–3, 5, 6
in Enschede, 126
February strike, 52–53
hiding onderduikers, 11–12, 54–58
resistance activities of, 39–41, 52–
53, 54–55, 59–63
Oversteegen, Truus
Battle of the Netherlands, 12–14,
15–16, 19
birth and early life of, 1–6
death of, 286
in Enschede, 126–27
February strike, 52–53
Hannie and, 187–88, 235–36
detention of Hannie, 260–63,
265–66
first meeting, 136–39

hiding onderduikers, 11–12, 54–58
housecleaning jobs of, 5–6, 11
Liberation Day, 264–66
loyalty test of Frans, 63–67
meeting Frans, 59–67
Noordwijkerhout camping trip,
31–32
post-war life of, 277–83, 285–86
relationship with sister, 58–59
resistance activities of, 39–41, 52–
54, 60–67, 73–78, 86–87,
111–17, 124–27, 140–43,
163, 181
Bakker assassination, 249–50
The Bunker sabotage, 230–33
Gerritsen assassination, 97–98
"Granny," 112–13, 114–17
Haarlem bridge bombing attempt, 226–30
hanging of flag, 124–26
IJmuiden bunker, 224–26
Krist assassination, 213–18,
242
Langendijk assassination attempt, 244–49
luring of SS officer, 88–94
Madame Sieval assassination
attempt, 250–53
Mussert and bicycle bells, 40–
41
parcel deliveries, 221–23
sidelining by Velsen group,
237–40
Smit assassination, 204–8
tracking V-2 missile
movements, 194–97
transport of Jewish children,
84–86, 149–60, 197
"tulip run," 223, 226
Willy, 142–43
Zirkzee assassination, 241–47
Overzet, Jan, 216, 216n

Pacifism, 28, 134
Paris, 195, 198
Patton, George, 223–24
Persoonsbewijzencentrale (PBC),
82–83
Pillar System, 49–50
Plekker, S.L.A., 205

Polak, Philine, 198, 199, 221–22
  befriending of Hannie, 29, 30
  in hiding, 99–100, 106, 121–22,
      134–35, 189–90, 199
  identity card for, 51, 79, 99
  Liberation Day, 266
  at University of Amsterdam, 39,
      47, 51
Poland, invasion of, 9, 11, 29
Political Investigation Service, 271–
      72, 277–78
Pos, H. J., 29
Posen speeches, 148–49
Protestant Reformation, 20–21

Raad van Verzet (RVV), 74–78, 110–
      11, 113–14, 202. *See also*
      Haarlem Raad van Verzet
  strikes, 123–24
Radio Oranje, 30–31, 120, 128, 174,
      198, 201–2, 205
Ragut, Willem, 182–88
Rauter, Hanns Albin, 35, 36, 43–44,
      123, 147–48
  reprisals against resistance activi-
      ties, 103–9, 127–28, 146–
      48, 170
Ravensbruck concentration camp,
      84
Red Cross, 29, 149–50, 153, 216–17,
      262
Rembrandt Theater, 163–64, 171
Resistance. *See* Dutch resistance
Reydon, H., 103–4
Rijksstraatweg, 254–55
Ritman, Willem, 169
Rommel, Erwin, 119
Roosendaal, 200
Rosy, 151–52, 155–56, 157, 159–60
Rotterdam, 152, 153
  bombing of, 16–17, 18, 29–30
Royal Netherlands Army, 9–10, 14,
      16
Ruhl, Emil, 169, 189–90, 268
  detainment and interrogation of
      Hannie, 255–57, 258, 260
Rusman, Cor, 73
  loyalty test of Hannie, 132–33
  resistance activities of, 114, 125,
      142, 163
    luring of SS officer, 89, 91–94

Rembrandt Theater bombing
    attempt, 163–64, 171, 189,
    190
  Willemse assassination, 204–8
Rutte, Mark, 286
RVV. *See* Raad van Verzet

Schaft, Aafje Talea Vrijer, 48
  Battle of the Netherlands, 29–30
  early life of daughter, 25–27
  hiding *onderduikers*, 120–22
  police raid on home, 189–90
  resistance activities of daughter,
      133–35, 165
  at Vught concentration camp,
      189, 190, 191–92
Schaft, Annie, 25
Schaft, Jannetje Johanna "Jo" "Joop"
      ("Hannie")
  arrest of, 254–56
  Battle of the Netherlands, 29–30
  Bonekamp and, 131–32, 138,
      171–73
    Ragut assassination, 182–84
    shooting and death of Jan,
        186–88, 190–92
  ceremony honoring, 275–77
  early education of, 24, 26–28
  early life of, 24–27
  execution of, 267–70, 271–72
  exhumation of body, 272–73
  gravesite of, 278–79
  growing carelessness of, 234–35,
      240–41
  imprisonment of, 265–66, 272
    efforts to release, 259–63
    interrogation and confession,
        255–59
  legacy of, 278–81, 283
  loyalty test of Frans, 132–33
  meeting Truus and Freddie, 136–
      39
  melancholy of, 196, 197–99
  nom de guerre of "Hannie," 130,
      130n
  political radicalization of, 30–31
  red hair of, 24, 26, 30, 130, 131,
      137, 188, 192, 256, 259
  resistance activities of, 46–48, 78,
      106, 130–34, 141–42, 163,
      165, 168, 234–35, 236

Bakker assassination, 249–50
The Bunker sabotage, 230–33
Faber assassination, 178–81, 256
Haarlem bridge bombing attempt, 226–30
hiding onderduikers, 99–100, 120–22
identity cards, 51, 72, 79, 82, 99–100, 167
IJmuiden bunker, 224–26
Krist assassination, 213–18, 242
Langendijk assassination attempt, 244–49, 256–57
mapping of German defenses, 161–62, 171
parcel deliveries, 221–23
Ragut assassination, 182–87, 256
Rembrandt Theater bombing attemp, 163–64, 171
sidelining by Velsen group, 237–40
tracking V-2 missile movements, 194–97
transfer of weapons depot, 174–77
"tulip run," 223, 226
Velsen-Noord plant bombing attempt, 143–45
Willemse assassination, 204–8, 256
Willy, 142–43
Zirkzee assassination, 241–47
return to Haarlem, 106, 118–19, 120–21, 146
at University of Amsterdam, 28–29, 30, 39, 47, 48, 51, 99–100, 101–2, 104–6
Schaft, Pieter, 48, 121, 165
Battle of the Netherlands, 29–30
ceremony for daughter, 275–76
early life of daughter, 25–27
execution of daughter, 269–70
hiding onderduikers, 120–22
police raid on home, 189–90
resistance activities of daughter, 133–35, 165
at Vught concentration camp, 189, 190, 191–92, 199
Schattenkampf (documentary), 285–86
Schlacthuisbuurt, 24
Schmitz, W.H.M., 267–69, 272
Scholten, Paul, 38
Schottenkampf (documentary), 67n
Schweitzer, Albert, 28
Seyffardt, Hendrik, 102–4, 110
Seyss-Inquart, Arthur, 33–38, 42–43, 45, 49, 96, 101, 123, 128, 201, 205, 211
Sicherheitpolizei (Security Police), 35–36
Sicherheitsdienst (SD), 35–36, 97, 165, 185
Siege of Stalingrad, 119
Sikkel, N. G., 219–22, 236–37, 239–40, 269, 283–84
Slomp, Frederick "Frits," 81–82
Smit, Harm, 203–8
Sobibor extermination camp, 199
Social Help in Practice, 4–5
Socialism, 2, 4, 26, 39–40, 134
Soviet partisans, 59, 60–61
Soviet Union
    Cold War, 277–78
    Operation Barbarossa, 47–48, 59, 60
    Siege of Stalingrad, 119
Spaarne River, 24
    Haarlem bridge bombing attempt, 226–30
Spanish Civil War, 7, 29
SS (Schutzstaffel), 35, 45, 53, 77, 103–4, 178
    Oversteegen girls luring of SS officer, 88–94
"Stumpers," 197

Tempelman, Kalei, 218
Ten Boom, Betsie, 83–84, 166
Ten Boom, Casper, 165–66
Ten Boom, Corrie, 83–84, 166
"Tiptoe to the tulips" (song), 13n
Trouw (The Faith), 59, 68–69, 73–74, 120
Truus Oversteegen. See Oversteegen, Truus

Tulip bulbs, eating, 223, 225, 226
Tulip trade, 21–22, 223
Twee Zussen in Verzet (documen-
    tary), 285

University of Amsterdam
    anti-Jewish measures, 38
    Jo "Hannie" at, 28–29, 30, 39, 47,
        48, 51, 99–100, 101–2, 104–
        6
    labor draft, 101–2, 104, 105–6
    loyalty pledge, 104–6
University of Delft, 39, 105
University of Utrecht, 101
Utrecht, 9, 10, 45

Van Biel, Dien, 100
Van Calsem, Annie, 29, 30–31, 46–
    48, 234–35
Van de Berg, Hans, 146–47
Van der Veen, Gerrit, 82–83, 275–76
Van der Voort, Cees, 237, 239, 241,
    249
Van der Wiel, Alexander, 73–78
Van der Wiel, Frans
    background of, 74
    as leader of Haarlem RVV, 74–78,
        107, 109, 111, 113–14, 123,
        141–42, 163, 178, 220
    loyalty test of Hannie, 132–33
        loyalty test of Oversteegen
        girls, 63–67
    meeting Oversteegen girls, 59–63
    resistance activities of, 73, 107,
        109, 111, 113–14, 127, 131,
        189
        The Bunker sabotage, 230–33
        Haarlem bridge bombing at-
            tempt, 226–30
        hiding onderduikers, 95, 96
        luring of SS officer, 88–90, 92–
            93
        Ragut assassination, 182, 182n
Van der Wiel, Sander, 236–37
Van Hall, Walraven, 238, 275–76
Van Ossietzky, Carl, 28
Van Rossem, Ada, 258, 267
Van Zoelen, Jan, 168–69

Velsen-Noord electric plant bomb-
    ing, 143–45
Velser Affaire, 283–84
Verbong, Ben, 283
Verleun, Jan, 103
Vlot, Cornelis, 218
Volkswagen Kubelwagen, 175
Von Benda-Beckman, Bas, 284
Von Braun, Wernher, 195
Von Rundstedt, Gerd, 203
Vrij Nederland (Free Netherlands),
    68, 120, 254
V-2 rocket, 162, 194–97
Vught concentration camp, 80, 115,
    129, 190, 191–92, 199

WA (weather department), 42, 110
Wagenaar, Gerben, 239
Wagenweg, 24, 63, 133
Wassenaar, 194–95
Weaponry, 61, 65, 75–76, 111–12,
    114, 172–73
Westerbork Labor Camp, 80, 99,
    115, 118, 135, 190, 193,
    199, 204, 280
Westergracht Bridge, 215, 216–17
Western Front, 203
"White hats," 126–27
Wilhelmina Hospital, 185, 188, 189
Wilhelmina, Queen, 15–16, 30, 201–
    2, 275–76
Willemse, Franciscus, 203–8
Winterswijk, 81–82
World War I, 8, 34–35
Wutrich, Johannes, 218

Yad Vashem, 281–82
Yellow stars, 81, 150
Ypkemeule, Henk, 130–32, 142

Zaandam, 45, 181
    Ragut assassination, 182–86
Zaan Raad van Verzet (RVV), 143,
    163, 171
Zentralstelle for Jewish Emigration,
    79–80, 81, 148–49
Zirkzee, Willem, 241–47
Zon, Willem van de, 236–37